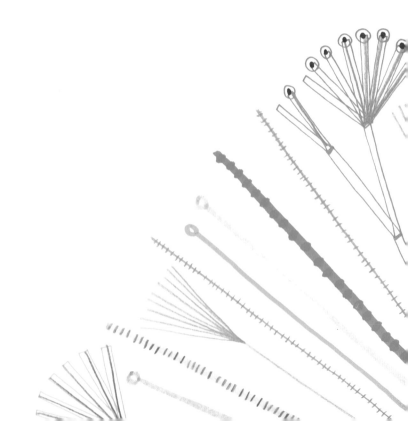

GIORGIA LUPI

Dear Data

STEFANIE POSAVEC

Princeton Architectural Press, New York

Published by
Princeton Architectural Press
A McEvoy Group company
37 East Seventh Street
New York, New York 10003

Visit our website at www.papress.com.

Designers: Giorgia Lupi and Stefanie Posavec
Color reproduction by Rhapsody

Special thanks to: Madisen Anderson, Janet Behning, Nicola Brower, Abby Bussel, Erin Cain,
Tom Cho, Barbara Darko, Benjamin English, Jenny Florence, Jan Cigliano Hartman, Lia Hunt, Mia
Johnson, Valerie Kamen, Simone Kaplan-Senchak, Stephanie Leke, Diane Levinson, Jennifer
Lippert, Kristy Maier, Sara McKay, Jaime Nelson Noven, Esme Savage, Rob Shaeffer, Sara
Stemen, Paul Wagner, Joseph Weston, and Janet Wong of Princeton Architectural Press —Kevin
C. Lippert, publisher

ISBN 978-1-61689-532-7
Library of Congress Cataloging-in-Publication Data is available from the publisher

To GABRIELE,
and MY PARENTS
CATIA and GIANNI

To STEVE,
AND MY PARENTS
MARILEE AND STEVEN

FOREWORD by maria popova

"MY EXPERIENCE IS WHAT I AGREE TO ATTEND TO," William James wrote at the dawn of modern psychology. And yet however perennial this insight may be, it is only a partial truth. Our experience is shaped as much by what we agree to take in as it is by what we refuse – what we choose to leave out – and both are only partly conscious choices. Our attention filters in a fraction of what goes on around us at any given moment and filters out, thanks to millions of years of evolution, the vast majority of the shimmering simultaneity with which the life of sensation and perception unfolds. This highly subjective, selective, imperfect filtration of reality guarantees that however many parallels two human beings may have between their lives, however much common ground, the paths by which they navigate their respective landscapes of experience will be profoundly divergent.

In their year-long visual correspondence project, Giorgia Lupi, an Italian woman living in New York, and Stefanie Posavec, an American woman living in London, capture the inherent poetry of that subjective selectivity. Each week, they jointly selected one aspect of daily life – from sleep to spending habits to mirror use – and depicted their respective experience of it in a hand-drawn visualization on the back of a postcard, then mailed it to the other. Out of these simple diurnal observations emerges the complexity of the human experience – nonlinear, contradictory, and always filtered through the discriminating yet imperfect lens of attention.

The creative constraint of the unifying themes only amplifies the variousness of possibility within each parameter. Despite the substantial similarities between the two women – both are information designers known for working by hand, both are only children, both have left their respective home-land to move across the Atlantic in pursuit of creative fulfillment, and they are the exact same

age – their attentional orientation toward each week's chosen subject is completely different, both in substance and in style. They deliberately used different visual metaphors and information design techniques for each week's theme, producing an immensely pleasurable duet of sensibilities – side by side, Posavec's signature spatial poetics and Lupi's mastery of shape and colour elevate one another to a higher plane of meaning and delight.

A twenty-first-century testament to Virginia Woolf's celebration of letter-writing as "the humane art," the project radiates a lovely countercultural charm. Ours is the golden age of Big Data, where human lives are aggregated into massive data sets in the hope that analysis of the aggregate will yield valid insight into the individual – an approach no more effective than taking an exquisite poem in English, running it through Google Translate to render into Japanese, and then Google-translating it back into English – the result may have the vague contours of the original poem's meaning, but none of its subtle magic and vibrant granular beauty.

Lupi and Posavec reclaim that poetic granularity of the individual from the homogenizing aggregate-grip of Big Data. What emerges is a case for the beauty of small data and its deliberate interpretation, analog visualization, and slow transmission – a celebration of the infinitesimal, incomplete, imperfect, yet marvelously human details through which we wrest meaning out of the incomprehensible vastness of all possible experience that is life.

MARIA POPOVA is a reader and a writer, and writes about what she reads on Brain Pickings *(brainpickings.org), which is included in the Library of Congress archive of culturally valuable materials. She has also written for* The New York Times, Wired UK, *and* The Atlantic, *among others, and is an MIT Fellow.*

INTRODUCTION

EVER SINCE WE WERE YOUNG, WE HAVE BEEN fascinated with collecting and organizing information from the world around us.

Stefanie remembers going to baseball games with her father, helping him fill out baseball scorecards, slowly compressing inning after inning of the game into pencilled notations on two sides of paper, and feeling excited at being able to capture a moment in time into something that could be neatly tucked away and re-lived at another date.

Giorgia remembers how, as a child, she loved to collect and organize all kind of items into transparent folders that she would then tag with maniacal care. Coloured pieces of papers, little stones, pieces of textiles from her grandmother's tailor-shop, buttons, sales receipts and many more formed her collections, and she remembers the pleasure of categorizing her treasures according to their colours, sizes and dimensions and drawing tiny labels to specify how to read them.

It was only later when we became adults that we realized we were collecting data, and that data was something that we could communicate with while working as information designers.

Unknowingly living almost parallel lives, when we bumped into each other at an arts festival we realized how similar they were. We were each living in a foreign country (Giorgia moved from Italy to New York, and Stefanie, who grew up in Denver, Colorado, now lives in London), we were the same age and were both only children. But, most importantly, we were visual designers who both loved drawing, and specifically drawing with data.

This book is the story of how we, Giorgia and Stefanie, became friends through revealing to each other the details of our daily lives. But we didn't do this by chatting in cafés and bars or on social media. Instead we started an old-fashioned correspondence with an unusual twist. Each week, for a year, we sent each other a postcard describing what had happened to the other during that week. But we didn't write what had happened – we drew it. And we didn't try to draw about everything that had happened to us: we selected a weekly theme.

Every Monday we chose a particular subject on which to collect data about ourselves for the whole week: how often we complained, or the times when we felt envious; when we came into physical contact and with whom; the sounds we heard around us. We then created a drawing representing this data

OUR NEW, SHARED ROUTINE FOR A YEAR

OBSERVE   COUNT   DRAW / EXPLAIN   POST!

... ACTIVITIES ...

... IDEAS ...

... THOUGHTS ...

... SURROUNDINGS ...

HOW TO READ IT?

... and fingers crossed!

on a postcard-sized sheet of paper, and dropped the postcard into an English post box (Stefanie) or an American mail box (Giorgia).

Over the fifty-two weeks, the collecting of data about our lives became a kind of ritual. We would spend the week noticing and noting down our activities or thoughts, before translating this information into a hand-drawn visualization. On the front of the postcard there would be a unique representation of our weekly data, and, on the other side (in addition to the necessary postage and address), we would squeeze in detailed keys to our drawings: the code to enable the recipient to decipher the picture, and to fantasize about what had happened to her new friend the week before.

We started *Dear Data* as a way to get know each other through our data, the material that is most familiar to us: but we soon found we were also becoming more in-tune with ourselves as we captured the life unfolding around us and sketched the hidden patterns we discovered in the details. By noticing our behaviour, we were influencing our behaviour.

We believe data collected from life can be a snapshot of the world in the same way that a picture catches small moments in time. Data can describe the hidden patterns found in every aspect of our lives, from our digital existence to the natural world around us. Every plant, every person, every interaction we take part in can be mapped, counted, and measured, and these measurements are what we call data. And once you realize that data can be gathered from every single being and thing on the planet, and you know how to find these invisible numbers, you begin to see these numbers everywhere, in everything.

Besides *finding* data in the world around us, we are all *creating* data just by living: our purchases, our movements through the city, our explorations across the internet, all contribute to the "data trail" we leave in our wake as we move through life. This data is being collected, counted, and computed – both on a massive scale by companies and institutions seeking insights and answers – and on a smaller scale by individuals seeking to understand more about themselves, using data to "quantify" the self and become more efficient, optimised humans.

EVERYTHING CAN BE MAPPED, COUNTED, AND MEASURED

Because of this, we are said to be living in the age of "Big Data", where algorithms and computation are seen as the new keys to universal questions, and where a myriad of applications can detect, aggregate, and visualize our data for us to help us become these efficient super-humans. We prefer to approach data in a slower, more analogue way. We've always conceived *Dear Data* as a "personal documentary" rather than a quantified-self project which is a subtle – but important – distinction. Instead of using data just to become more efficient, we argue we can use data to become more humane and to connect with ourselves and others at a deeper level.

We hope this book will inspire you in many ways: to draw (even if you don't think of yourself as an artist), to slow down and appreciate the small details of your life, and to make connections with other people. You'll find our fifty-two cards in this book, along with the thoughts we had while conceiving and crafting them. They have not been edited: they appear exactly as they did when originally received through the mail, highlighting a year of learning, doubts and indecision as well as love, affection and humour.

Bearing all the scuff-marks of their journey across the ocean, together they form a personal data-diary that first we shared with each other, and now we share with you.

We'll also unfold what we've learned from this year of collecting our daily data, expanding upon how we gained meaning from what we collected and on our artistic process. Starting this year with nervousness and trepidation, we ended it feeling confident in capturing and drawing the moments of our lives: it doesn't take much to get started.

We see data as a creative material like paint or paper, an outcome of a very new way of seeing and engaging with our world. We hope this book will inspire you to see your world through a new lens, where everything and anything can be a creative starting point for play and expression.

GIORGIA LUPI   Stefanie Posavec

STEFANIE'S

desk in

LONDON

data-gathering notebook

120 130 140 150 mm

week one
a week of
CLOCKS

This was the first week of *Dear Data* – Giorgia and Stefanie were excited, and a bit scared at the same time: would they be able to create something compelling?

The topic of the first week might seem impersonal: how often did they check the time? But by adding anecdotal details about these moments, they started to tell each other the stories of their days through their data.

EVERY SINGLE TIME GIORGIA CHECKED THE TIME in THE week

7:22
I am so late!

11:15
THIS IS INSANE!
I officially Stop
wearing my
wrist watch.

7:17
I am
Texting
Stefanie!

12:30
SUPER
HUNGRY!

6:15
I am
BoRed.

7:30
I am
waiting
for the bus
and it's
Raining!!

SECOND ATTEMPT
NEW YORK, NY 100
GIORGIA LUPI
Brooklyn
-NY-
07 OCT 2014

" DEAR DATA
WEEK 01: WHAT'S the time?

HOW TO READ IT :

1AM
12 AM
M t W T F S S
- days of the week

- each symbol represents every moment I glanced at the clock, grouped by hours of the day.
- - - - - -
Different symbols and attributes represent WHY and HOW I checked the time.

SYMBOLS

o on purpose : wanted to know what the time was.

• just glanced : on a phone, mac or else

⊠ Because I thought of this project.

x I thought " Don't look!" But I did.

I Because I was Bored

II Because I was Hungry

Δ Heard somebody saying the time aloud.

ATTRIBUTES

˙ f**ck! I'm late!

˳ oh, ok. I'm fine.

• analog support (i.e. wrist watch)

⦙ alarm clock rang.

• glanced at the clock while texting or emailing with Stefanie. ☺

0012280001

SEND TO:

STEFANIE POSAVEC

~~EEEEEEEEEEEE~~

LONDON ~~HHHHHHHHH~~

[UK]

ENGLAND

Drawing her first postcard, Giorgia had an idea for her whole collection: from now on every time she tracks something related to Stefanie, or to *Dear Data*, she uses a special pen to represent it!

• pink ink pen!

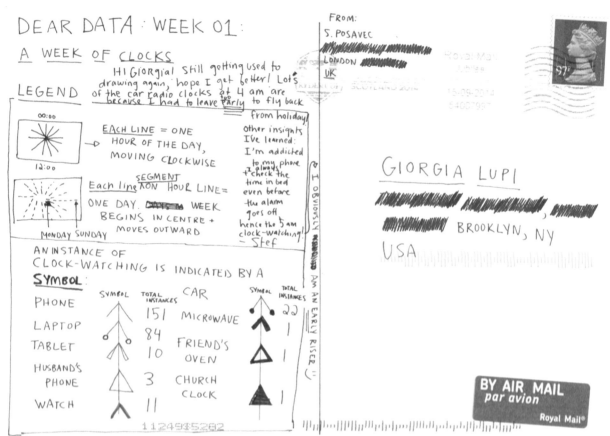

DEAR DATA · WEEK 01:

A WEEK OF CLOCKS

HI GIORgia! Still getting used to drawing again, hope I get better! Lots of the car radio clocks at 4 am are because I had to leave early to fly back from holiday!

LEGEND

00:00

12:00

EACH LINE = ONE HOUR OF THE DAY, MOVING CLOCKWISE

SEGMENT
Each line ~on HOUR LINE = ONE DAY. ~~DAYS IN~~ WEEK BEGINS IN CENTRE + MOVES OUTWARD

MONDAY SUNDAY

AN INSTANCE OF CLOCK-WATCHING IS INDICATED BY A

SYMBOL:

Other insights I've learned: I'm addicted to my phone + always check the time in bed even before the alarm goes off hence the 5 am clock-watching! — Stef

I OBVIOUSLY ~~AM~~ AM AN EARLY RISER !!

	SYMBOL	TOTAL INSTANCES		SYMBOL	TOTAL INSTANCES
PHONE		151	CAR		22
LAPTOP		84	MICROWAVE		1
TABLET		10	FRIEND'S OVEN		1
HUSBAND'S PHONE		3	CHURCH CLOCK		1
WATCH		11			

1 1 2 4 9 3 5 2 8 2

FROM:
S. POSAVEC
LONDON
UK

GIORGIA LUPI
BROOKLYN, NY
USA

BY AIR MAIL
par avion
Royal Mail®

This week Giorgia and Stefanie tried gathering data in small notebooks (tedious), but soon switched to making notes on their phones (much easier). Stefanie's favourite clock to capture: a bell tolling the time in a town in Devon.

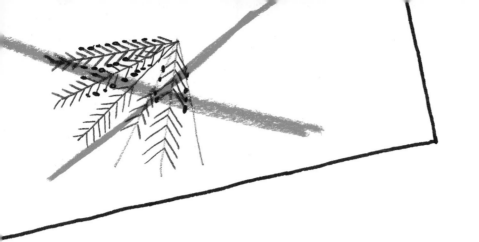

STEFANIE:

"I'm TERRIBLE at drawing!"

"Well, you'll be better after a year, right?"

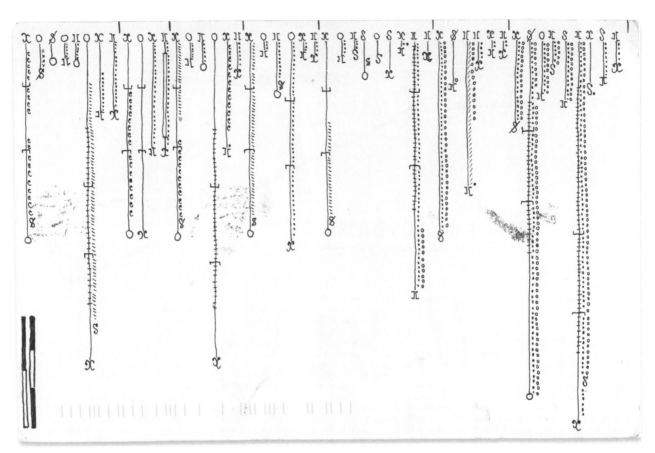

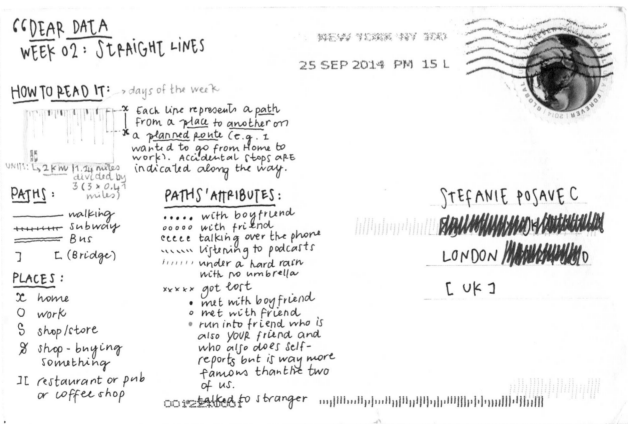

"DEAR DATA
WEEK 02: STRAIGHT LINES

HOW TO READ IT: → days of the week

Each line represents a path from a place to another on a planned route (e.g. I wanted to go from Home to work). Accidental stops are indicated along the way.

UNITS: L 2 km /1.24 miles divided by 3 (3 × 0.41 miles)

PATHS:
——— walking
+++++ subway
=== Bus
] [(Bridge)

PLACES:
x home
O work
S shop/store
⊗ shop - buying something
][restaurant or pub or coffee shop

PATHS' ATTRIBUTES:
•••• with boyfriend
ooooo with friend
eeeee talking over the phone
˄˄˄˄˄ listening to podcasts
¦¦¦¦¦¦ under a hard rain with no umbrella
xxxx got lost
• met with boyfriend
○ met with friend
• run into friend who is also your friend and who also does self-reports but is way more famous than the two of us.
talked to stranger

STEFANIE POSAVEC

LONDON

[UK]

The treat of the week was running into our common friend and famous self-tracker Nick Felton (www.feltron.com) — a nice excuse for Giorgia to use her pink ink pen.

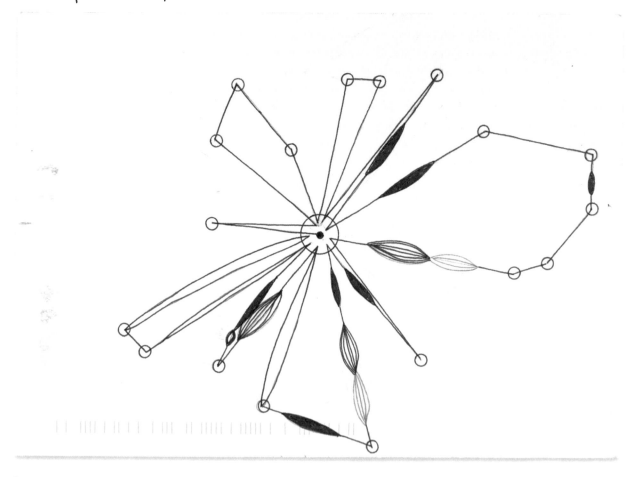

DEAR DATA : WEEK 02
A WEEK OF PUBLIC TRANSPORTATION

HI GIORGIA, THIS ISN'T MY BEST DRAWING,
PROBABLY BECAUSE I WALK ALOT, SO THERE
ISN'T MUCH OTHER TRANSPORT HAPPENING (EXCEPT FOR
THE ONE TIME I RAN TO CATCH A BUS!) STEF

FROM:
S. POSAVEC ~~~~~~~~
~~~~~~~~~~ ~~~~~~
LONDON ~~~~~~~
UK

97P

LEGEND

LOCATIONS

⊙ — HOME

THE BEGINNING OF THE WEEK OF
TRANSPORT : ALL TRANSPORT MOVES
CLOCKWISE

○ — a location OTHER THAN HOME

GIORGIA LUPI

~~~~~~~~~~~ ~~~~~~~~~~, ~~~~~~
~~~~~~~~~ BROOKLYN, NY ~~~~~~~
USA

TRANSPORT : lines between locations are textured
with different patterns

WALKING ————
RUNNING ⬭
CAR ⬭
BUS ⬭
UNDERGROUND ⬭
OVERGROUND ⬭
TRAIN ⬭

NOTE: DISTANCE OF
LINES MEANS
NOTHING, AS I
COULDN'T FIGURE
OUT HOW TO PLAN+
CALCULATE BY HAND
OH, WELL :")

BY AIR MAIL
par avion
Royal Mail®

This was the only week Giorgia and Stefanie used a phone app to track their data: it felt too impersonal,
so they agreed to only gather data that computers couldn't track for the rest of the project.

PUBLIC
TRANSPORT
DATA

SOCIAL MEDIA
NETWORKS

BROWSING
HISTORY

"DRAWING FROM LIFE" NOW INCLUDES DRAWING OUR

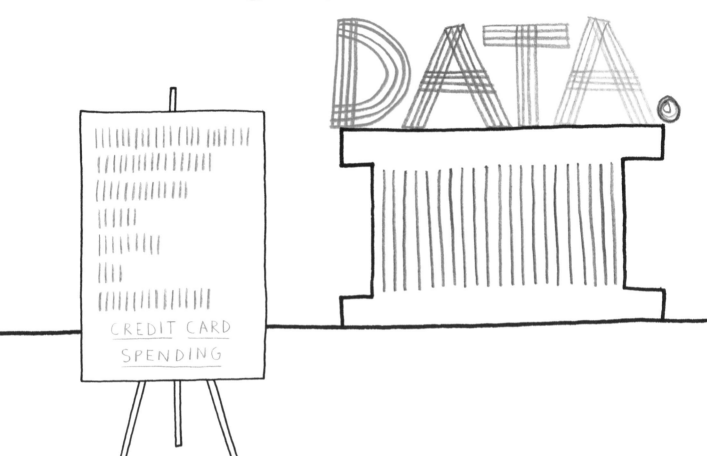

DATA

CREDIT CARD
SPENDING

a week of
"Thank you!"

How often do we say "thank you" to the people
we meet (and the people we love)?

This week, Giorgia and Stefanie wanted to see how
kind and gracious they are to others, and realized
they should probably be more thankful to their
friends and families than to strangers.

THANK you!

THANK you!

THANK you!

THANK you!

THANK you!

THANK you!

THANK you!

THANK you!

THANK you!

THANK you!

THANK you!

GIORGIA'S Thank-you (s)
To and fROM BOYFRIEND

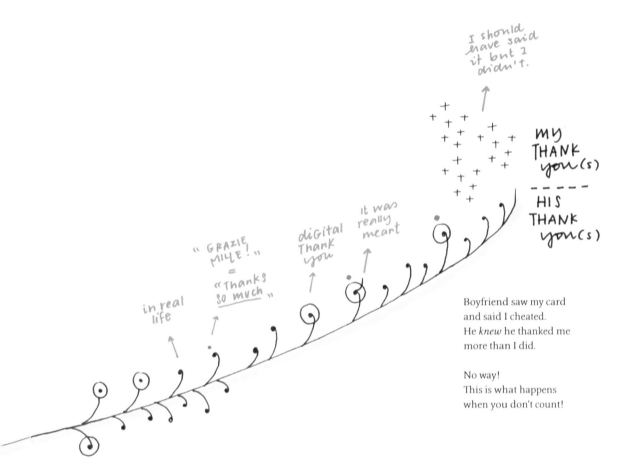

I should have said it but I didn't.

my
THANK
you (s)
- - - - -
HIS
THANK
you (s)

it was
really
meant

digital
Thank
you

" GRAZIE
MILLE ! "
=
"Thanks
so much "

in real
life

Boyfriend saw my card
and said I cheated.
He *knew* he thanked me
more than I did.

No way!
This is what happens
when you don't count!

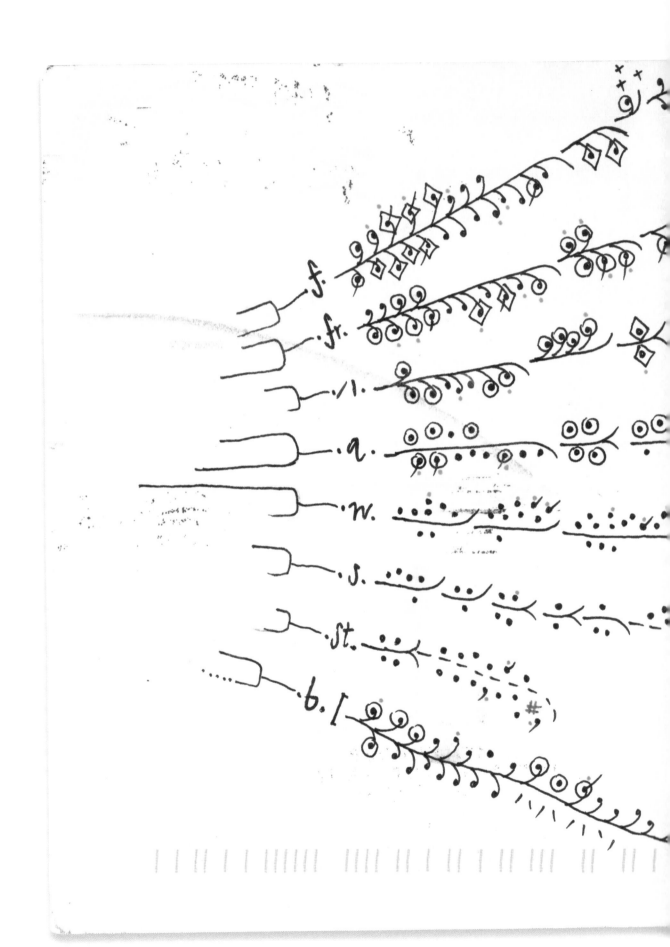

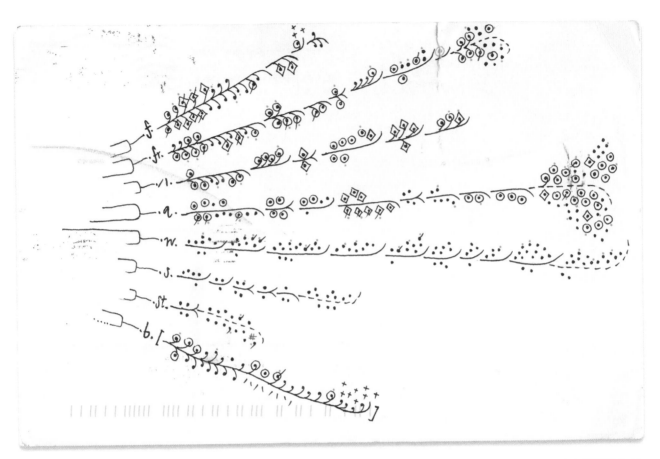

66 DEAR DATA
WEEK 03: thank you so much!

HOW TO READ IT:

Each branch represents a category of people I said thank you to.

→ Dots ABOVE the branch: I said thank you

→ Dots BELOW the branch: they said thank you to me.

aggregated information per category.

δ = family
fr = friends
√ = Accurat
a = acquaintances
w = waiter/tress
s = shop assistant
st = stranger
b = boyfriend

connected DOTS = Italian "GRAZIE"
flying DOTS = English "thank you".

ATTRIBUTES
- real life
- digital (texts, emails....)
- over the phone
- a really MEANT thank you
- "thanks a lot".... "t. very much"....
- ++ should have said more
- ,,,, boyfriend saw the postcard and says he's sure he said more
- thank you to Stefanie!
- Spanish "GRACIAS"
- # MTA machine really appreciated my metro card refill and thanked me digitally.

Each DIVISION indicates a singular person. Curves go up and down indicating who thanked the most (me - up, other person - down)

FROM:
G. LUPI

NEW YORK
NY 100
07 OCT 201... BROOKLYN,
PM 15 L   NY   USA

SEND TO:
STEFANIE POSAVEC
~~EAST~~ ~~MOUNT~~
LONDON ~~MMMMM~~
[UK]
ENGLAND ANK

Giorgia realized she is a compulsive thanker of waitresses and waiters. When you have it all visualized, it really jumps out at you. (And then she also figured she should eat at home more often...!)

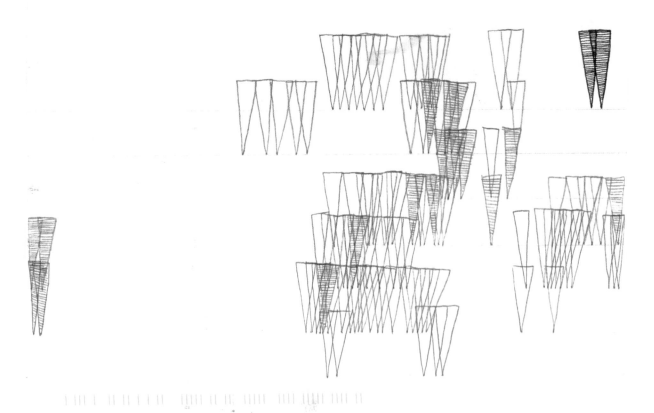

DEAR DATA: WEEK 03
A WEEK OF THANK YOUS

Hi GIORGIA! SO THIS WEEK WAS A
CHALLENGE: THANK-YOUS ARE A CHALLENGE,
PARTICULARLY WITHIN CLOSE RELATIONSHIPS:
I'M SURE I MISSED THANK-YOUS ~~SPENT~~ TO MY
HUSBAND. BUT THIS WAS AN UNUSUAL WEEK:
I WAS TRAVELLING FOR WORK TO HELSINKI, SO
I SPENT MORNINGS IN MY HOTEL ROOM AND
REALLY DIDN'T ~~SPEND~~ THANK ~~AS~~ ANYONE BUT
SHOP WORKERS + AIRPORT WORKERS!

LEGEND   DATA GATHERED ON ALL ☺
                VERBAL THANK-YOUS, ON   STEP
                PHONE OR IN PERSON.

                CLOSENESS OF RELATIONSHIP
                WITH THANK-YOU RECIPIENT:

EACH DAY
REPRESENTED
BY A HORIZONTAL   TOTAL   ACQUAINTANCE/   VERY CLOSE
LINE. EACH   STRANGER   WE'VE BEEN   RELATIONSHIP
THANK-YOU PLACED   FORMALLY   (MY HUSBAND)
ON LINE ACCORDING   INTRODUCED
TO TIME OF THANK-YOU. (ROUGH TIME APPROXIMATIONS DUE
                        TO IMPERFECT HAND DRAWING THIS!)

FROM:
S POSAVEC
▓▓▓▓▓▓▓▓▓▓ ▓▓▓▓▓▓▓▓
LONDON ▓▓▓▓▓▓▓
UK

GIORGIA LUPI
▓▓▓▓▓▓▓▓▓ ▓▓▓▓▓▓▓▓▓, ▓▓▓▓▓▓
BROOKLYN, NY ▓▓▓▓▓▓
USA

Stefanie's favourite thank-yous from this week: whispering *kiitos* to shopkeepers
in Finland because she didn't feel comfortable speaking Finnish.

DOING THE
"WORKINGS OUT"
CREATES MORE
OPPORTUNITIES
FOR PERSONAL
DISCOVERY,

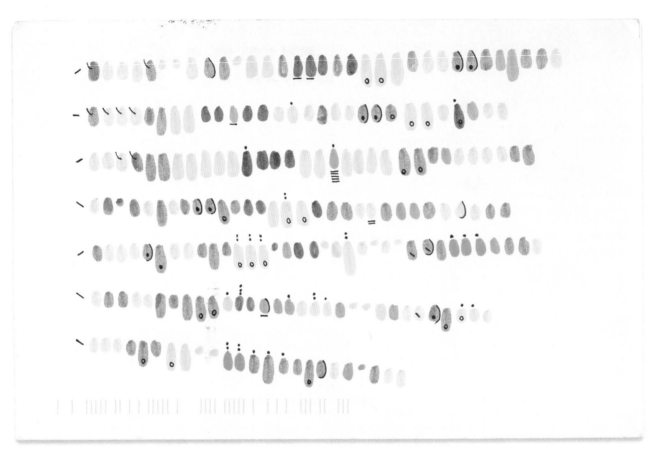

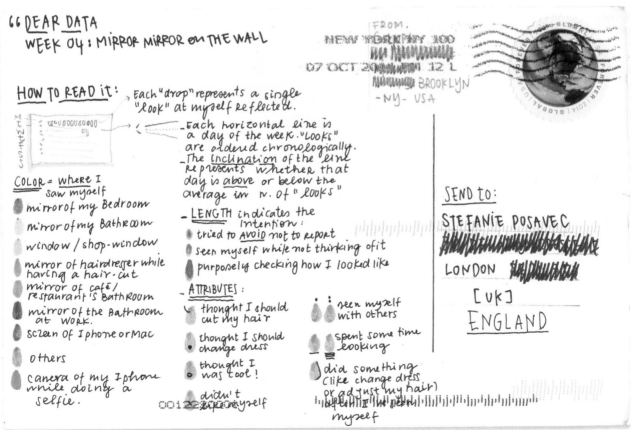

66 DEAR DATA
WEEK 04 : MIRROR MIRROR ON THE WALL

HOW TO READ IT:

→ Each "drop" represents a single "look" at myself reflected.

→ Each horizontal line is a day of the week. "Looks" are ordered chronologically.
- The inclination of the line represents whether that day is above or below the average in n. of "looks"

- LENGTH indicates the intention :
  ● tried to AVOID not to report
  ● seen myself while not thinking of it
  ● purposely checking how I looked like

COLOR = where I saw myself
● mirror of my Bedroom
● mirror of my Bathroom
● window / shop-window
● mirror of hairdresser while having a hair-cut
● mirror of café / restaurant's Bathroom
● mirror of the Bathroom at WORK.
● screen of Iphone or Mac
● others
● camera of my Iphone while doing a selfie.

- ATTRIBUTES :
  ﹨ thought I should cut my hair
  thought I should change dress
  thought I was cool !
  didn't see myself

  ⫶ seen myself with others
  spent some time looking
  did something (like change dress or adjust my hair)
  myself

FROM.
NEW YORK NY 100
07 OCT 20 12 L
BROOKLYN
- NY- USA

SEND TO:
STEFANIE POSAVEC

LONDON
[UK]
ENGLAND

Without telling each other, Giorgia and Stefanie both drew a colourful postcard. Giorgia started noticing how she is still somehow influenced by the previous week's topic: thinking about it for a second every time she said "thank you"!

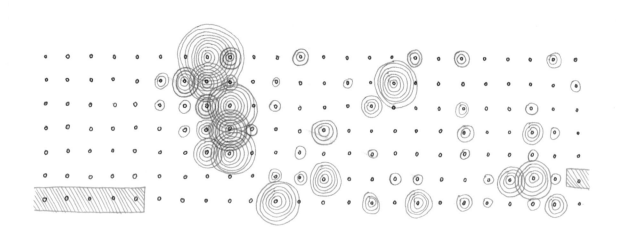

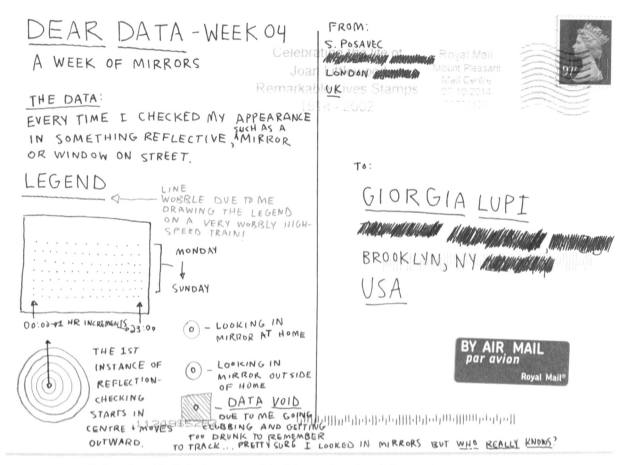

DEAR DATA - WEEK 04

A WEEK OF MIRRORS

THE DATA:
EVERY TIME I CHECKED MY APPEARANCE
IN SOMETHING REFLECTIVE, SUCH AS A MIRROR
OR WINDOW ON STREET.

LEGEND

LINE WOBBLE DUE TO ME DRAWING THE LEGEND ON A VERY WOBBLY HIGH-SPEED TRAIN!

MONDAY
↓
SUNDAY

00:00→1 HR INCREMENTS→23:00

THE 1ST INSTANCE OF REFLECTION-CHECKING STARTS IN CENTRE + MOVES OUTWARD.

○ - LOOKING IN MIRROR AT HOME

○ - LOOKING IN MIRROR OUTSIDE OF HOME

- DATA VOID DUE TO ME GOING CLUBBING AND GETTING TOO DRUNK TO REMEMBER TO TRACK... PRETTY SURE I LOOKED IN MIRRORS BUT WHO REALLY KNOWS?

FROM:
S. POSAVEC
LONDON
UK

TO:
GIORGIA LUPI
BROOKLYN, NY
USA

BY AIR MAIL
par avion
Royal Mail®

On Saturday night Stefanie went to a club while carrying a disco ball covered with hundreds of tiny mirrors yet somehow forgot to enter this into her data (though you can likely guess the reason).

IT IS ONLY
BY ADDING
PERSONAL
CONTEXT
THAT YOU GET
CLOSER TO REAL
MEANING

WE SHOULDN'T EXPECT ANY APP TO TELL US SOMETHING NEW ABOUT OURSELVES.

20.
19.   21.
16. 17. 18.   22.   ...
15.   ...   ...
14.   ...
13.

12.

WHAT I
WAS DOING

DID SOMETHING
SPECIAL HAPPEN?

WHO WAS I WITH?

HOW DID I feel?

FOR FIFTy-TWO WEEKS, WE EMPHASIZED THE OBSERVATION OF OUR DATA AS PERSONAL STORIES.

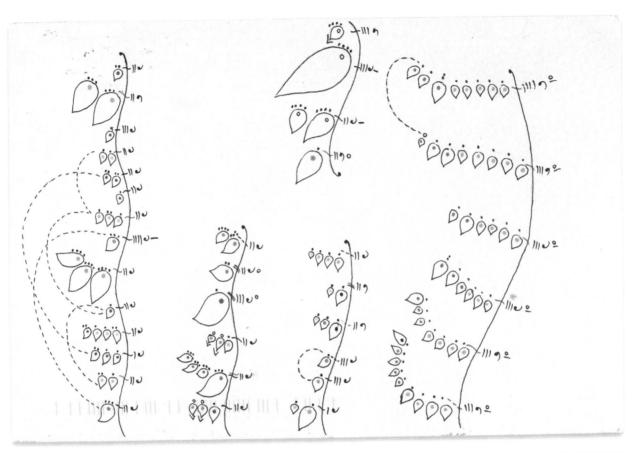

ᏅᏅ DEAR DATA
WEEK 05: THINGS I (WE) BOUGHT

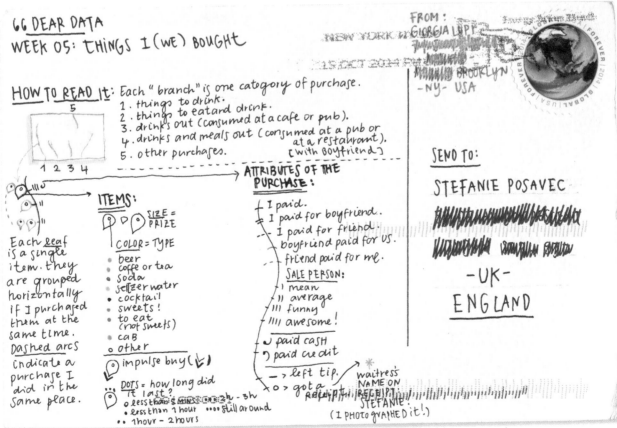

HOW TO READ It: Each "branch" is one category of purchase.
1. things to drink.
2. things to eat and drink.
3. drinks out (consumed at a cafe or pub).
4. drinks and meals out (consumed at a pub or at a restaurant).
5. other purchases.   [with boyfriend]

1 2 3 4

Each leaf is a single item. they are grouped horizontally if I purchased them at the same time. Dashed arcs indicate a purchase I did in the same peace.

ITEMS:
SIZE = PRIZE

COLOR = TYPE
• beer
• coffe or tea
• soda
• seltzer water
• cocktail
• sweets !
• to eat (not sweets)
• caB
◦ other

ⓘ impulse buy (⤵)

DOTS = how long did It last?
◦ less than 5 MINS   ••• 2h - 3h
• less than 1 hour   •••• still around
•• 1 hour - 2 hours

ATTRIBUTES OF THE PURCHASE:
┼ I paid.
┼ I paid for boyfriend.
-- I paid for friend.
┼ boyfriend paid for us.
┼ friend paid for me.

SALE PERSON:
) mean
)) average
))) funny
)))) awesome!

↶ paid cash
↷ paid credit

— > left tip.
↷ ◦ > got a receipt.

⁕ waitress' NAME ON RECEIPT: STEFANIE (I photographed it!)

SEND TO:

STEFANIE POSAVEC
~~~~~~~~~~~~~~~~~~~
~~~~~~~~~~~~~~~~~~~
-UK-
ENGLAND

Giorgia learns that being honest with your data-gathering includes being honest with the number of drinks. Argh. (Disclaimer: she shared some with her boyfriend!)

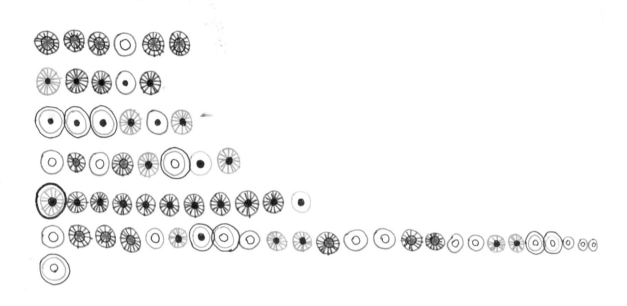

DEAR DATA - WEEK 05

A WEEK OF THINGS I BUY

FROM:
S. POSAVEC
~~~~~~~~~~~~~
LONDON
ENGLAND

LEGEND

AM ———→ PM

M	o o o o
T	o o o o o o
W	o o o o
Th	o o o o
F	o o o
S	o o o o
S	o o o o

NOTES ON DATA:

- ONLY INCLUDES ITEMS PURCHASED THROUGH DAY: NO RENT, GYM, ETC.
- ROUGH PRICE ESTIMATE DUE TO VARIOUS 'MULTI-BUY' DEALS/ TRANSPORT PRICE CAPS.

OOPS! ~~ran out of room~~ TOP 54 PURCHASES (MOST EXPENSIVE)
① TRAIN FROM LDN-SHEFFIELD
② POLISH FOOD DINNER W/FRIENDS
③ VANS TRAINERS
④ BEAUTY TREATMENT (WAY... AHEM)

EACH ITEM PURCHASED IS REPRESENTED BY A CIRCLE:

TYPE OF PURCHASE:

TRANSPORT LEISURE PERSONAL APPEARANCE FOOD ALCOHOL

PAYMENT TYPE:

CASH   CARD

NECESSITY OF PURCHASE:

NECESSARY FOR LIFE   NOT NECESSARY, JUST FOR FUN

COST OF ITEM:

UNDER $10 $10.01-$49.99 $50+

DUE TO FACT I AM LEFT-HANDED + SMUDGE EVERYTHING SMUDGES ON FRONT OF CARD

TO:

GIORGIA LUPI

~~~~~~~~~~~~~~~~~~~
BROOKLYN, NY ~~~~~
USA

[AIRMAIL]

TOTAL SPENT £320.17

Stefanie learns that being honest with your data-gathering includes being very open
about your personal beauty treatments, even if they are slightly embarrassing!

STEFANIE'S BATTLE AGAINST
LEFT-HAND SMUDGES

A PERFECT
POSTCARD

Hooray!

Three seconds later:

A PERFECT
POSTCARD

NOOOOOOOOOOOO
OOOOOOOOOOOOO
OOOOOOOOOOOOO
OOOOOOOOOOOOO
OOOOOOOOOOOOO
OOOOOOOOOOOOO
OOOOOOOOOOOOO
OOOOOOOOOOOOO
OOOOOOOOOOOOO
OOOOOOOOOOOOO
OOOOOOOOOOOO

WEEK SIX

A WEEK OF

PHYSICAL CONTACT

Living in a big city full of people, we are bumped into and jostled on a regular basis. But how often do we intentionally give or receive physical contact?

This week, Giorgia and Stefanie decided to collect data on physical contact, ranging from perfunctory handshakes with professional acquaintances to contact that was slightly more... "intimate".

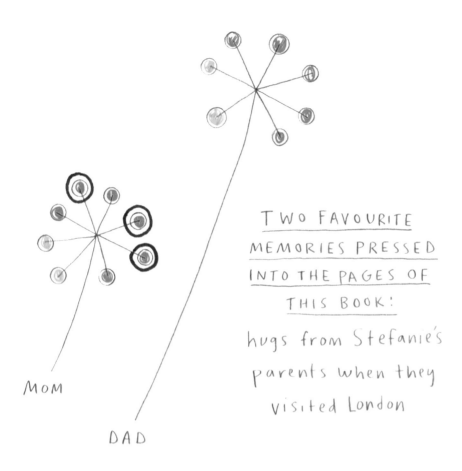

MOM

DAD

TWO FAVOURITE
MEMORIES PRESSED
INTO THE PAGES OF
THIS BOOK:

hugs from Stefanie's
parents when they
visited London

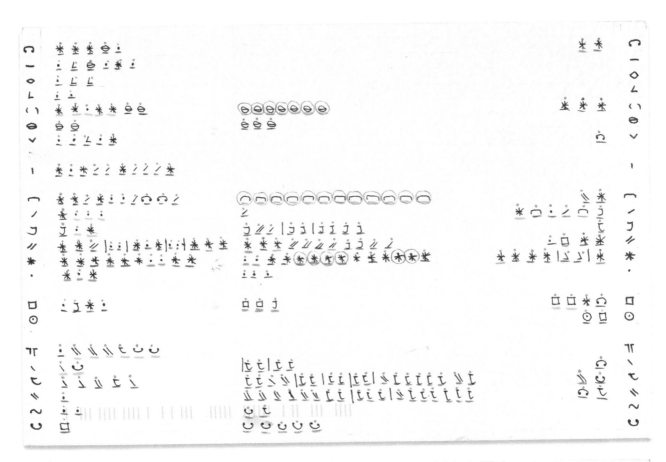

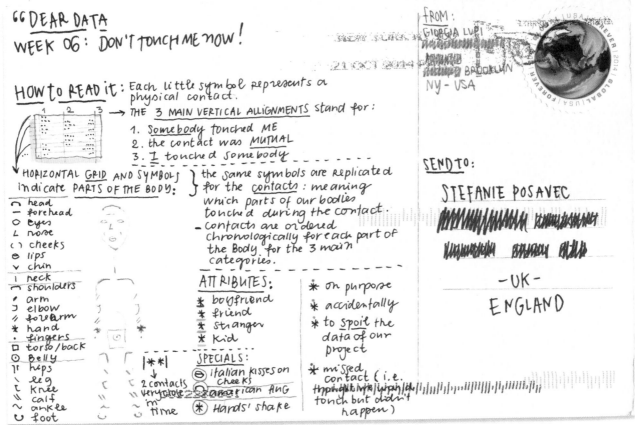

"DEAR DATA
WEEK 06: DON'T TOUCH ME NOW!

HOW to READ it: Each little symbol represents a physical contact.

→ THE 3 MAIN VERTICAL ALLIGNMENTS stand for:
1. Somebody touched ME
2. the contact was MUTUAL
3. I touched somebody

↓ HORIZONTAL GRID AND SYMBOLS indicate PARTS OF THE BODY:
} the same symbols are replicated for the contacts: meaning which parts of our bodies touched during the contact.
- contacts are ordered chronologically for each part of the body for the 3 main categories.

⌒ head
— forehead
○ eyes
L nose
() cheeks
⊖ lips
∨ chin
| neck
⌐ shoulders
ɔ arm
ɔ elbow
// forearm
✳ hand
⌐ fingers
□ torso/back
⊙ belly
‖ hips
⌐ leg
⌐ knee
~ calf
~ ankle
∪ foot

ATTRIBUTES:
✳ boyfriend
✳ friend
✳ stranger
✳ kid

SPECIALS:
⊖ italian kisses on cheeks
2 contacts 3 american hug
✳ hands' shake
time

✳ on purpose
✳ accidentally
✳ to spoil the data of our project
✳ missed contact (i.e. the action to touch but didn't happen)

FROM:
GIORGIA LUPI
BROOKLYN
NY - USA

SEND TO:
STEFANIE POSAVEC
-UK-
ENGLAND

Giorgia wanted to try something different here and she mocked-up a "body-shape" to represent her physical contacts. She didn't really like the aesthetic of the outcome, but still thinks it has a valid structure!

32

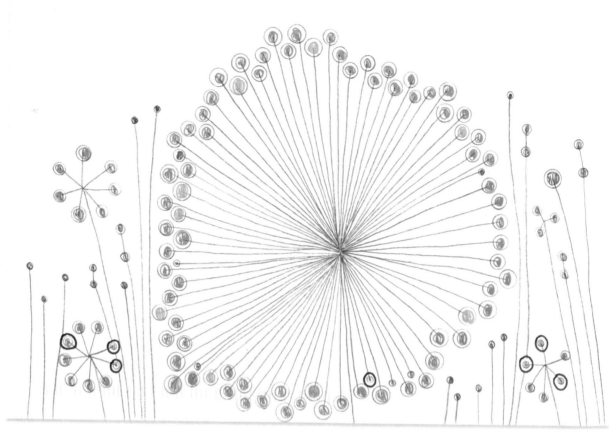

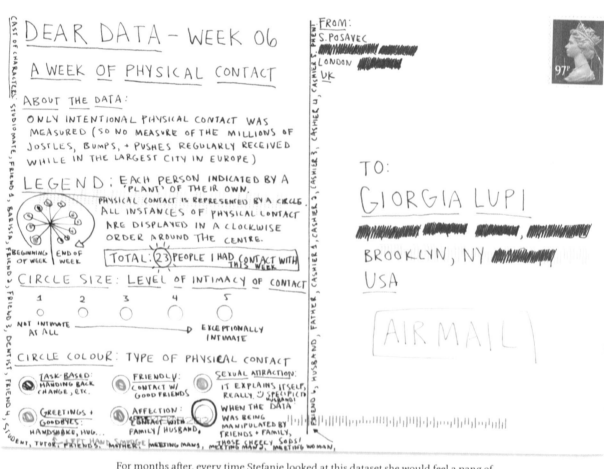

For months after, every time Stefanie looked at this dataset she would feel a pang of
homesickness, and miss her parents: a perfect example of how data can inspire emotion.

When your friends and family don't take your data collection seriously.

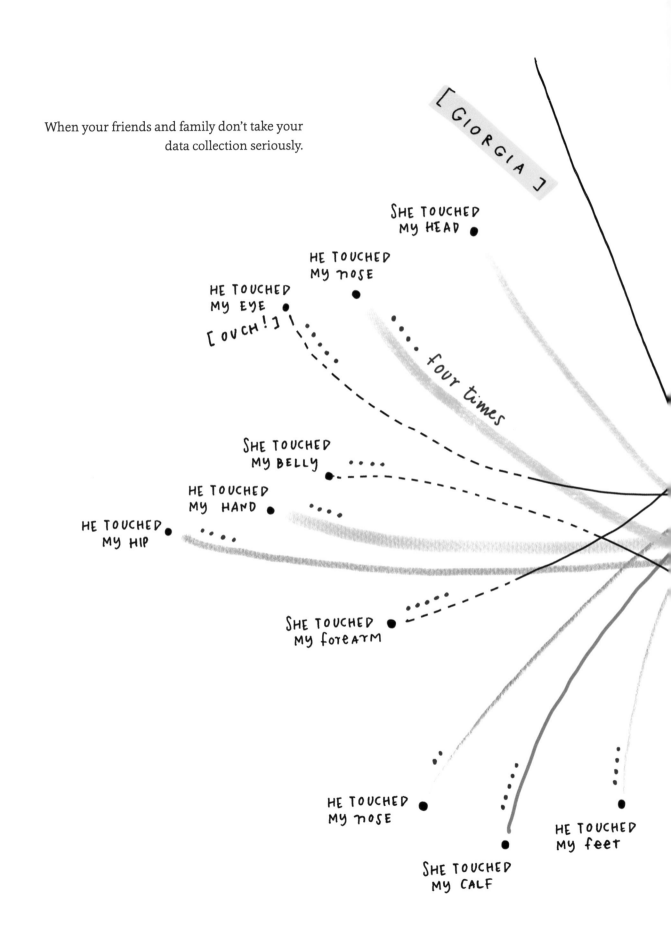

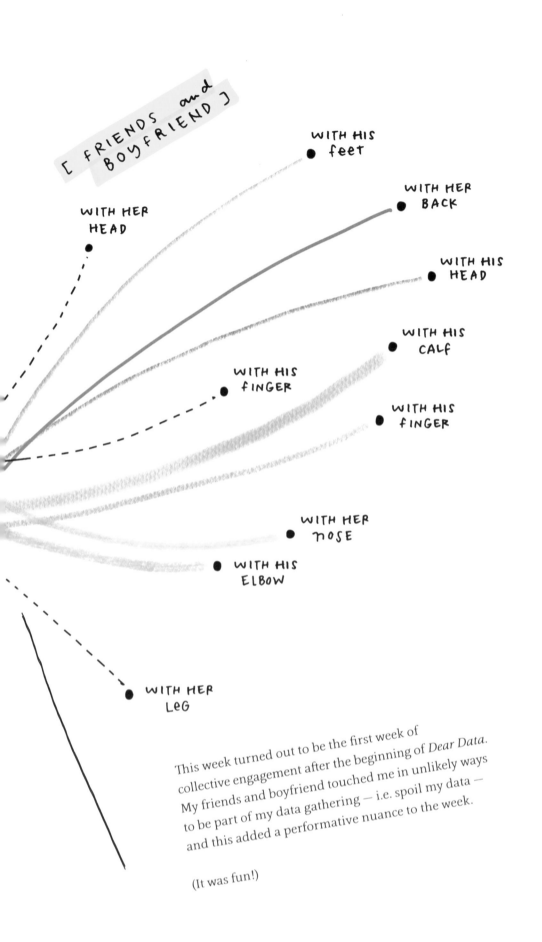

[FRIENDS and BOYFRIEND]

WITH HIS
• feet

WITH HER
• BACK

WITH HER
HEAD
•

WITH HIS
• HEAD

WITH HIS
• CALF

WITH HIS
• FINGER

WITH HIS
• FINGER

WITH HER
• nose

WITH HIS
• ELBOW

WITH HER
• LEG

This week turned out to be the first week of collective engagement after the beginning of *Dear Data*. My friends and boyfriend touched me in unlikely ways to be part of my data gathering — i.e. spoil my data — and this added a performative nuance to the week.

(It was fun!)

week seven

a week of

CQMPLAINTS

How often do we complain, what do we rant about, and how many of our complaints are unnecessary?

This week's postcards were delivered in person, as the following week, Stefanie and Giorgia hung out together in New York.

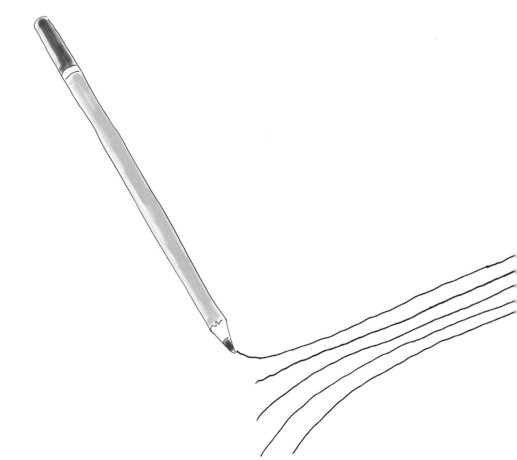

GIORGIA DRAWING THE REPETITIVE MELODIES OF HER PROTESTS

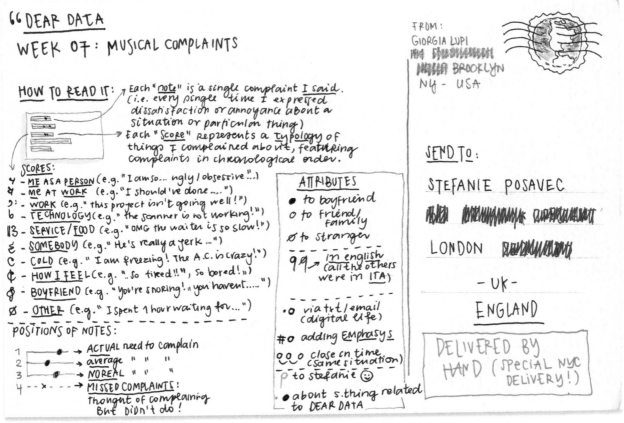

What better visual reference than a musical score to show the repetitiveness of Giorgia's protests and the "level" of complaint: whether they are justified or totally out of place.

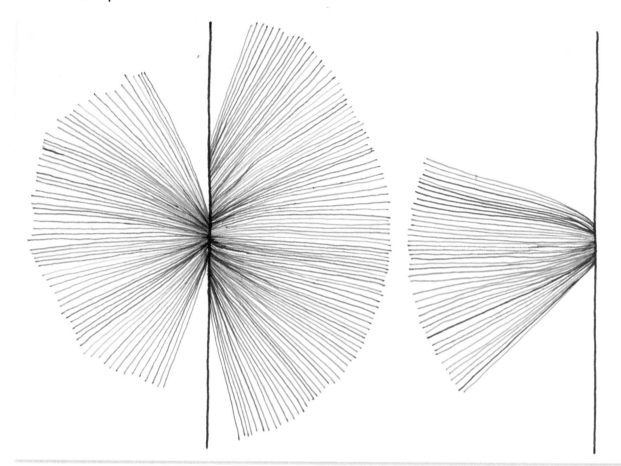

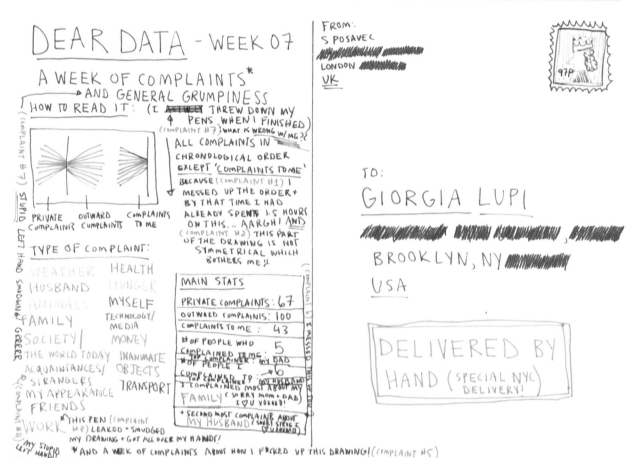

DEAR DATA - WEEK 07

A WEEK OF COMPLAINTS*
→ AND GENERAL GRUMPINESS

HOW TO READ IT: (I ~~ACTUAL~~ THREW DOWN MY
4 PENS WHEN I FINISHED)
(COMPLAINT #7) WHAT IS WRONG W/ ME??

(COMPLAINT #7) STUPID LEFT HAND SMUDGING GRRRRR

PRIVATE COMPLAINTS   OUTWARD COMPLAINTS   COMPLAINTS TO ME

ALL COMPLAINTS IN
CHRONOLOGICAL ORDER
EXCEPT 'COMPLAINTS TO ME'
BECAUSE (COMPLAINT #1) I
MESSED UP THE ORDER +
BY THAT TIME I HAD
ALREADY SPENT 1.5 HOURS
ON THIS... AARGH! AND
(COMPLAINT #2) THIS PART
OF THE DRAWING IS NOT
SYMMETRICAL WHICH
BOTHERS ME!!

TYPE OF COMPLAINT:

(COMPLAINT #3) MY STUPID LEFT HAND!!

WEATHER   HEALTH
HUSBAND   HUNGER
ANIMALS   MYSELF
FAMILY   TECHNOLOGY/
               MEDIA
SOCIETY/   MONEY
THE WORLD TODAY   INANIMATE
ACQUAINTANCES/   OBJECTS
STRANGERS   TRANSPORT
MY APPEARANCE
FRIENDS
WORK

*THIS PEN (COMPLAINT #4) LEAKED + SMUDGED
MY DRAWING + GOT ALL OVER MY HANDS!

*AND A WEEK OF COMPLAINTS ABOUT HOW I F*CKED UP THIS DRAWING! (COMPLAINT #5)

(COMPLAINT #6 I MESSED THIS)

MAIN STATS
PRIVATE COMPLAINTS:	67
OUTWARD COMPLAINTS:	100
COMPLAINTS TO ME:	43
# OF PEOPLE WHO COMPLAINED TO ME:	5
TOP COMPLAINER: MY DAD	
# OF PEOPLE I COMPLAINED TO:	6
TOP COMPLAINEE: MY HUSBAND	

I COMPLAINED MOST ABOUT MY
FAMILY (SORRY MOM + DAD)
I ♥ U XOXOX!

+ SECOND MOST COMPLAINS ABOUT
MY HUSBAND (SORRY STEVE
♥ U XOXOXO)

FROM:
S POSAVEC
~~████████████~~
LONDON ~~██████~~
UK

97P

TO:
GIORGIA LUPI
~~████████████████████████~~
BROOKLYN, NY ~~██████~~
USA

DELIVERED BY
HAND (SPECIAL NYC
DELIVERY!)

Note the hand-drawn stamps: these postcards were delivered in person in New York!

che freddo! questo posto fa vomitare! I can't stand her any more! Era colpa tua che russavi! Voglio andare via ora! Questo cab mi fa venire il vomito! che schifo questo posto! ma come potevi pensare che andasse bene? they are just crazy with the A.C.! Ho sonno! Cosa sono tutti quegli scottex in giro? Dai sistema la tua roba non la posso vedere così! No va beh ma è uno st***o! Ma come si fa a comportarsi così? Dio se odio Google-drive! It's not working again, I mean, we pay for it! THIS place is so f***ing cold! No sul serio sto morendo di freddo fai qualcosa! Ma è colpa sua se non sta funzionando! I haven't been preparing enough and It will be a disaster! NON ho niente da mettermi per il talk! NON RUSSARE!!! Smettila di RUSSARE non ce la faccio più! Non ho dormito nulla ed è tutta colpa tua! E quando pensavi di farlo? E' ancora in ritardo! I am so much not an interesting person, I can only talk about my work. It was ok but I could have done better. I wasn't at my best I could have been better. Questo posto è freddissimo voglio andare via!! che freddo! Sto congelando! Madonna ma ha dei problemi sta cameriera! Ma cosa avevi in mente, perché gli hai scritto? Non riesco a lavorare così! Non ho chiuso occhio sono stanchissima! ma dai sti Americani hanno dei problemi però eh?! He was so out of place! Questa luce fa ca***e! I don't want to go! I so much don't want to go! Non funziona la mail ancora! uffa che p***e! cioè ha servito prima loro di noi non è giusto! Si gela! Questa birra sa di verdura! che schifo c'è il cilantro, bleah! che casino adesso mi metto a urlare anche io! we've ordered 10 minutes ago and our drinks aren't here yet! Can you turn the heater up because it's really freezing in here! sono così fuori forma uffa! ti sei dimenticata ancora! ma come non è possibile che non ce l'abbiano! tira la tenda della doccia quante volte te lo devo dire! Che freddo! No va beh sto gelando! ce ne andiamo per favore? Eh ma cosa pensavi che fosse un bel locale? Il cameriere non ci c**a! yes we were here before them!

che freddo! questo posto fa vomitare! I can't stand her any more! Era colpa tua che russavi! Voglio andare via ora! Questo cab mi fa venire il vomito! che schifo questo posto! ma come potevi pensare che andasse bene? they are just crazy with the A.C.! Ho sonno! Cosa sono tutti quegli scottex in giro? Dai sistema la tua roba non la posso vedere così! No va beh ma è uno st***o! Ma come si fa a comportarsi così? Dio se odio Google-drive! It's not working again, I mean, we pay for it! THIS place is so f***ing cold! No sul serio sto morendo di freddo fai qualcosa! Ma è colpa sua se non sta funzionando! I haven't been preparing enough and It will be a disaster! NON ho niente da mettermi per il talk! NON RUSSARE!!! Smettila di russare così? Dio se odio Google-drive! It's not working again, I only talk about my work. It was ok but I could have done better. I wasn't at my best I could have been better. Questo posto è freddissimo voglio andare via!! che freddo! Sto congelando! Madonna ma ha dei problemi sta cameriera! Ma cosa avevi in mente, perché gli hai scritto? Non riesco a lavorare così! Non ho chiuso occhio sono stanchissima! ma dai sti Americani hanno dei problemi però eh?! He was so out of place! Questa luce fa ca***e! I don't want to go! I so much don't want to go! Non funziona la mail ancora! uffa che p***e! cioè ha servito prima loro di noi non è giusto! si gela! Questa birra sa di verdura! che schifo c'è il cilantro, bleah! che casino adesso mi metto a urlare anche io! we've ordered 10 minutes ago and our drinks aren't here yet! Can you turn the heater up because it's really freezing in here! sono così fuori forma uffa! ti sei dimenticata ancora! ma come non è possibile che non ce l'abbiano! tira la tenda della doccia quante volte te lo devo dire! Che freddo! No va beh sto gelando! Ce ne andiamo per favore? Eh ma cosa pensavi che fosse un bel locale? Il cameriere non ci c**a! yes we were here before them! this isn't fair! I hate technology, why it's not working?! I have no idea why but it has been off the whole day, someone should come and repair it! I have been waiting here 15 minutes! I am really tired! Sono stanchissima!! why it's always so f***ing cold in here?! I mean I am wearing my coat! I can't believe we have to do this! Gli avevo chiesto di consegnarmi i files ieri, come sempre è in ritardo! ma cosa ci vuole a tenere la luce più bassa?! La paghiamo 80 dollari all'ora e non piega nemmeno la laundry! Che freddo! Ma cosa pensavi quando gli hai scritto? Ti sei dimenticato ancora! SHE WAS 45 MINUTES LATE, AGAIN!! Non ce la faccio più la prossima volta non la chiamo, giuro! Che freddo! Non serve a niente questo networking, lo sapevo! Come te lo devo dire di non lasciare la roba in giro?! Che freddo! I won't come to this place anymore, it's freezing! La birra non sa di niente!

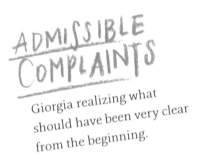

ADMISSIBLE COMPLAINTS

Giorgia realizing what should have been very clear from the beginning.

STEFANIE'S
MAIN
COMPLAINT:

A
LEAKY
PEN!

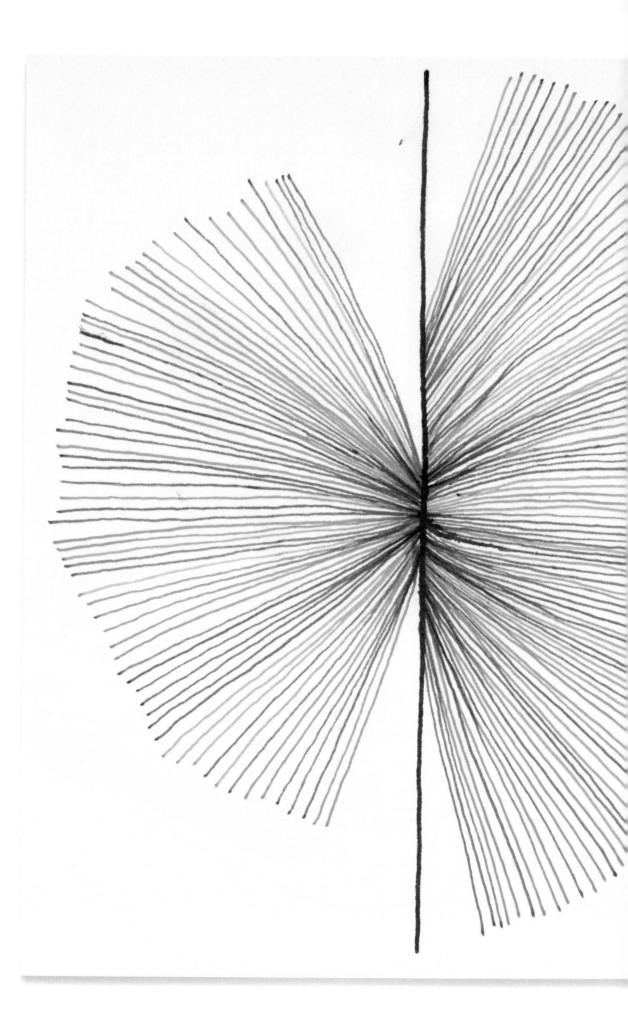

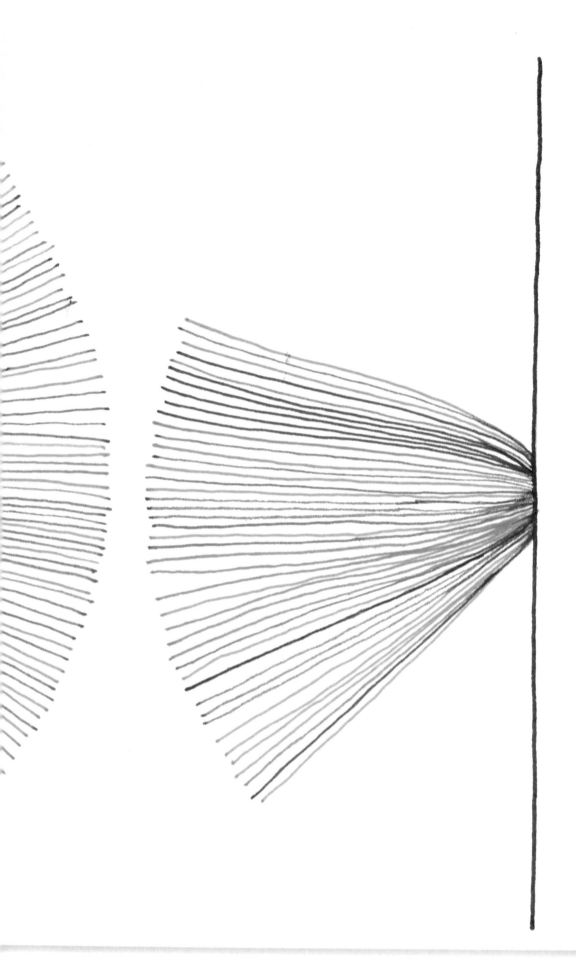

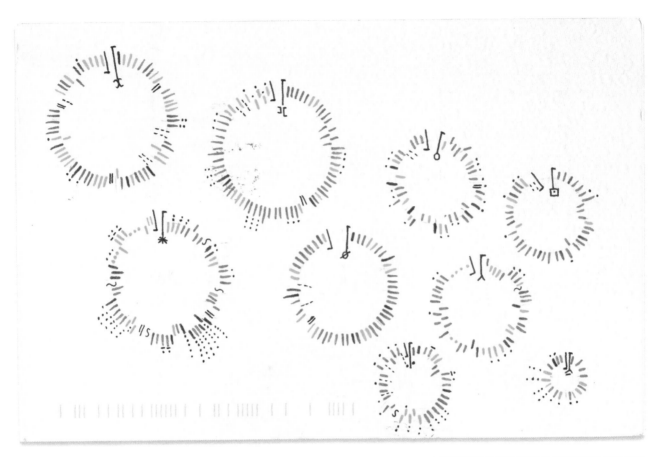

66 DEAR DATA
WEEK 08: PHONE ADDICTION!

HOW TO READ IT:

— Every circle represents a PLACE or SITUATION where I checked my phone, somehow ordered from left to right according to How many times I did it in that place.

— Every single LINE is a SINGLE TIME I interacted with my phone, ordered chronologically per each peace.

PLACES/sit.:

x while walking
* while working
JE while waiting for sthing or S.body
∅ in the Bathroom
o on the conch
⊡ on the bed
∧ other places at home
'/. café/restaurants shops....
⌒ public transportation

COLORS; the reason why I picked it:
— text/email
— social media
— other APPS
— check the time
— check the weather
— phone call
— text with somebody who was in the room
— to charge it
— text/email with YOU
• take pictures of our postcards!
··· dots = while with other people (how many)
•| = used others'phone

ATTRIBUTES:
→ outside = I picked it PURPOSELY
↪ INSIDE = Because of an alert
~ turned the phone facing the table not to see it
--- didn't picked it Because I didn't want to report
= thought it was ringing but wasn't!

NEW YORK FROM: GIORGIA LUPI BROOKLYN -NY- USA 05 NOV 2014

SEND TO:
STEFANIE POSAVEC
- UK -
ENGLAND

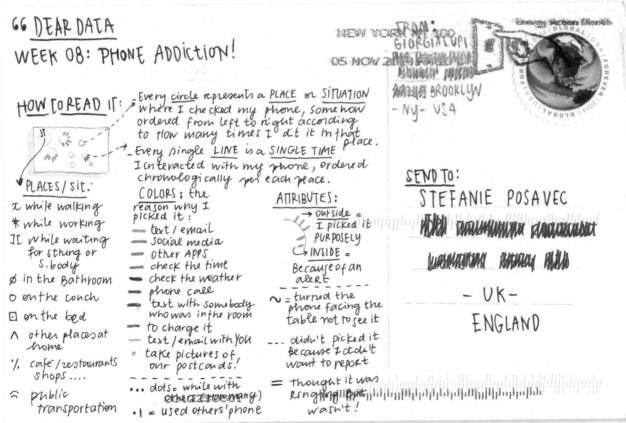

Yes, Giorgia realizes she does need to cut the cord with her phone (as do most of us). She was interested in the correlations between where she checks her phone and what she does with it, so the structure of her drawing reflects that.

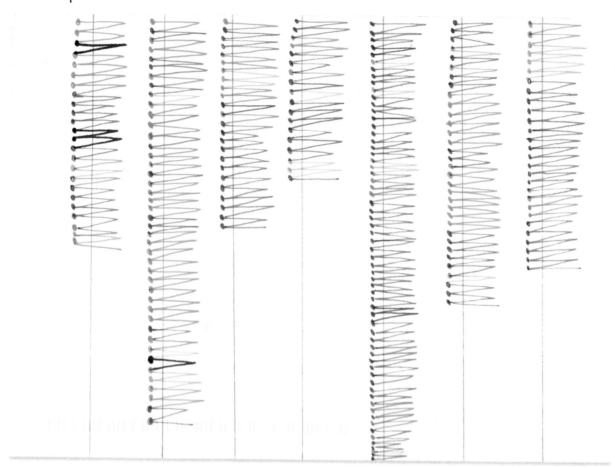

DEAR DATA - WEEK 08

A WEEK OF PHONE ADDICTION

THE DATA: I TRACKED EVERY TIME **I** PICKED UP MY PHONE IN THE FIRST INSTANCE. (MULTIPLE INTERACTIONS NOT TRACKED)

HOW TO READ IT:

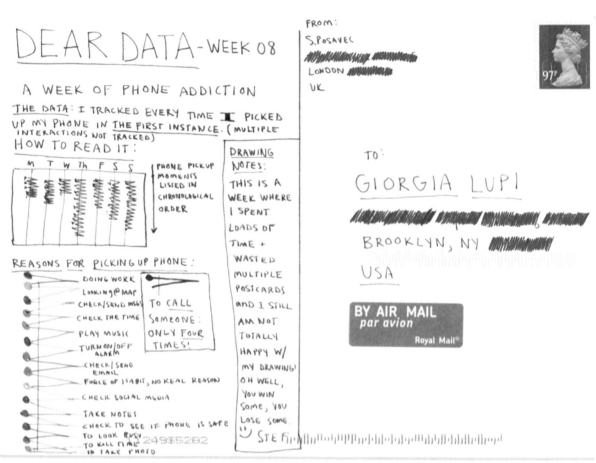

PHONE PICKUP MOMENTS LISTED IN CHRONOLOGICAL ORDER

REASONS FOR PICKING UP PHONE:
- DOING WORK
- LOOKING @ MAP
- CHECK/SEND msgs
- CHECK THE TIME
- PLAY MUSIC
- TURN ON/OFF ALARM
- CHECK/SEND EMAIL
- FORCE OF HABIT, NO REAL REASON
- CHECK SOCIAL MEDIA
- TAKE NOTES
- CHECK TO SEE IF PHONE IS SAFE
- TO LOOK BUSY
- TO KILL TIME
- TO TAKE PHOTO

TO CALL SOMEONE: ONLY FOUR TIMES!

DRAWING NOTES:

THIS IS A WEEK WHERE I SPENT LOADS OF TIME + WASTED MULTIPLE POSTCARDS AND I STILL AM NOT TOTALLY HAPPY W/ MY DRAWING! OH WELL, YOU WIN SOME, YOU LOSE SOME. ☺ STEF

FROM:
S. POSAVEC
~~████████~~
LONDON ~~████~~
UK

TO:

GIORGIA LUPI
~~████████████████████████~~
BROOKLYN, NY ~~████~~
USA

BY AIR MAIL
par avion
Royal Mail®

On Tuesday and Saturday Stefanie was mostly airborne and listening to music, as can be seen in her data drawing.

WEEK NINE

A WEEK OF

Giorgia & Stefanie

This week Stefanie had the opportunity to travel to North America for work: a perfect excuse to visit New York City, and also meet Giorgia in person for the third time ever.

NEW YORK

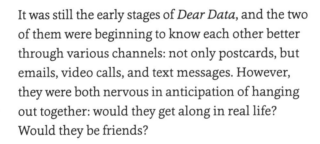

It was still the early stages of *Dear Data*, and the two of them were beginning to know each other better through various channels: not only postcards, but emails, video calls, and text messages. However, they were both nervous in anticipation of hanging out together: would they get along in real life? Would they be friends?

To commemorate this in-person meeting, Giorgia suggested they spend the week tracking all their interactions with each other, ranging from digital interactions to the times they spent time together in person.

I hope we'll like hanging out with each other...

STEFANIE'S THOUGHTS DURING
HER FLIGHT ACROSS THE ATLANTIC

LONDON

I'm excited to
meet Giorgia for
the THIRD time!

Ok NOW I'm
starting to become
a little nervous...

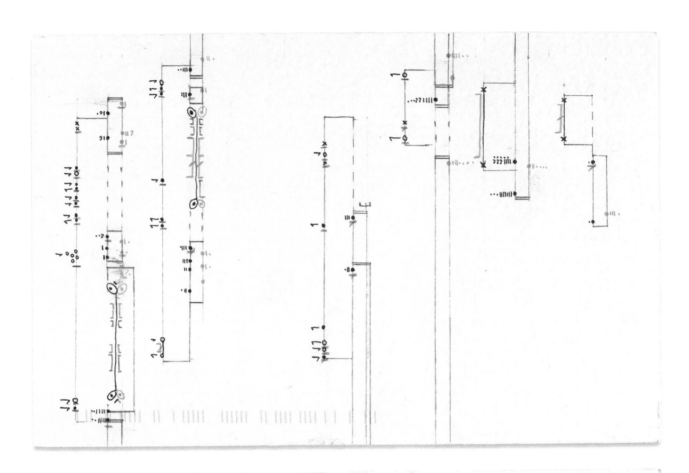

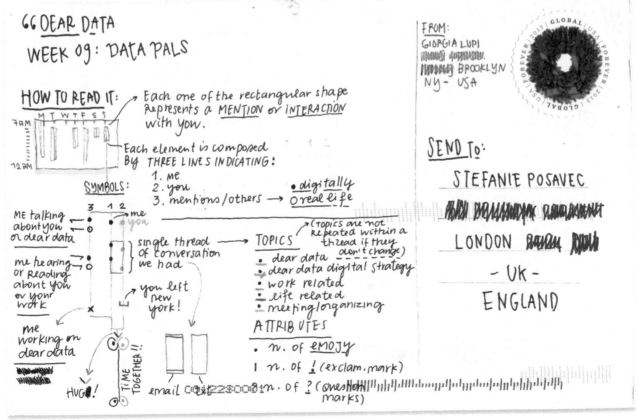

Giorgia's card ended up as a weird technical drawing. She still believes it has some insights, even if it is a little hard to read.

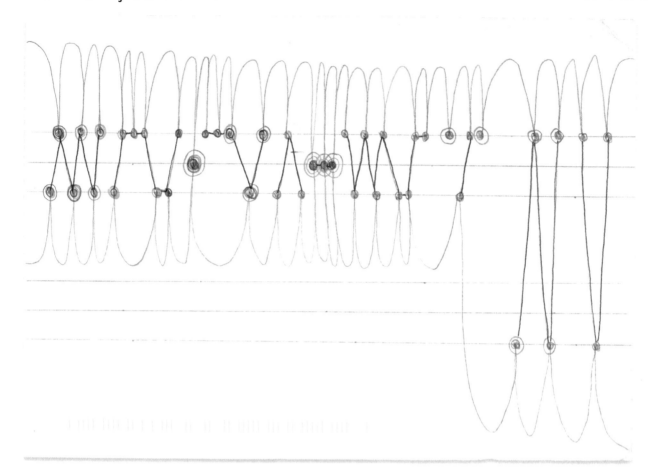

DEAR DATA — WEEK 09

A WEEK OF ~~THE~~ INTERACTION : NYC!!

THE DATA: TAKEN MAINLY FROM PHONE/EMAIL RECORDS + MEMORY (NOTE: WHILE INTERACTIONS ARE IN CHRONOLOGICAL ORDER THERE MAY BE INACCURACIES DUE TO CLOCKS CHANGING IN AUTUMN + INTERNATIONAL TRAVEL CAUSING ISSUES W PHONE CLOCK)

FROM:
SPOSAVEC
~~████████~~
~~████████~~
LONDON ~~████~~
UK

97p

HOW TO READ IT:

M ——————→ F

NYC
LDN

INTERACTION SYMBOLS ARE PLACED ON LINES REPRESENTING LOCATION OF GIORGIA OR STEF AT THAT TIME.
GIORGIA COMMUNICATING
— ELECTRONICALLY IN NYC OR LDN
— IN PERSON IN RESPECTIVE CITIES
— STEFANIE COMMUNICATING ELECTRONICALLY FROM NYC/LDN

TO:
GIORGIA LUPI
~~████████████ ████████████ ████~~
BROOKLYN, NY ~~████████~~
USA

— EACH PERSON'S INTERACTIONS ARE CONNECTED BY ARCHED PENCIL LINE.

— INTERACTIONS FROM SAME EMAIL/MSG 'CHAIN' ARE LINKED

TYPE OF INTERACTION

○ TEXT ◎ EMAIL ◉ IN PERSON!

REASON FOR INTERACTION

● DEAR DATA   ● TEXT/COMMS PROBLEMS
● ~~DRINKING~~   ● WALKING ON BRIDGE
● PLANNING TO MEET UP   ● STEF SPEAKING!

↑ DETAIL

BY AIR MAIL
par avion
Royal Mail®

"Stef speaking": Stefanie was talking about her work as a designer in the workspace that Giorgia works in.

we have been writing with Data

In our correspondence, we didn't speak English or Italian — we spoke Data.

DEAR STEFANIE,

GIORGIA

week TeN

a week of

to-do lists

For this week, Giorgia and Stefanie tracked their
to-do lists, their ways of addressing their tasks,
and how much they *really* got done by the end
of the week.

Analysing the way each of them organizes their
lists tells us a lot about her personality and her
way of planning her time.

GIORGIA'S WEEK

MONDAY

DONE!

REPHRASED

HANDED TO
SOMEONE ELSE

LOWERED
IN PRIORITY

MOVED TO
A DIFFERENT LIST

TUESDAY

ERASED
THE
TASK

WEDNESDAY

RE WROTE
MY TASKS
ON PAPER

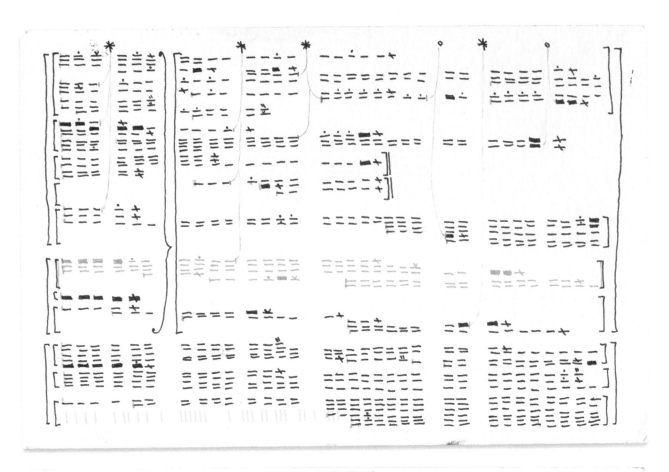

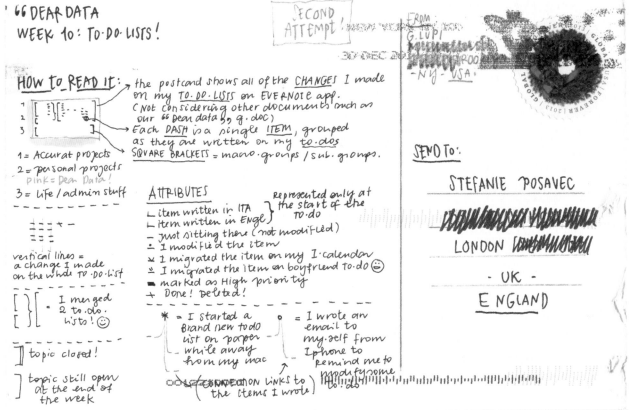

With her drawing Giorgia wanted to show Stefanie how many times she modifies items on her lists without actually doing them, and how many tasks are sitting there for ever, without any action. Argh!

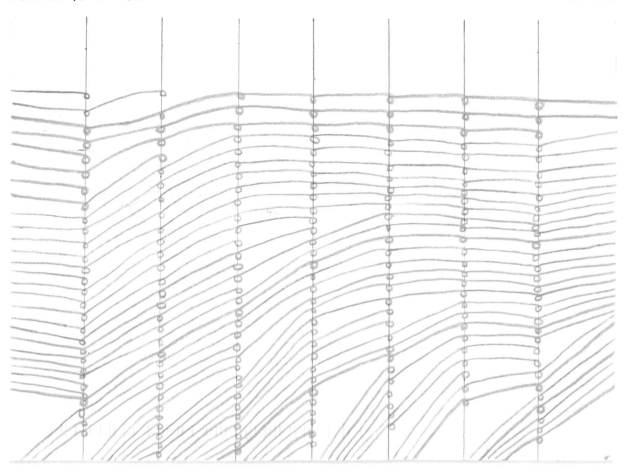

DEAR DATA — WEEK 10

A WEEK OF TO-DOs

(OR: A TO-DO LIST <u>NEVER</u> <u>DIES</u>.)

<u>THE DATA</u>: ALL CONTENTS OF MY TO-DO NOTEBOOK FOR 7 DAYS.

<u>HOW TO READ IT</u>:

KEY STATS: 61 ITEMS ON LIST / ONLY 33 COMPLETED !! (OOPS)

- ALL THINGS-TO-DO IN CHRONOLOGICAL ORDER (AS THEY WERE WRITTEN IN MY NOTEBOOK)

- THINGS-TO-DO LINES LOOP AROUND EACH DAY LINE UNTIL THE TASK IS COMPLETED, THEN IT STOPS. IF THE TASK WASN'T COMPLETED IT CONTINUES OFF THE RIGHT-HAND SIDE OF THE PAGE.

<u>COLOURS</u>

— DEAR DATA TASKS: OOPS, SORRY FOR NOT DOING ALL OF THESE GIORGIA!

— COMMUNICATION / EMAILS TO WRITE

— PERSONAL / HOUSE-BASED ADMIN

— WISHFUL THINKING (EX: get tickets for a GALLERY, etc.)

— THINGS TO DO FOR FRIENDS

— THINGS TO DO FOR WORK

FROM:
S. POSAVEC
~~xxxxxxxx~~
LONDON
~~xxxxxxxx~~

97P

TO:

GIORGIA LUPI
~~xxxxxxxxxxxx~~
BROOKLYN, NY ~~xxxxx~~
USA

AIRMAIL

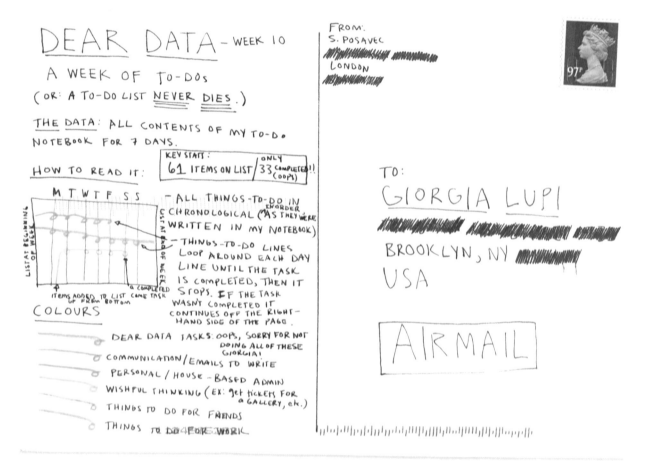

After this week of data-gathering, Stefanie realized that her to-do list never decreases, but always achieves a sort of stasis: in short, she may as well stop worrying about getting everything done, because the list will never, ever die.

EVERYONE SECRETLY STORES DATA

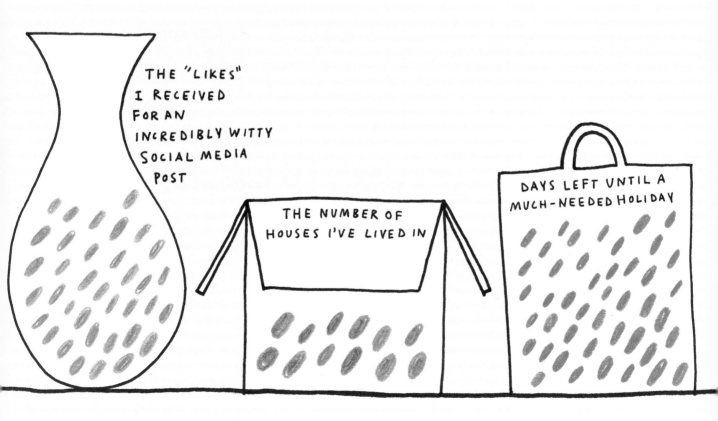

(EVEN IF THEY DON'T ADMIT TO IT)

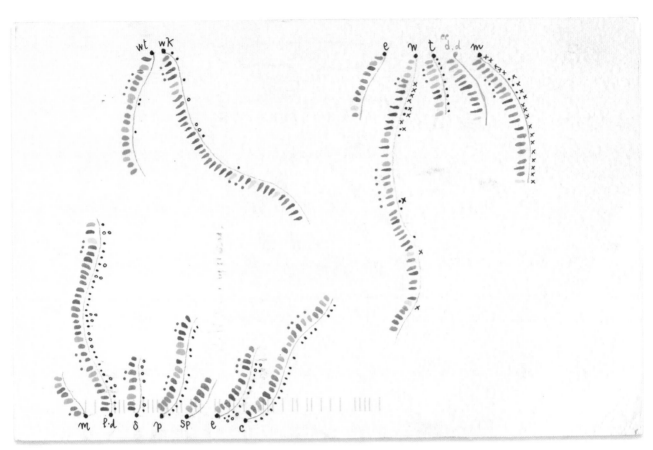

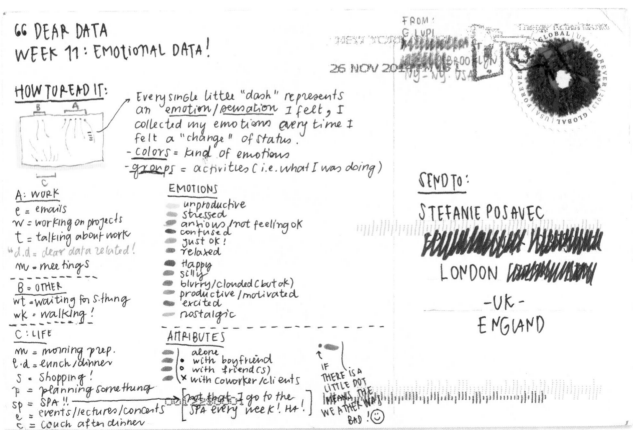

66 DEAR DATA
WEEK 11: EMOTIONAL DATA!

HOW TO READ IT:

Every single little "dash" represents an emotion/sensation I felt, I collected my emotions every time I felt a "change" of status.
- COLORS = kind of emotions
- groups = activities (i.e. what I was doing)

A: WORK
e = emails
w = working on projects
t = talking about work
d.d = dear data related!
m = meetings

B: OTHER
wt = waiting for s.thing
wk = walking!

C: LIFE
m = morning prep.
l.d = lunch/dinner
S = shopping!
p = planning something
sp = SPA !!
e = events/lectures/concerts
c = couch after dinner

EMOTIONS
unproductive
stressed
anxious/not feeling ok
confused
just ok!
relaxed
happy
silly
blurry/clouded (but ok)
productive/motivated
excited
nostalgic

ATTRIBUTES
· alone
· with boyfriend
○ with friend(s)
× with coworker/clients

[not that I go to the SPA every week! H4!]

IF THERE IS A LITTLE DOT MEANS THE WEATHER WAS BAD! ☺

FROM:
G. LUPI
... St
BROOKLYN
NY - NY. USA
26 NOV 2014

SEND TO:
STEFANIE POSAVEC
LONDON
- UK -
ENGLAND

By adding contextual details, such as if the weather was nice, or what she was doing at the time,
Giorgia was able to add interesting correlations to her "emotions" collection.

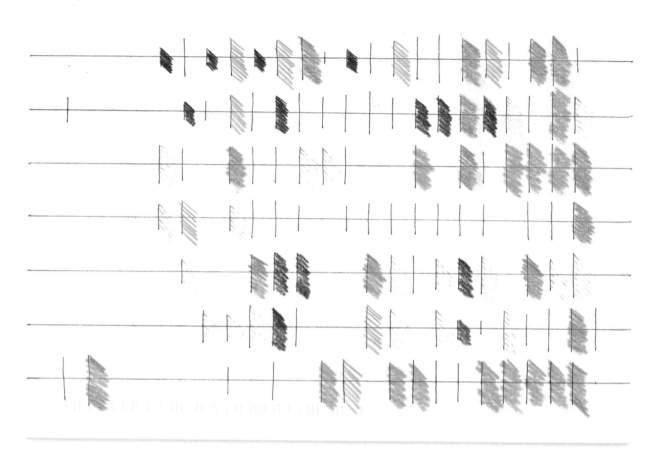

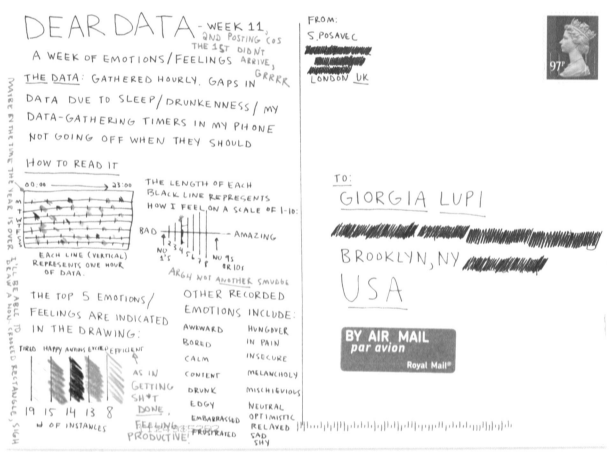

DEAR DATA - WEEK 11, 2ND POSTING COS THE 1ST DIDNT ARRIVE, GRRRR

A WEEK OF EMOTIONS / FEELINGS

THE DATA: GATHERED HOURLY. GAPS IN DATA DUE TO SLEEP/DRUNKENNESS / MY DATA-GATHERING TIMERS IN MY PHONE NOT GOING OFF WHEN THEY SHOULD

HOW TO READ IT

00:00 ——————→ 23:00

EACH LINE (VERTICAL) REPRESENTS ONE HOUR OF DATA.

THE LENGTH OF EACH BLACK LINE REPRESENTS HOW I FEEL ON A SCALE OF 1-10:

BAD ————————— AMAZING
1 2 3 4 5 6 7 8
NO 1'S   NO 9S OR 10S

ARGH NOT ANOTHER SMUDGE

THE TOP 5 EMOTIONS / FEELINGS ARE INDICATED IN THE DRAWING:

TIRED HAPPY ANXIOUS EXCITED EFFICIENT
19   15   14   13   8
OF INSTANCES

EFFICIENT AS IN GETTING SH*T DONE. FEELING PRODUCTIVE!

OTHER RECORDED EMOTIONS INCLUDE:

AWKWARD   HUNGOVER
BORED   IN PAIN
CALM   INSECURE
CONTENT   MELANCHOLY
DRUNK   MISCHIEVIOUS
EDGY   NEUTRAL
EMBARRASSED   OPTIMISTIC
FRUSTRATED   RELAXED
               SAD
               SHY

MAYBE BY THE TIME THE YEAR IS OVER I'LL BE ABLE TO DRAW A NON-CROSSED RECTANGLE, SIGH

FROM:
S. POSAVEC
~~███████████~~
~~███████████~~
LONDON UK

97ᴾ

TO:
GIORGIA LUPI
~~████████████████~~
BROOKLYN, NY ~~████~~
USA

BY AIR MAIL
par avion
Royal Mail®

A busy work-week for Stefanie, hence how tired she was. She was at a house party on Saturday (note the late hours on Sunday morning). On Sunday evening she spent a few happy hours with old friends from her hometown.

DATA CAN MAKE US MORE HUMAN

THIS IS me, me AND me ONLY.

THIS IS ME,
ME AND ME
ONLY.

and HELP CONNECT WITH
OURSELVES and
OTHERS at a
DEEPER LEVEL

week Twelve

a week of

people

How much time do we spend alone during a week, and how much with people we know? How many times are we surrounded by complete strangers?

For this week Giorgia and Stefanie captured how many people were in their vicinity every hour on the hour: since they both live in big cities, they wanted to find a way of recording the moments where they are surrounded by strangers.

GIORGIA TRACKING HER ENCOUNTERS IN NEW YORK REALIZING SHE COULDN'T ADD ANY DETAILS :-

1.
– WOMAN
– 20/30 y.o.
– WEARING A NICE BLUE DRESS
– PRETTY!
– 37TH Str. and 1St. AVENUE

2.
– WOMAN
– 20/25 y.o.
– WEARING a STRIPED DRESS

3.
– WOMAN
– 15/20 y.o.
– yellow DRESS

4.
– MAN

5.
– MAN

6.
– MAN

7.
– WOMAN

8.
– WOMAN

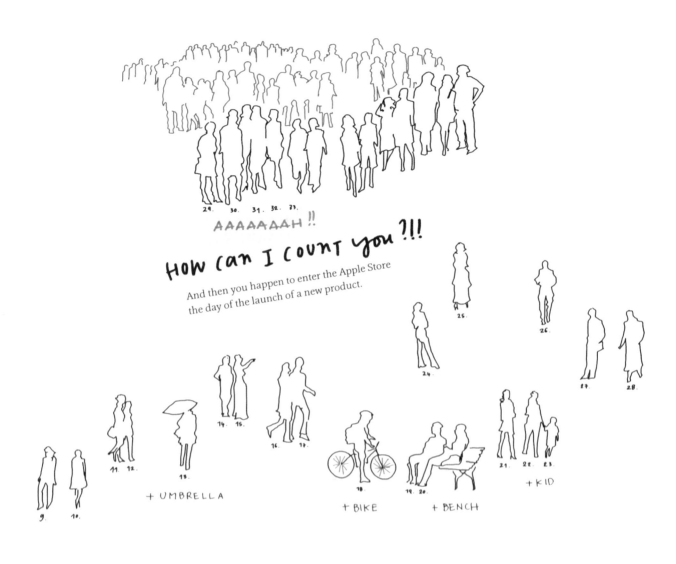

AAAAAAAH !!

HOW can I count you ?!!

And then you happen to enter the Apple Store
the day of the launch of a new product.

+ UMBRELLA

+ BIKE

+ BENCH

+ KID

66 DEAR DATA

WEEK 12 : HOW MANY PEOPLE?

HOW TO READ IT : I collected data every HOUR for every day
of the week.
→ every little line is a person I was
able to see in the moment of the
data collection. The dot [·] indicates
I was alone.

{ } curly Brackets = Beginning and End of the day

[ ] Square brackets = each collection moment.

[→→ people ABOVE the line = I knew them !
[→→ people BELOW the line = I didn't know them !

COLORS = people take the
color of the activity / situation
I was in :
||| home
||| walking
||| working
||| hanging out
||| lunch /dinner out
||| public place (store ...)   OO1220OO1 ☺
||| working on Dear Data !

ATTRIBUTES
¦→ boyfriend
¦→ person I know for sure
      is Italian
¦→ person YOU know !
Featuring Nick Felton,
Jer Thorpe, Marius Watz,
Jen Lowe , Sha Hwang

FROM :
GIORGIA LUPI
O4 DEC
BROOKLYN
NY- USA

SEND TO:
STEFANIE POSAVEC

LONDON

- UK -

ENGLAND

It's nice to see what state the postcards get to their destination in ... Sometimes they are perfect,
while others they are scuffed, crumpled, cut, and this time even watered.

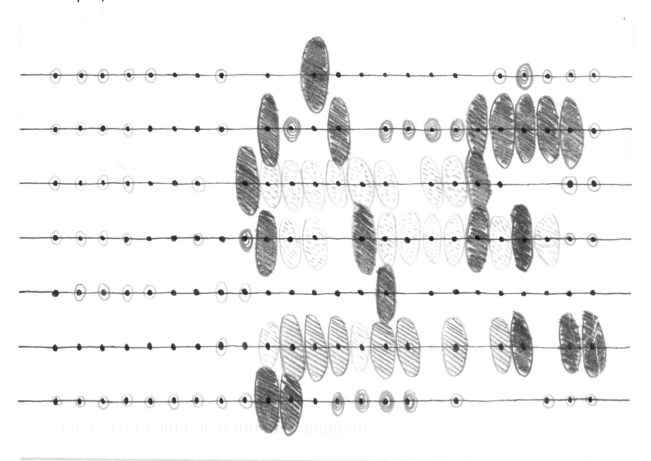

DEAR DATA – WEEK 12

A WEEK OF PEOPLE

THE DATA: I TRACKED THE NUMBER OF
PEOPLE IN MY VICINITY (SO THE # OF PEOPLE
IN THE ROOM I WAS IN, OR THE # OF PEOPLE
IN ANY ENCLOSED SPACE) THIS WAS HARD TO
GATHER, HENCE ME RESORTING TO REPRESENTING
THE DATA THROUGH USING BANDING. NOTE: SOME
DATA IS MISSING DUE TO MY HAPHAZARD DATA
                                                        GATHERING!
HOW TO READ IT: (NOT MUCH SLEEP THIS WEEK)

BLACK DOTS EACH REPRESENT
AN HOUR WHERE THERE IS DATA.

NUMBER OF PEOPLE IN MY SPACE/VICINITY:

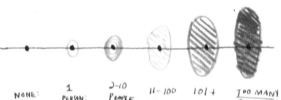

NONE: 1   2-10   11-100   101+   TOO MANY
JUST   PERSON: PEOPLE   TO COUNT
ME   (GENERALLY   (ON STREET,
        MY HUSBAND!)   PUBLIC TRANSPORT, ETC.)

FROM:
S. POSAVEC
LONDON
UK

TO:
GIORGIA LUPI

BROOKLYN, NY
USA

BY AIR MAIL
par avion
Royal Mail®

Wednesday and Thursday, Stefanie was teaching a two-day workshop in a small room, and on Friday she was
speaking in front of a crowd of people . . . both of which are seen in the drawing's patterns.

PERFECT
POSTCARD!

GIORGIA IS
SO PROUD!

posted: Dec 1st,
NEW YORK

THE NON-LINEAR MYSTERIOUS JOURNEY OF OUR CARDS ACROSS THE ATLANTIC.

This is the point at which we realized our postcards live lives of their own, and we have a third party collaborating in *Dear Data*: the Postal Service of two countries.

Our cards carry not only a visual representation of our weeks, but also one of their travels across the ocean.

TO: STEFANIE POSAVEC

ROYAL MAIL

TO: STEFANIE POSAVEC

TO: STEFANIE POSAVEC

WAIT, WASN'T IT THE ATLANTIC?

RECEIVED: JAN 2ND, LONDON

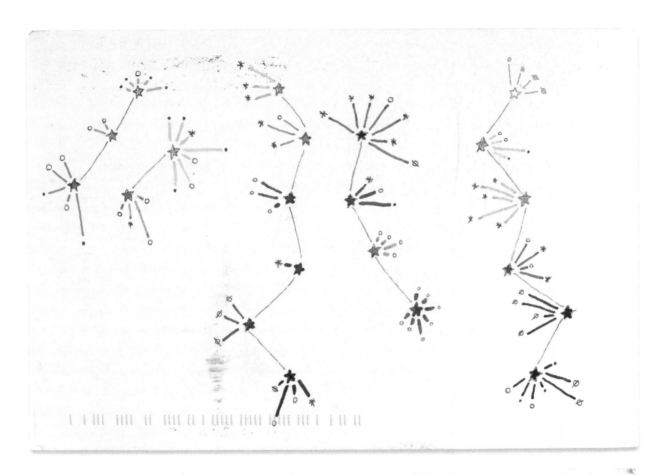

66 DEAR DATA

WEEK 13: I WISH I......

HOW TO READ IT:
- every "constellation" is a group of desires I felt during the week.
- every STAR (color) is a specific type of desire
- every LINE is THE desire I felt.

1. Food and beverages
a = food
- chocholate!
- sweets!
- I'm Hungry!
b = beverages
- coffee
- Beer! Drink!

2. life, general
a = physical
- eaten less, I'm exploding!
- feel more relaxed
- sleep!
- Being different
- Having all figured out
- other
b. external
- weather related
- escape from a situation
- Be Home already
- Be there (a place) already

3. work
- Dear Data related
- feel more productive
- work less!
- be less anxious
- knowing it will be ok!
- Other work related

ATTRIBUTES
line length = How much do I need it?
- not really
- nice to have!
- I need it!!
- So badly!!

SYMBOLS =
Did I get it?
- yes! Right away!
○ yes but later
✳ not at all ☹
ø still don't know if it'll come true!

FROM: TRIBOROUGH/NY/P1 BKLYN-QNS-S ... BROOKLYN -NY- USA

SEND TO:
STEFANIE POSAVEC
LONDON
-UK-
ENGLAND

Giorgia feels that desires are projections of a present we'd like to change, in the near or far future, so she drew constellations: dots that the viewer sees as aligned only from a specific point of view.

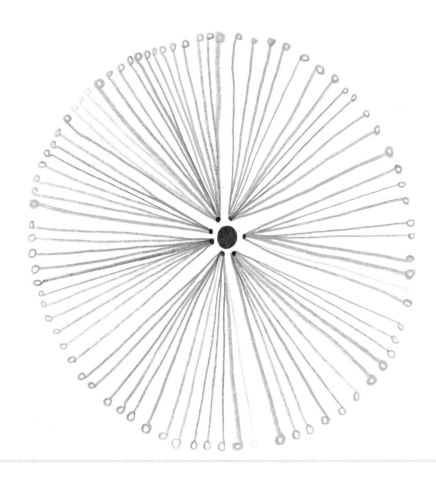

DEAR DATA - WEEK 13

A WEEK OF DESIRES*

OR: A WEEK OF HOW SELF-CENTRED I AM, HA!

THE DATA: I TRACKED WHENEVER
I FELT I REALLY DESIRED/WANTED
SOMETHING. TRIED TO BE AS HONEST
AS POSSIBLE.*

*THOUGH I'VE FOUND WAYS OF OBSCURING SOME
NEEDS/DESIRES... A DATA VIS IS NEVER
NEUTRAL, RIGHT? I LIKE A BIT OF MYSTERY...

HOW TO READ IT:

EACH DESIRE IS REPRESENTED
BY A COLOURED LINE. DESIRES
ARE DIVIDED INTO DAYS, AND
ARE ORGANISED IN
CHRONOLOGICAL ORDER.

DESIRES:*

APPEARANCE - RELATED:
TO LOOK BETTER, ETC.

FOOD/DRINK : COFFEE
ALCOHOL,
DINNER,...

WORK - RELATED:
TO COME UP W/IDEA,
BE A BETTER DESIGNER

CLEANER AIR FOR THE WORLD/
NEW CLOTHING: NEW
COAT, SCARF, CARDIGAN

HAPPINESS FOR ALL

BASIC HUMAN NEEDS:
SEX / EXERCISE / SLEEP /
NEEDING THE BATHROOM... I
WILL LEAVE IT TO
EVERYONE ELSE TO GUESS!"

BUS DESIRES: I ALWAYS
WANT MY BUS TO TURN UP!

CONFIDENCE

DESIRES RELATING TO
FRIENDS

DESIRE RELATING TO
HUSBAND

WORLD PEACE

ENDING HUNGER   I ACCEPT THIS LIST IS NOT ENTIRELY ACCURATE.

BY AIR MAIL
par avion
Royal Mail®

"Basic human needs": intentionally obscured to save Stefanie some embarrassment. Look closely, because
some of her desires in the legend aren't found in the actual drawing...

STEFANIE'S LEGEND TAMPERING*

ORIGINAL

*in the hopes Giorgia won't look too closely

TYPES OF DESIRES

 Self-centred desires and wants

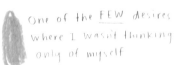 One of the <u>FEW</u> desires where I wasn't thinking only of myself

 FAKE worldly and noble desires that will hopefully make me seem like less of an awful person

week fourteen
a week of
"SCHEDULES."

At week fourteen Giorgia and Stefanie decided to
observe how they spent their time, focusing on their
schedule and thus mapping their (productive!)
activities, even though they interpreted the week's
theme differently.

Giorgia collected every single work *task* she performed during the week: emails sent, video calls,
meetings, problems she solved, talks delivered,
projects reviewed, and so much more, to give Stefanie
an idea of her days at work. While Stefanie tracked
everything she *did* — for every waking hour.

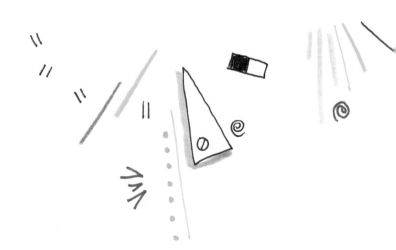

GIORGIA REPRESENTING HER CHAOTIC DAYS

"The positioning and rotation of the elements are an absolutely random and direct function of the aesthetic composition I want to create."

(AND TAKING SOME ARTISTIC FREEDOM FOR ONCE)

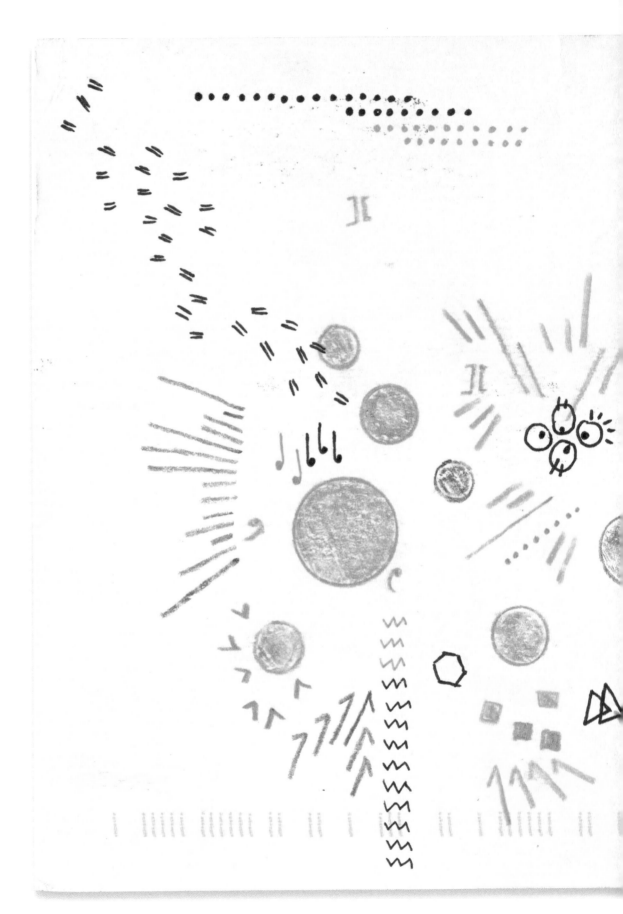

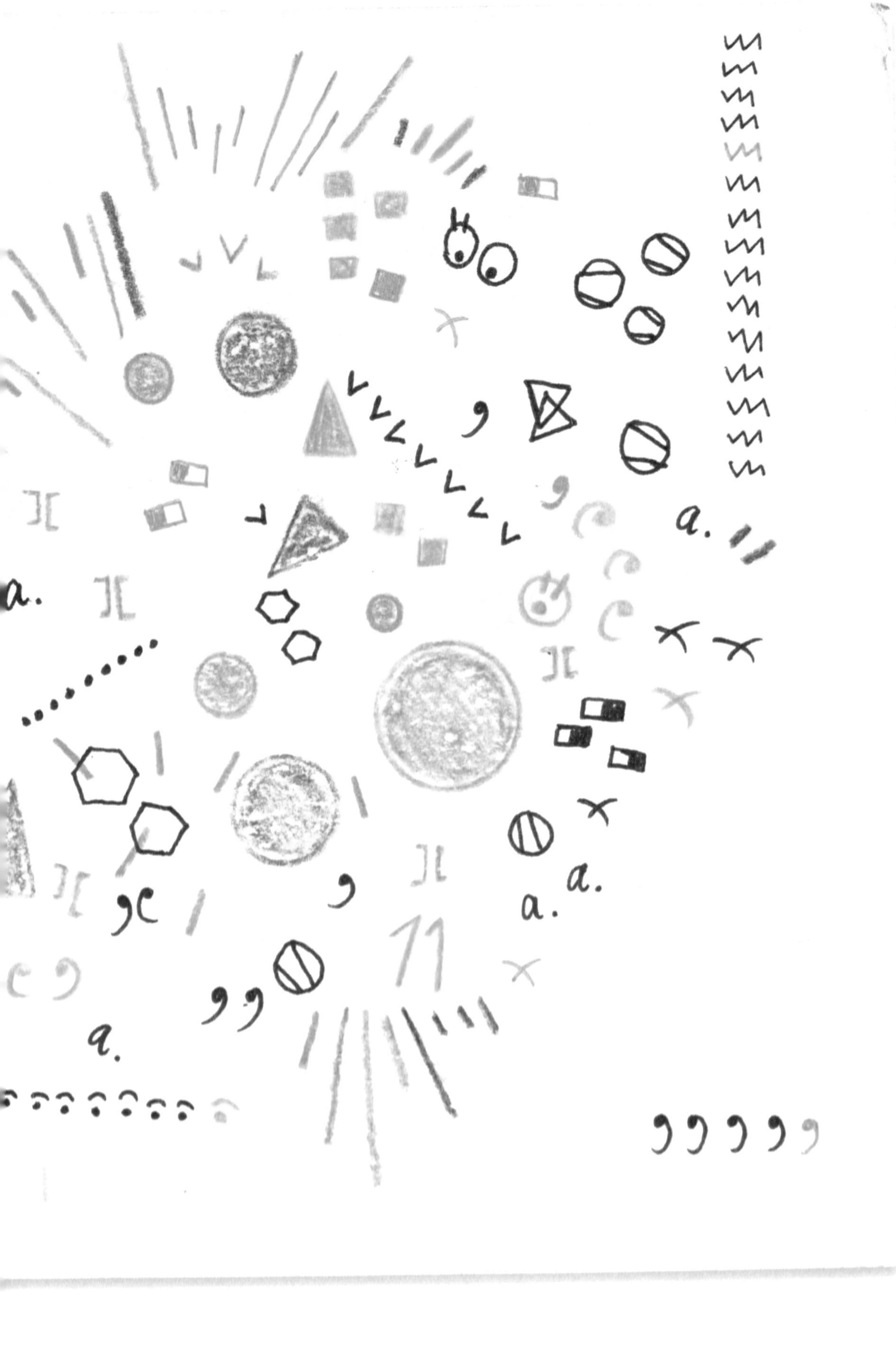

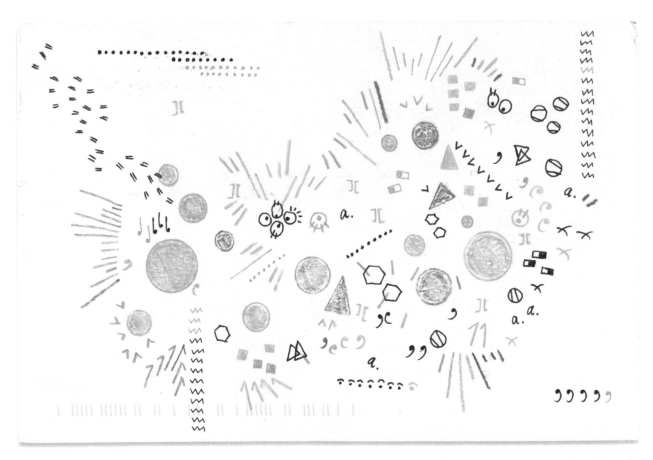

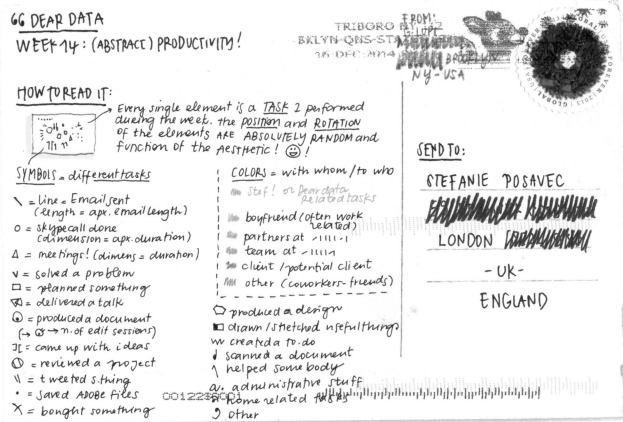

Giorgia has always been fascinated by abstract art, and she used it as her main reference: she mixed pens, pencils and markers and plain shapes with more unconventional ones, to compose a futuristic poster of her week of work tasks.

DEAR DATA - WEEK 14

<u>A WEEK OF SCHEDULES:</u>
HOW I SPENT MY TIME

<u>THE DATA:</u> I TRACKED AS MUCH OF MY
SCHEDULE AS I COULD, DOWN TO THE
MINUTE. IT'S AS COMPLETE OF A PICTURE
AS POSSIBLE (SOME HOURS ARE MISSING, OH WELL)

<u>HOW TO READ IT:</u>

[EACH LINE] ON THE 'HEAD' OF THE
'PLANT' REPRESENTS 20 MINUTES
(DATA ROUNDED UP/DOWN ACCORDINGLY)
[EACH PLANT] REPRESENTS ONE
WAY I SPEND MY TIME.

<u>WAYS I SPENT MY TIME</u> (RECORDED IN HOURS + MINS.)

SLEEPING   50:31   PERSONAL MAINTENANCE   8:31
                         (SHOWER, MAKEUP, CHANGE)
WORKING   INTERNET/EMAIL WORK + PERSONAL 8:00
(projects, meetings) 27:03
                         CONSUMING TRAD. MEDIA   7:00
                         (FILM, TV, PAPER)
TRAVELLING TO   16:12   SHOPPING (GROCERIES - CLOTHES) 5:37
GET SOMEWHERE   CLEANING/TIDYING HOUSE   2:47
(BUS, train, walking)   ATTENDING LIVE PERFORMANCE   1:49
                         SPENDING TIME W/   1:44
DRINKING/EATING 13:21
  SOCIALLY   TENDING TO FINANCES   0:52   & TRYING TO OFFER MY HUSBAND SOME DATA PRIVACY HERE :)
PREPARING/EATING MEAL 12:51   SOMETHING GIORGIA-RELATED! 0:47 YOU WILL SEE SOON...

FROM:
S POSAVEC
LONDON
UK

97

TO:
GIORGIA LUPI
BROOKLYN, NY
USA

BY AIR MAIL
par avion
Royal Mail®

Stefanie sent Giorgia a present ("something Giorgia-related") for being so hospitable while she was visiting her in New York.

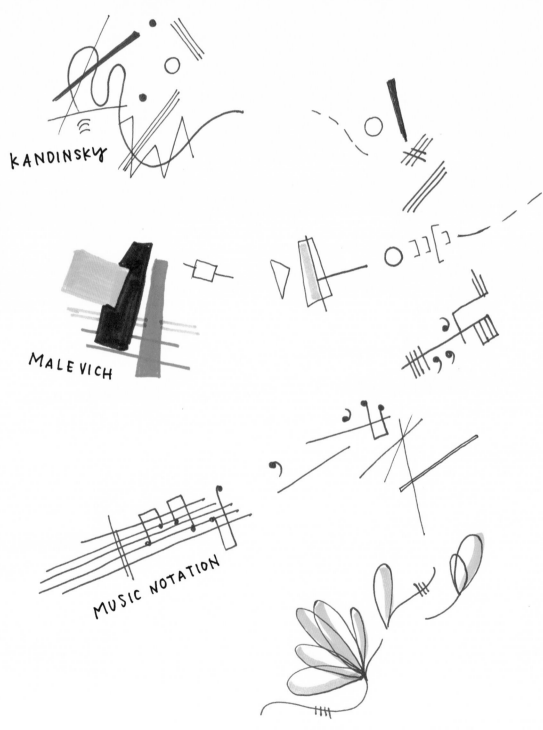

KANDINSKY

MALEVICH

MUSIC NOTATION

OBJECTS IN THE WORLD

TO LEARN TO DESIGN
YOU HAVE TO
LEARN HOW
TO SLEEP

WEEK FIFTEEN

A WEEK OF

Compliments

Hands on hearts, Stefanie and Giorgia aren't vain, they promise! However, this week, they decided to investigate more closely the compliments that came their way (and also gave in return), so as to appreciate and savour the kind words and thoughts that their friends and family had given them.

A BOUQUET OF
COMPLIMENTS
GIVEN TO STEFANIE

83

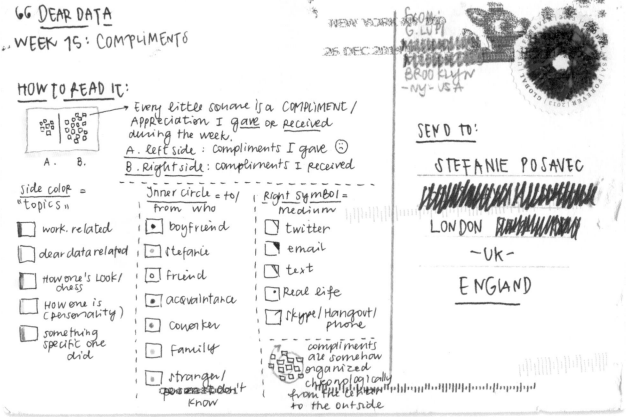

66 DEAR DATA

WEEK 15: COMPLIMENTS

HOW TO READ IT:

→ Every little square is a COMPLIMENT /
Appreciation I gave or received
during the week.
A. left side: compliments I gave ☺
B. Right side: compliments I received

A.   B.

side color =
"topics"

☐ work. related

☐ dear data related

☐ How one's Look/
dress

☐ How one is
(personality)

☐ something
specific one
did

Inner circle = to/
from who

☐ boyfriend

☐ stefanie

☐ friend

☐ acquaintance

☐ coworker

☐ family

☐ stranger/
person I don't
know

Right symbol =
medium

☐ twitter

☐ email

☐ text

☐ Real life

☐ skype/Hangout/
phone

compliments
are somehow
organized
chronologically
from the center
to the outside

NEW YORK NY 100   FROM:
                   G. LUPI
25 DEC 2014   ▨▨▨▨▨▨
                   ▨▨▨▨▨▨
                   BROOKLYN
                   -NY- USA

SEND TO:

STEFANIE POSAVEC

▨▨▨▨▨▨▨▨▨▨▨▨▨

LONDON ▨▨▨▨▨▨▨

-UK-

ENGLAND

Giorgia's drawing reflects her negligence. She divided the space into two separate parts: the compliments she gave and
the ones she received: tiny symbols and lots of white space for the ones she *should* have said.

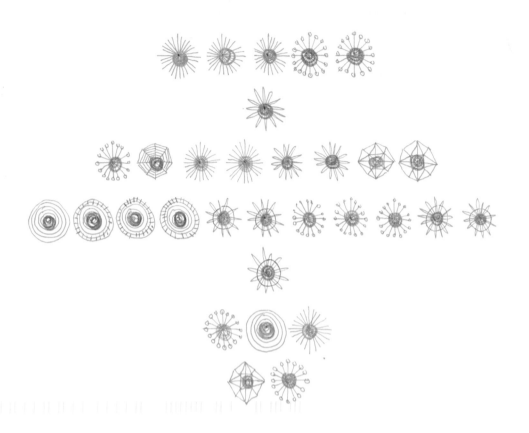

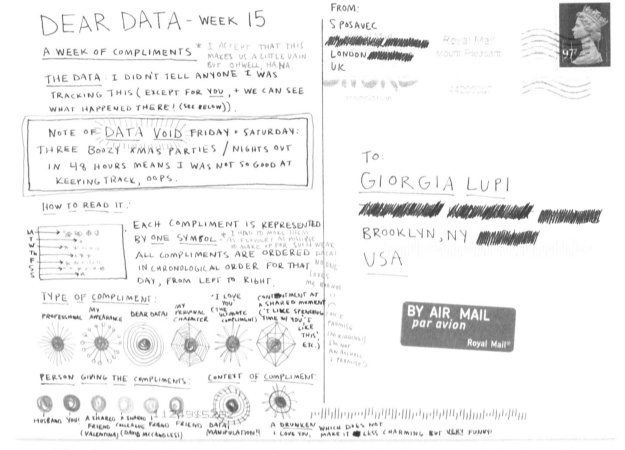

DEAR DATA - WEEK 15

A WEEK OF COMPLIMENTS   * I ACCEPT THAT THIS MAKES US A LITTLE VAIN BUT OH WELL, HA HA.

THE DATA: I DIDN'T TELL ANYONE I WAS TRACKING THIS (EXCEPT FOR YOU , + WE CAN SEE WHAT HAPPENED THERE ! (SEE BELOW)).

NOTE OF DATA VOID FRIDAY + SATURDAY: THREE BOOZY XMAS PARTIES / NIGHTS OUT IN 48 HOURS MEANS I WAS NOT SO GOOD AT KEEPING TRACK, OOPS.

HOW TO READ IT:

EACH COMPLIMENT IS REPRESENTED BY ONE SYMBOL * I HAD TO MAKE THEM AS FLOWERY AS POSSIBLE TO MAKE UP FOR SUCH WEAK DATA!
ALL COMPLIMENTS ARE ORDERED IN CHRONOLOGICAL ORDER FOR THAT DAY, FROM LEFT TO RIGHT.
NO ONE LOVES ME BOO HOO !!

TYPE OF COMPLIMENT:

PROFESSIONAL   MY APPEARANCE   DEAR DATA!   MY PERSONAL CHARACTER   'I LOVE YOU' (THE ULTIMATE COMPLIMENT)   COMPLIMENT AT A SHARED MOMENT ('I LIKE SPENDING TIME W/ YOU' 'I LIKE THIS' ETC.)   (OK I PROMISE I'M KIDDING!) I'M NOT AN ALCOHOLIC I PROMISE!)

PERSON GIVING THE COMPLIMENTS: CONTEXT OF COMPLIMENT:

HUSBAND YOU! A SHARED FRIEND (VALENTINA) A SHARED COLLEAGUE FRIEND (DAVID MCCANDLESS) FRIEND   DATA MANIPULATION!!   A DRUNKEN 'I LOVE YOU', WHICH DOES NOT MAKE IT ANY LESS CHARMING BUT VERY FUNNY!

FROM:
S POSAVEC
LONDON
UK

Royal Mail
Mount Pleasant

TO:
GIORGIA LUPI

BROOKLYN, NY

USA

BY AIR MAIL
par avion
Royal Mail®

Stefanie drew each compliment in an elaborate, flowery style to indicate how they are as appreciated (and potentially sometimes as superficial a sentiment) as a bouquet of flowers.

SMALL DATA
IS THE NEW
BIG DATA

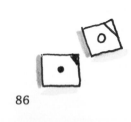

THE VERY
FEW COMPLIMENTS
I MADE
THIS WEEK.

week sixteen
a week of
our CLOSETS

GIORGIA,
IN THE U.K.
WE USE
WARDROBES!

This week Giorgia and Stefanie decided to take an "archaeological" approach to getting to know each other. Just once in the week they would analyze their closets (or wardrobes!) and categorize and quantify them.

They wanted to see beyond tracking activities and into how their personalities are expressed.

Giorgia walked to her closet with many questions:

NEVER WORN

WHAT DO I ACTUALLY WEAR?

WHAT AM I ASHAMED TO OWN?

WHAT SHOULD I GET RID OF?

HOW MANY DRESSESS OF THE SAME TYPE?

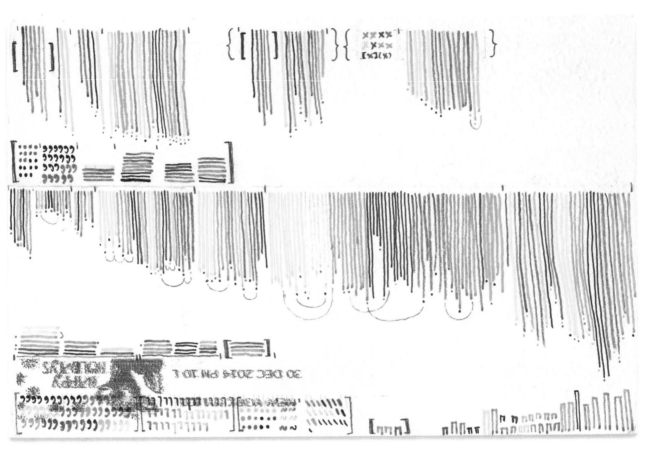

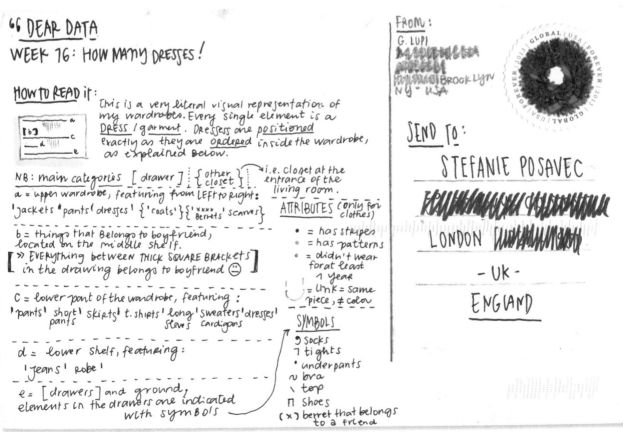

66 DEAR DATA
WEEK 16: HOW MANY DRESSES!

HOW TO READ it:

This is a very literal visual representation of my wardrobe. Every single element is a DRESS / garment. Dresses are positioned exactly as they are ordered inside the wardrobe, as explained below.

NB: main categories [drawer] { other closet } i.e. closet at the entrance of the living room.

a = upper wardrobe, featuring from LEFT to right:
'jackets' 'pants' 'dresses' { 'coats' } { 'xxxx berrets' 'scarves' }

b = things that Belongs to boyfriend, located on the middle shelf.
[» EVERYTHING between THICK SQUARE BRACKETS in the drawing belongs to boyfriend ☹]

c = lower part of the wardrobe, featuring :
'pants' 'short pants' 'skirts' 't.shirts' 'long sleeves' 'sweaters cardigans' 'dresses'

d = lower shelf, featuring:
'jeans' 'robe'

e = [drawers] and ground, elements in the drawers are indicated with symbols

ATTRIBUTES (only for clothes)

- • = has stripes
- • = has patterns
- • = didn't wear for at least 1 year
- ⌣ = link = same piece, ≠ color

SYMBOLS
- 9 socks
- 7 tights
- • underpants
- ∿ bra
- \ top
- ⊓ shoes
- (×) berret that belongs to a friend

FROM :
G. LUPI
~~█████████~~
~~█████████~~
~~████~~ BROOKLYN
NY - USA

GLOBAL | USA FOREVER 2013

SEND TO:

STEFANIE POSAVEC
~~█████████████~~
LONDON ~~█████████~~
- UK -
ENGLAND

Since everything in her closet is well ordered, colour coded and folded according to *her* rules, Giorgia pushed this point and literally represented it visually, to show Stefanie how obsessive she is.

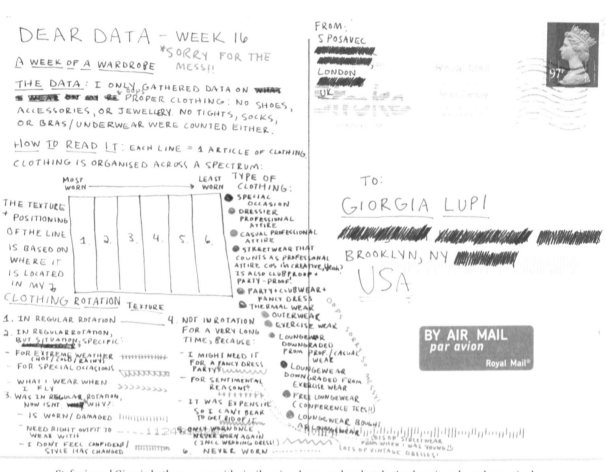

DEAR DATA - WEEK 16
*SORRY FOR THE MESS!!
A WEEK OF A WARDROBE

THE DATA: I ONLY GATHERED DATA ON ~~WHAT I WEAR ON MY FEET~~ PROPER CLOTHING: NO SHOES, ACCESSORIES, OR JEWELLERY. NO TIGHTS, SOCKS, OR BRAS/UNDERWEAR WERE COUNTED EITHER.

HOW TO READ IT: EACH LINE = 1 ARTICLE OF CLOTHING.
CLOTHING IS ORGANISED ACROSS A SPECTRUM:

THE TEXTURE + POSITIONING OF THE LINE IS BASED ON WHERE IT IS LOCATED IN MY CLOTHING ROTATION

MOST WORN ———→ LEAST WORN

| 1. | 2. | 3. | 4. | 5. | 6. |

TEXTURE

TYPE OF CLOTHING:
● SPECIAL OCCASION
● DRESSIER PROFESSIONAL ATTIRE
● CASUAL PROFESSIONAL ATTIRE
● STREETWEAR THAT COUNTS AS PROFESSIONAL ATTIRE COS I'M CREATIVE, YEAH? IS ALSO CLUBPROOF + PARTY-PROOF!
● PARTY + CLUBWEAR + FANCY DRESS
● THERMAL WEAR
● OUTERWEAR
● EXERCISE WEAR
● LOUNGEWEAR DOWNGRADED FROM PROF./CASUAL WEAR
● LOUNGEWEAR DOWNGRADED FROM EXERCISE WEAR
● FREE LOUNGEWEAR (CONFERENCE TEES!!)
● LOUNGEWEAR BOUGHT AS LOUNGEWEAR

1. IN REGULAR ROTATION ———————
2. IN REGULAR ROTATION, BUT SITUATION-SPECIFIC:
- FOR EXTREME WEATHER (HOT/COLD/RAIN) +++++++++
- FOR SPECIAL OCCASIONS ∪∪∪∪∪∪∪∪
- WHAT I WEAR WHEN I FLY >>>>>>>>>>
3. WAS IN REGULAR ROTATION, NOW ISN'T ~~WHY?~~ WHY?:
  - IS WORN/DAMAGED |||||||||||||||
  - NEED RIGHT OUTFIT TO WEAR WITH - - - - - -
  - I DON'T FEEL CONFIDENT/ STYLE HAS CHANGED +++++++++

4. NOT IN ROTATION FOR A VERY LONG TIME, BECAUSE:
- I MIGHT NEED IT FOR A FANCY DRESS PARTY ++++++++++
- FOR SENTIMENTAL REASONS +++++++++
- IT WAS EXPENSIVE SO I CAN'T BEAR TO GET RID OF IT

5. ~~ONLY WORN ONCE~~ NEVER WORN AGAIN (INCL WEDDING DRESS!) ∿∿∿∿∿

6. NEVER WORN ....

LOTS OF STREETWEAR FROM WHEN I WAS YOUNG!!
LOTS OF VINTAGE DRESSES!

FROM:
S POSAVEC
LONDON
UK

TO:
GIORGIA LUPI
BROOKLYN, NY
USA

BY AIR MAIL
par avion
Royal Mail®

Stefanie and Giorgia both came up with similar visual approaches, but that's where it ends: embarrassingly, all Stefanie's clothing during this survey was crammed into a filing cabinet!

GIORGIA'S CLOTHES

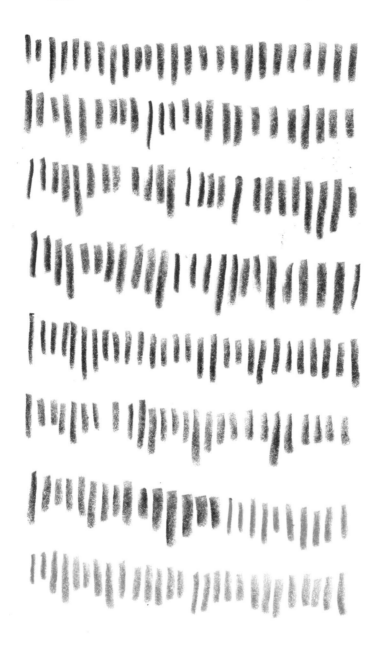

| = WHAT I ACTUALLY WEAR

Once I had drawn my postcard, I walked back to my
closet with a throwaway bag. When I was finished
I had four bags full of clothes I haven't worn for the
past year. Hooray to *Dear Data*!

BOYFRIEND'S CLOTHES

| = WHAT HE ACTUALLY WEARS

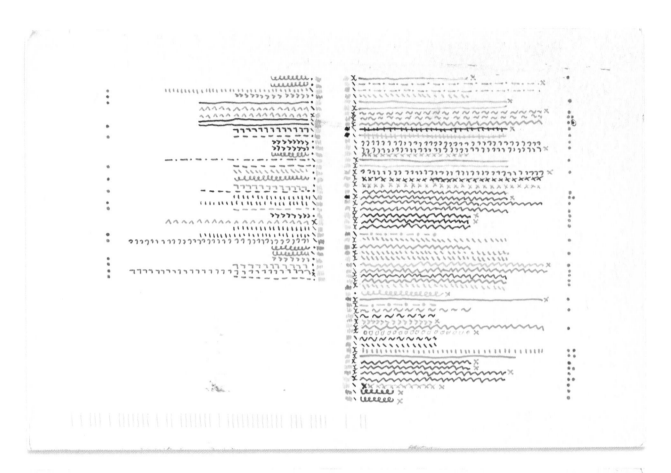

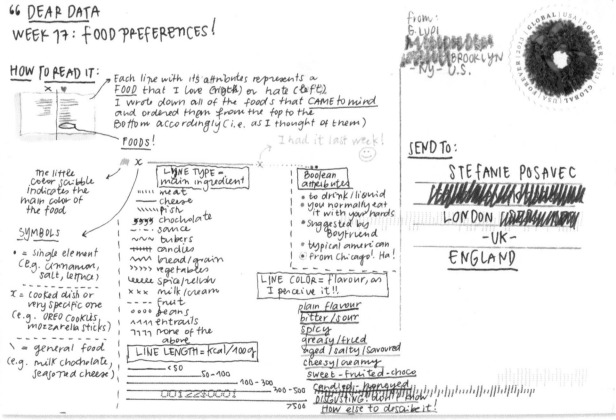

Giorgia calls herself a selective (picky) eater. She always eats the same things and dislikes many types of food, so she played with it in her postcard. She also kept things a little mysterious and made it in to a guessing game for Stefanie.

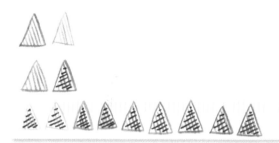

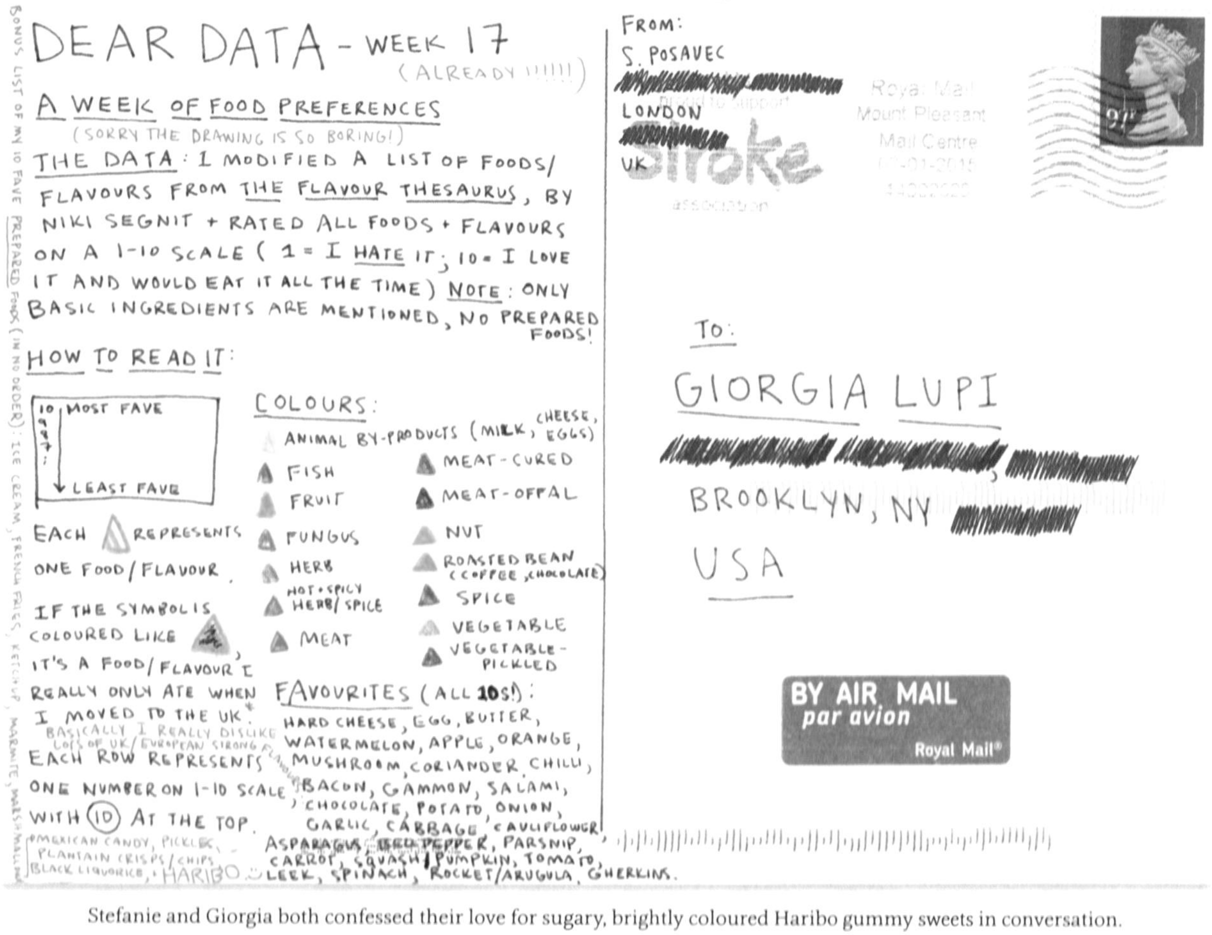

DEAR DATA - WEEK 17

DEAR DATA - WEEK 17
(ALREADY !!!!!!)

A WEEK OF FOOD PREFERENCES
(SORRY THE DRAWING IS SO BORING!)

THE DATA: I MODIFIED A LIST OF FOODS/
FLAVOURS FROM THE FLAVOUR THESAURUS, BY
NIKI SEGNIT + RATED ALL FOODS + FLAVOURS
ON A 1-10 SCALE (1 = I HATE IT; 10 = I LOVE
IT AND WOULD EAT IT ALL THE TIME) NOTE: ONLY
BASIC INGREDIENTS ARE MENTIONED, NO PREPARED
FOODS!

HOW TO READ IT:

FAVOURITES (ALL 10s!):
HARD CHEESE, EGG, BUTTER,
WATERMELON, APPLE, ORANGE,
MUSHROOM, CORIANDER, CHILLI,
BACON, GAMMON, SALAMI,
CHOCOLATE, POTATO, ONION,
GARLIC, CABBAGE, CAULIFLOWER,
ASPARAGUS, BELL PEPPER, PARSNIP,
CARROT, SQUASH, PUMPKIN, TOMATO,
LEEK, SPINACH, ROCKET/ARUGULA, GHERKINS.

(left margin, rotated):
BONUS LIST OF MY 10 FAVE PREPARED FOODS (IN NO ORDER): ICE CREAM, FRENCH FRIES, KETCHUP, MARMITE, MAYO, MALT, AMERICAN CANDY, PICKLES, PLANTAIN CRISPS/CHIPS, BLACK LIQUORICE, HARIBO.

(center notes):
EACH ▲ REPRESENTS
ONE FOOD/FLAVOUR.

IF THE SYMBOL IS
COLOURED LIKE ▲,
IT'S A FOOD/FLAVOUR I
REALLY ONLY ATE WHEN
I MOVED TO THE UK.
BASICALLY I REALLY DISLIKE
LOTS OF UK/EUROPEAN STRONG

EACH ROW REPRESENTS
ONE NUMBER ON 1-10 SCALE,
WITH ⑩ AT THE TOP.

COLOURS:
▲ ANIMAL BY-PRODUCTS (MILK, CHEESE, EGGS)
▲ FISH   ▲ MEAT-CURED
▲ FRUIT   ▲ MEAT-OFFAL
▲ FUNGUS   ▲ NUT
▲ HERB   ▲ ROASTED BEAN (COFFEE, CHOCOLATE)
▲ HOT + SPICY HERB/SPICE   ▲ SPICE
▲ MEAT   ▲ VEGETABLE
                ▲ VEGETABLE-PICKLED

FROM:
S. POSAVEC
LONDON
UK

Royal Mail
Mount Pleasant
Mail Centre

TO:

GIORGIA LUPI

BROOKLYN, NY

USA

BY AIR MAIL
par avion
Royal Mail®

Stefanie and Giorgia both confessed their love for sugary, brightly coloured Haribo gummy sweets in conversation.

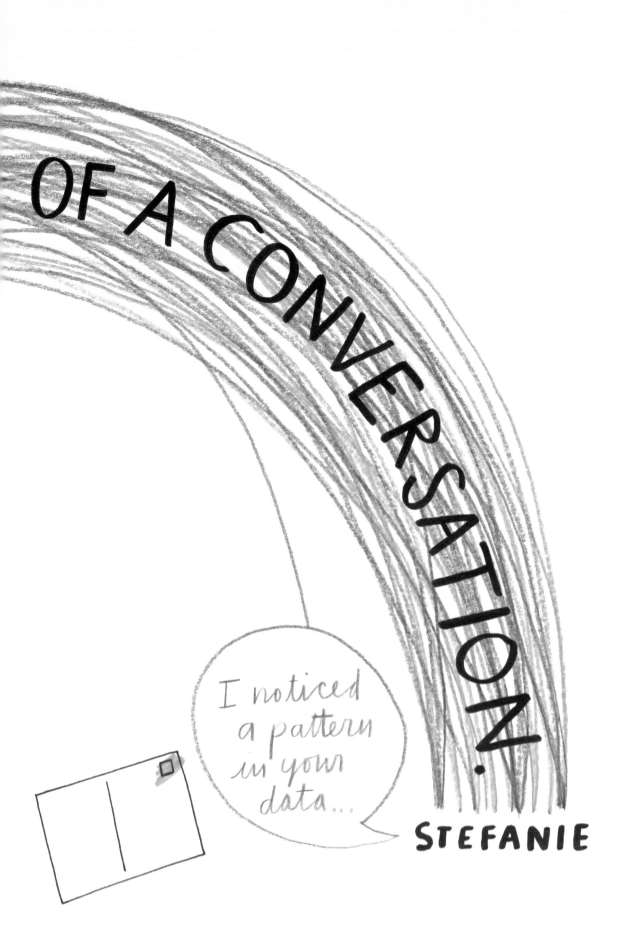

OF A CONVERSATION.

STEFANIE

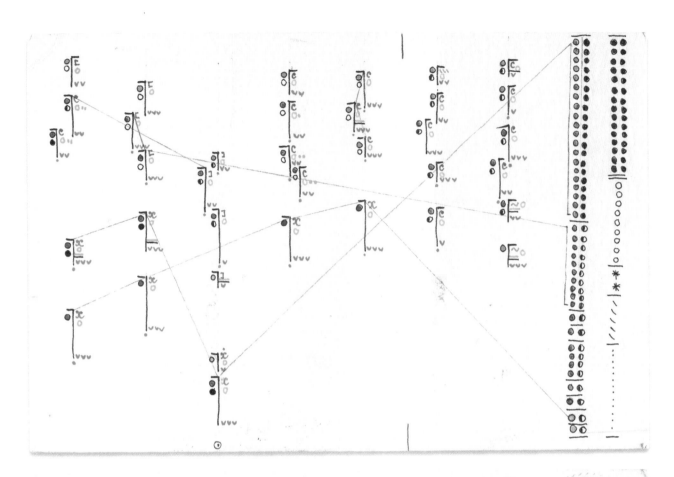

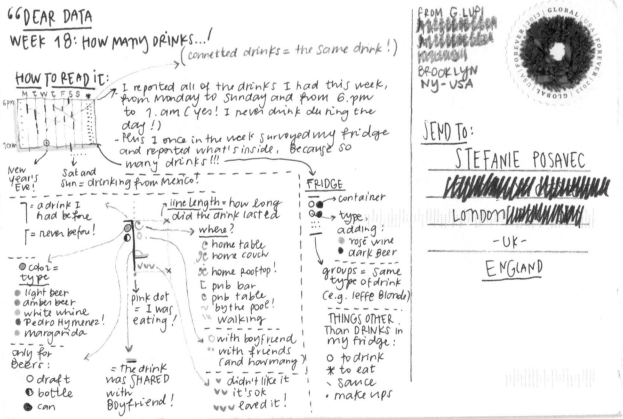

"DEAR DATA
WEEK 18: HOW MANY DRINKS...!
→ (connected drinks = the same drink!)

HOW TO READ IT:

- I reported all of the drinks I had this week, from monday to sunday and from 6.pm to 7.am (yes! I never drink during the day!)
- Plus I once in the week surveyed my fridge and reported what's inside, because so many drinks!!!

New year's Eve!

Sat and Sun = drinking from Mexico!

⌐ = a drink I had before
⌐ = never before!

● color = type
● light beer
● amber beer
○ white wine
● Pedro Hymenez!
● margarida

only for Beers:
○ draft
◐ bottle
● can

pink dot = I was eating!

= the drink was SHARED with Boyfriend!

line length = how long did the drink lasted
where?
C home table
X home couch
X home rooftop!
⊏ pnb bar
C pnb table
~ by the pool!
walking

○ with boyfriend
•• with friends (and how many)

v didn't like it
vv it's ok
vvv loved it!

FRIDGE
● container
● type,
adding:
● rosé wine
● dark beer

groups = same type of drink (e.g. leffe Blonde)

THINGS OTHER than DRINKS in my fridge:
○ to drink
✳ to eat
\ sauce
• make ups

FROM G.LUPI
▓▓▓▓▓▓▓
▓▓▓▓▓▓▓
▓▓▓▓▓
BROOKLYN
NY-USA

SEND TO:
STEFANIE POSAVEC
▓▓▓▓▓▓▓▓▓▓▓
LONDON▓▓▓▓▓
-UK-
ENGLAND

If last week's food preferences didn't humiliate Giorgia enough, here is an even more disgracing set of data. She almost only drinks beers, but never before 6.00 pm: the timeline begins at 6.00 pm, reflecting her drinking rigidity!

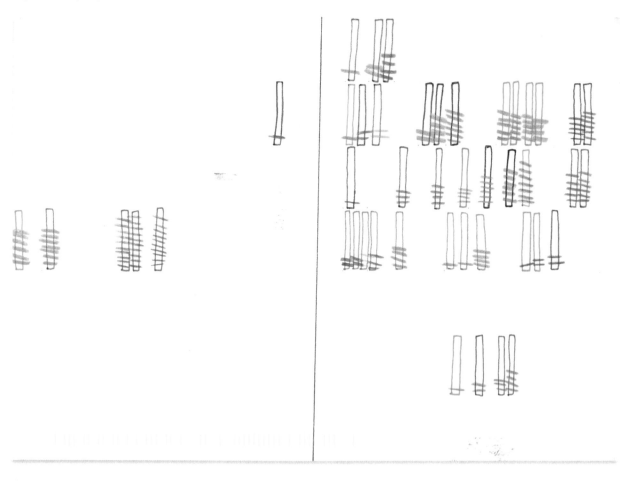

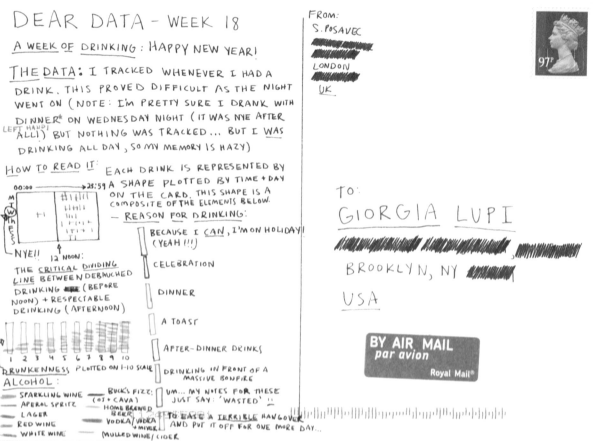

DEAR DATA - WEEK 18

A WEEK OF DRINKING : HAPPY NEW YEAR!

THE DATA: I TRACKED WHENEVER I HAD A
DRINK. THIS PROVED DIFFICULT AS THE NIGHT
WENT ON (NOTE: I'M PRETTY SURE I DRANK WITH
DINNER* ON WEDNESDAY NIGHT (IT WAS NYE AFTER
ALL!) BUT NOTHING WAS TRACKED ... BUT I WAS
DRINKING ALL DAY, SO MY MEMORY IS HAZY)
*LEFT HAND?

HOW TO READ IT: EACH DRINK IS REPRESENTED BY
A SHAPE PLOTTED BY TIME + DAY
ON THE CARD. THIS SHAPE IS A
COMPOSITE OF THE ELEMENTS BELOW.
— REASON FOR DRINKING:

THE CRITICAL DIVIDING
LINE BETWEEN DEBAUCHED
DRINKING (BEFORE
NOON) + RESPECTABLE
DRINKING (AFTERNOON)

BECAUSE I CAN, I'M ON HOLIDAY!!
(YEAH !!!)

CELEBRATION

DINNER

A TOAST

AFTER-DINNER DRINKS

DRINKING IN FRONT OF A
MASSIVE BONFIRE

UM ... MY NOTES FOR THESE
JUST SAY: 'WASTED' !!

TO EASE A TERRIBLE HANGOVER
AND PUT IT OFF FOR ONE MORE DAY...

DRUNKENNESS PLOTTED ON 1-10 SCALE

ALCOHOL :
SPARKLING WINE
APEROL SPRITZ
LAGER
RED WINE
WHITE WINE

BUCK'S FIZZ:
(OJ + CAVA)
HOME BREWED
BEER
VODKA/VODKA
+MIXER
(MULLED WINE/CIDER)

FROM:
S. POSAVEC
~~~~~~
~~~~~~
LONDON
~~~~~~
UK

97ᵖ

TO:
GIORGIA LUPI
~~~~~~~~~~~~~~~~~~~
BROOKLYN, NY ~~~~~~
USA

BY AIR MAIL
par avion
Royal Mail®

Stefanie's drinking rules are more relaxed than Giorgia's: any time after noon is socially acceptable (except for
one beer at 10 am this week on a train with friends: she drank the beer so she could enter it in her data!)

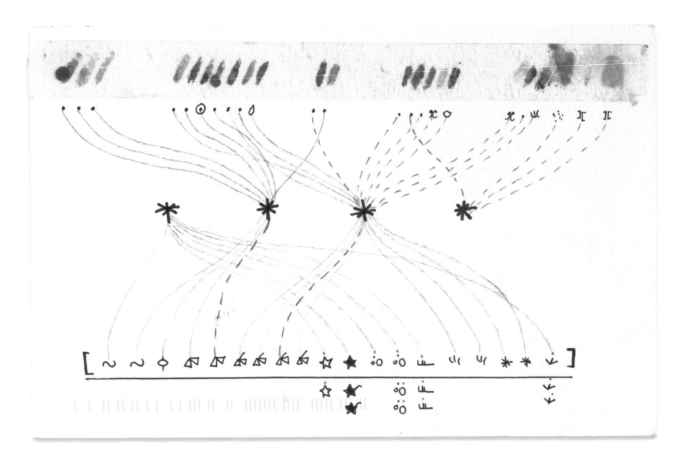

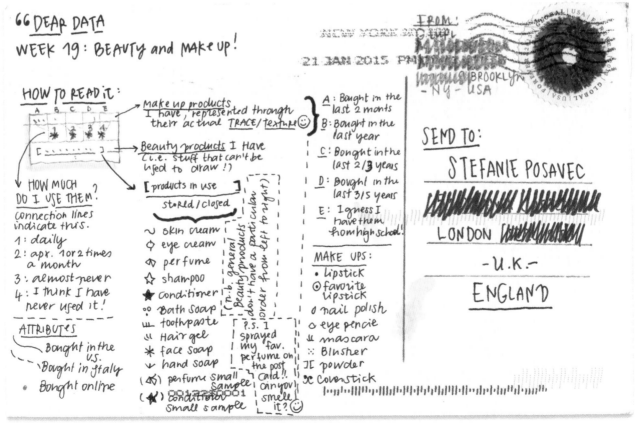

66 DEAR DATA
WEEK 19: BEAUTY and MAKE UP!

HOW TO READ iT:

→ Make up products I have, represented through their actual TRACE/texture ☺

→ Beauty products I Have (i.e. stuff that can't be Used to draw !)

[products in use]

Stored / closed

↓ HOW MUCH DO I USE THEM?
Connection lines indicate this.
1: daily
2: apr. 1 or 2 times a month
3: almost never
4: I think I have never used it!

ATTRIBUTES
— Bought in the U.S.
--- Bought in Italy
• Bought online

~ skin cream
◇ eye cream
⬦ perfume
☆ shampoo
★ conditioner
∘∘ Bath soap
⊔ toothpaste
ᴞ Hair gel
✳ face soap
↓ hand soap
(⬦) perfume small Sample
(★) conditioner small sample

(n.b. general Beauty products don't have a particular order from left to right)

P.S. I sprayed my fav. perfume on the post card!! can you smell it? ☺

A: Bought in the last 2 monts
B: Bought in the last year
C: Bought in the last 2/3 years
D: Bought in the last 3/5 years
E: I guess I have them from high school!

MAKE UPS:
• lipstick
⊙ favorite lipstick
∘ nail polish
◇ eye pencie
ᴜ mascara
∷ Blusher
Ⅱ powder
✕ coverstick

FROM:
NEW YORK
21 JAN 2015 PM
BROOKLYN
- NY - USA

SEND TO:
STEFANIE POSAVEC
~~~~~~~~~~~~~~~~
LONDON ~~~~~~~
- U.K. -
ENGLAND

Giorgia's main data story runs around the sixteen similar-coloured lipsticks that she still keeps on buying but almost never wears. Since she wanted Stefanie to see how similar they are, she used them as her markers.

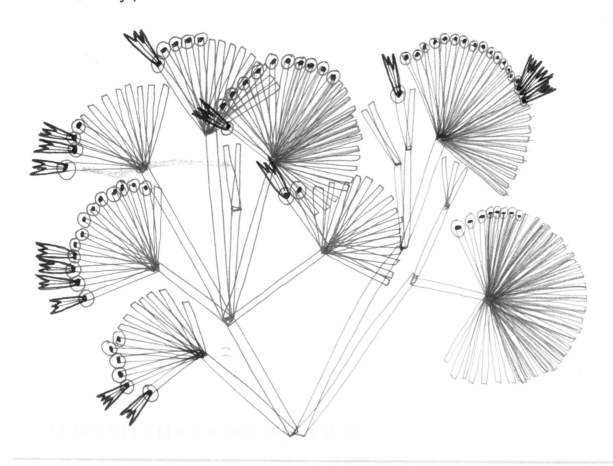

For Stefanie, honest data-gathering means writing down all of the embarrassing beauty products you use,
no matter how much she winces every time she reads her postcard.

Week twenty:
A week of
INTERESTING
THINGS

Stefanie was concerned that in this year of
drawing she and Giorgia weren't testing themselves
and pushing themselves to learn more drawing
techniques, so for this week they worked with a new
material to represent their data: collaged paper.

This week the pair gathered data on the people,
objects and ideas that piqued and excited their
interest as they went about their daily routine.

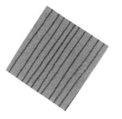

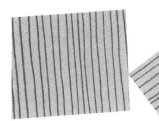

103

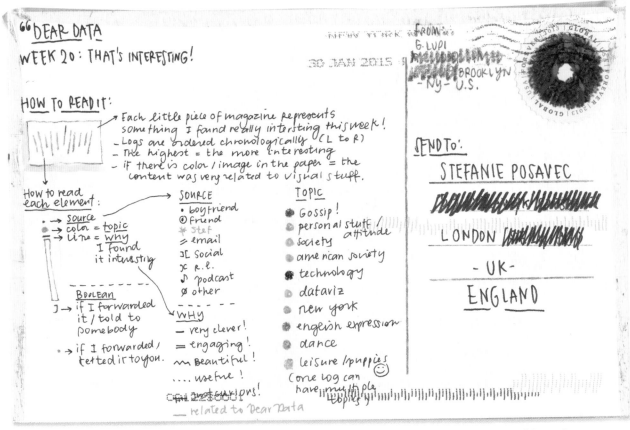

How fun is it that they both experimented with collage without telling each other? Given the topic of the week,
Giorgia cut apart an issue of the *New Yorker* to use as her drawing material. (Sorry!)

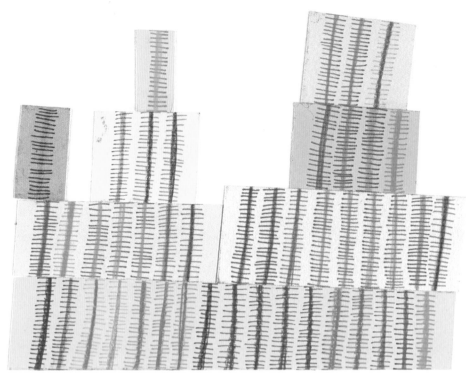

This postcard wasn't mailed by Stefanie, but rather was handed to someone in a university mailroom to post, making Stefanie blush: what would this person think about this snippet of data shoved into their hands?

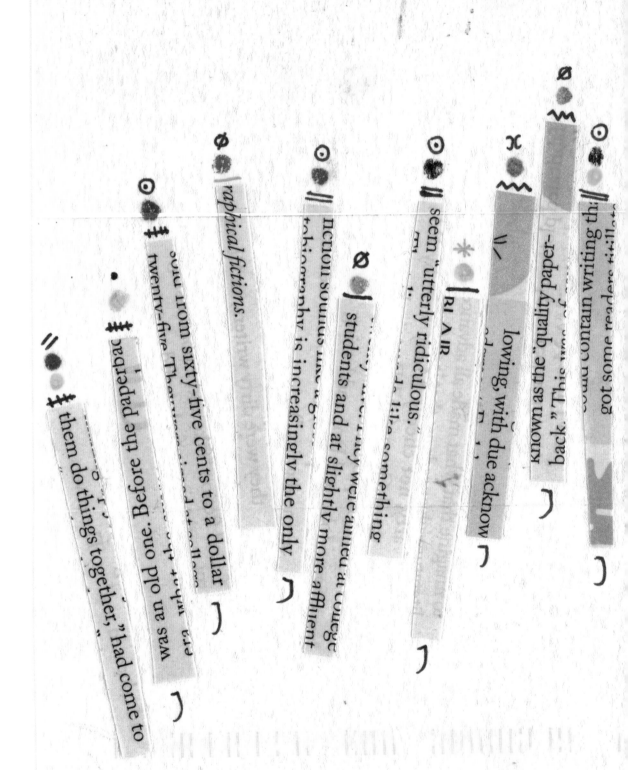

By 1954, Anchor was selling six

books were priced to break even at

argument was an early success. The

in "Re-Covering Mo

ernism") that pulp mag

had trouble reading and writing and 'guring and

things, and not a private immersion i

were rack-size—in effect,

upmarket rack

owitz is right (she is fo

With the idea that a boo

backs, he considered the sight of boo

locking quality paper—

SIDE VIEW OF HOW STEFANIE'S POSTCARDS
ARRIVE IN GIORGIA'S MAILBOX:

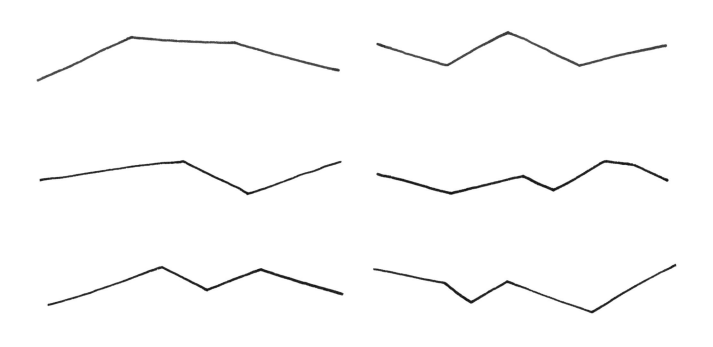

SIDE VIEW OF HOW <u>GIORGIA'S POSTCARDS</u> ARRIVE THROUGH <u>STEFANIE'S MAILSLOT</u> (SIGH):

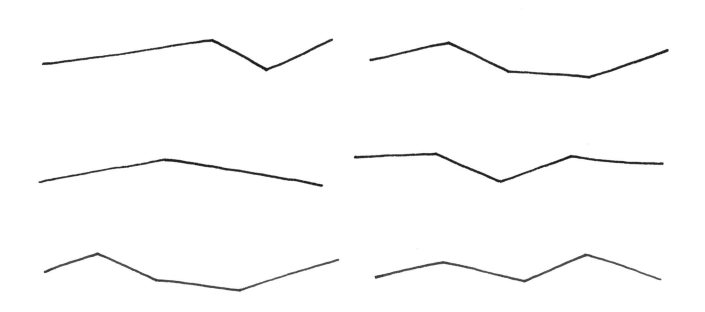

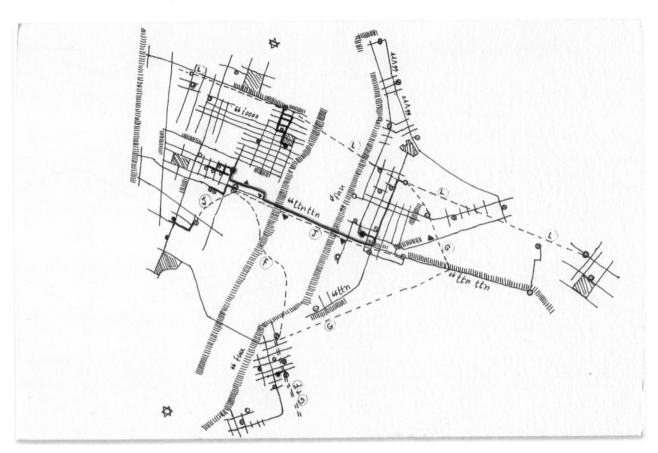

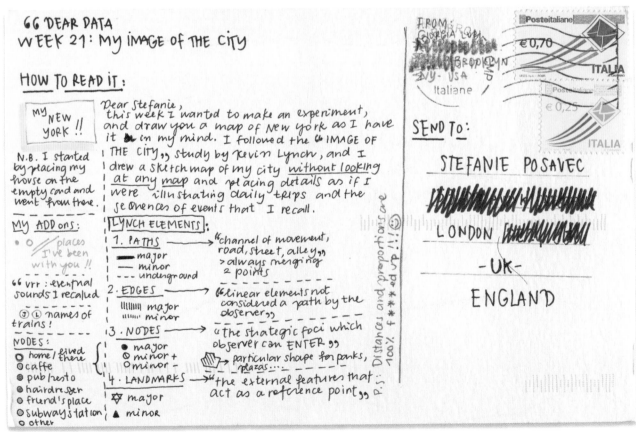

66 DEAR DATA
WEEK 21: MY IMAGE OF THE CITY

HOW TO READ IT:

MY NEW YORK !!

N.B. I started by placing my house on the empty card and went from there.

MY ADD ons:
• ○ ⫽ places I've been with you !!

66 vrr : eventual sounds I recalled

ⓙ ⓛ names of trains !

NODES:
○ home / lived there
◍ caffe
● pub /resto
◐ hairdresser
◑ friend's place
◎ subway station
○ other

Dear Stefanie,
this week I wanted to make an experiment, and draw you a map of New York as I have it ~ in my mind. I followed the 66 IMAGE OF THE CITY ,, study by Kevin Lynch, and I drew a sketch map of my city without looking at any map and placing details as if I were illustrating daily trips and the sequences of events that I recall.

LYNCH ELEMENTS :

1. PATHS ——→ "channel of movement, road, street, alley ,, > always merging 2 points
━━ major
── minor
--- underground

2. EDGES ——→ "linear elements not considered a path by the observer ,,
⊞⊞⊞ major
⊞⊞⊞ minor

3. NODES ——→ "the strategic foci which observer can ENTER ,,
● major
◉ minor +
○ minor -
↗ particular shape for parks, plazas....

4. LANDMARKS ——→ "the external features that act as a reference point ,,
✦ major
▲ minor

P.S. Distances and proportions are 100% f*** ed up !!!

FROM
Giorgia Lupi
~~~~~~~
BROOKLYN
NY - USA
Italiane

Posteitaliane
€ 0,70
ITALIA

Posteitaliane
€ 0,25
ITALIA

SEND TO:

STEFANIE POSAVEC
~~~~~~~~~~~~~~~~~~
LONDON ~~~~~~~
- UK -
ENGLAND

Giorgia and Stefanie didn't track any daily activity this week — instead, they reflected upon an experience and retrieved data about it later, telling each other about their relationship with their cities.

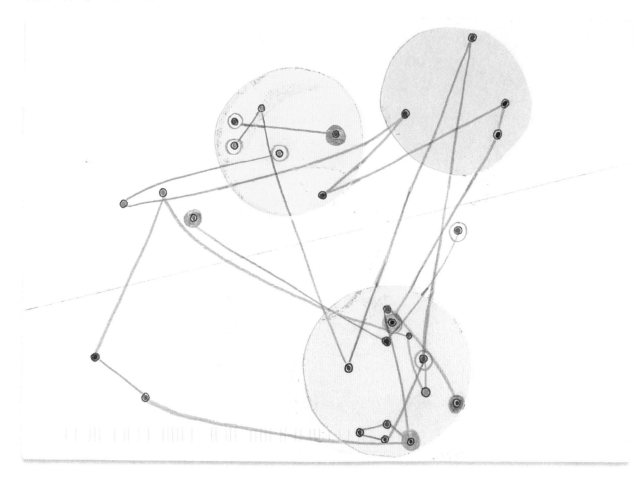

DEAR DATA - WEEK 21

A WEEK ABOUT MY LONDON

THE DATA: THE MOST IMPORTANT, MEMORABLE LOCATIONS WHILE I'VE LIVED IN LONDON (SINCE 2001 ON + OFF!), TAKING IN EVERYTHING FROM STUDY, TO MARRIAGE, + THEN CITIZENSHIP.

HOW TO READ IT

① A STYLISED MAP OF LONDON IS DRAWN ON THE CARD:

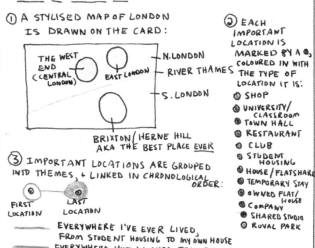

THE WEST END (CENTRAL LONDON) — N. LONDON — EAST LONDON — RIVER THAMES — S. LONDON

BRIXTON / HERNE HILL AKA THE BEST PLACE EVER

② EACH IMPORTANT LOCATION IS MARKED BY A ⊙, COLOURED IN WITH THE TYPE OF LOCATION IT IS:
- ⊙ SHOP
- ⊙ UNIVERSITY/ CLASSROOM
- ⊙ TOWN HALL
- ⊙ RESTAURANT
- ⊙ CLUB
- ⊙ STUDENT HOUSING
- ⊙ HOUSE / FLATSHARE
- ⊙ TEMPORARY STAY
- ⊙ OWNED FLAT/ HOUSE
- ⊙ COMPANY
- ⊙ SHARED STUDIO
- ⊙ ROYAL PARK

③ IMPORTANT LOCATIONS ARE GROUPED INTO THEMES, + LINKED IN CHRONOLOGICAL ORDER:

FIRST LOCATION   LAST LOCATION

—— EVERYWHERE I'VE EVER LIVED, FROM STUDENT HOUSING TO MY OWN HOUSE
—— EVERYWHERE I'VE WORKED, FROM TOPSHOP TO URBAN OUTFITTERS TO PENGUIN TO FREELANCE!
—— EVERYWHERE I'VE STUDIED (AIU + ST. MARTINS)
—— ALL MAJOR LOCATIONS IN MY MARRIAGE: 1ST MEETING, 1ST HOOKUP, 1ST DATE, PROPOSAL, WEDDING... 1ST HOUSE!
—— CITIZENSHIP: CITIZENSHIP TEST TO CEREMONY TO CELEBRATORY DINNER (DINNER BY HESTON BLUMENTHAL)

FROM:
S POSAVEC
~~~~~~
LONDON ~~~~~~
UK

Stroke
association

Royal Mail
Mount Pleasant
Mail Centre
02-02-2015
23900324

97P

TO:

GIORGIA LUPI

~~~~~~ ~~~~~~ ~~~~~~
BROOKLYN, NY, ~~~~~~
USA

AIRMAIL

In her adopted city, Stefanie has become an aggressively patriotic South Londoner, due to how many happy life memories have happened for her in Brixton and Herne Hill.

GIORGIA'S NEW YORK with closed EYES

Instead of drawing a map of New York,
I drew my mental image of it.

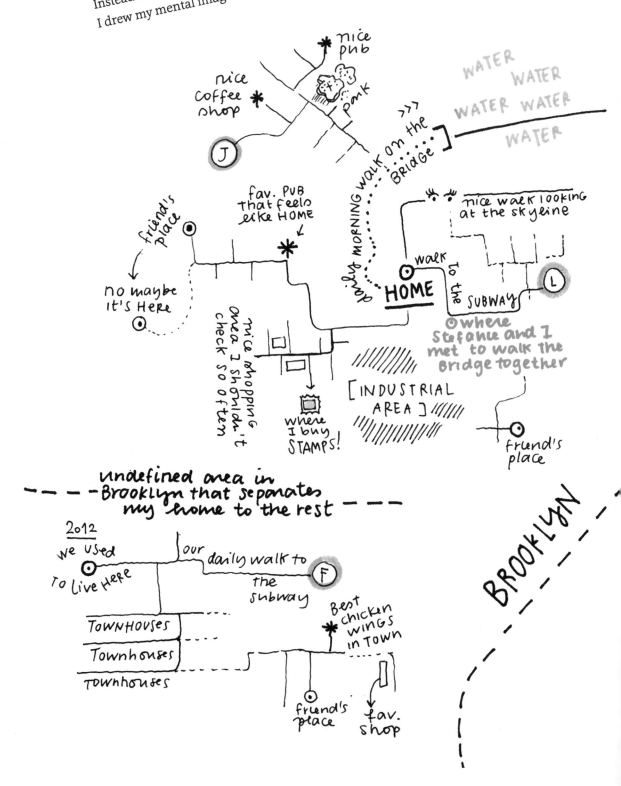

nice pub

nice coffee shop *

park

WATER WATER WATER WATER WATER

J

daily MORNING walk on the BRIDGE

>>>

nice walk looking at the skyline

friend's place ◉

fav. PUB that feels like HOME

no maybe it's HERE ◉

nice shopping area I shouldn't check so often

walk to the SUBWAY

HOME

L

◉ where Stefanie and I met to walk the Bridge together

where I buy STAMPS!

[INDUSTRIAL AREA]

friend's place ◉

undefined area in Brooklyn that separates my home to the rest

2012 we used to live HERE ◉

our daily walk to the subway

F

TOWNHOUSES

TOWNHOUSES

Townhouses

Best chicken wings in Town *

friend's place ◉

fav. shop

BROOKLYN

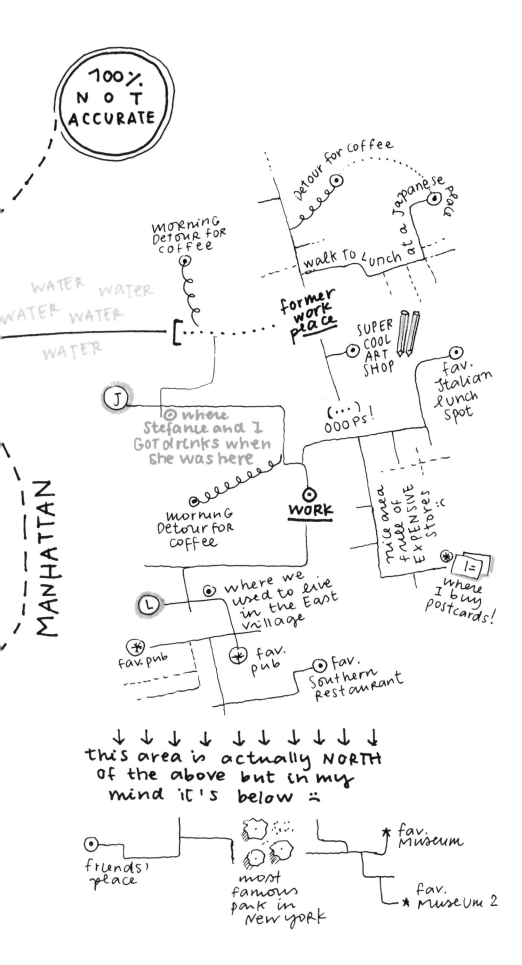

Following the work of urban sociologist Kevin Lynch, I created my image of the city following my perception of the ways I go about walking in New York every day, with my mundane little encounters and memories. I wasn't in New York while drawing this postcard, I was far away at my parents' in Italy: what better way to really "imagine" my city in my mind!

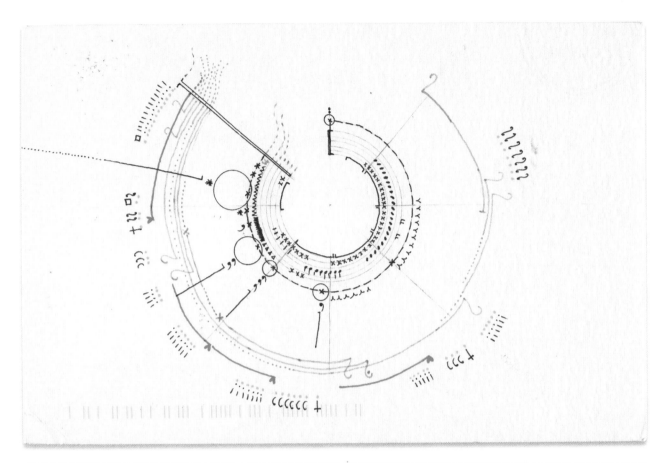

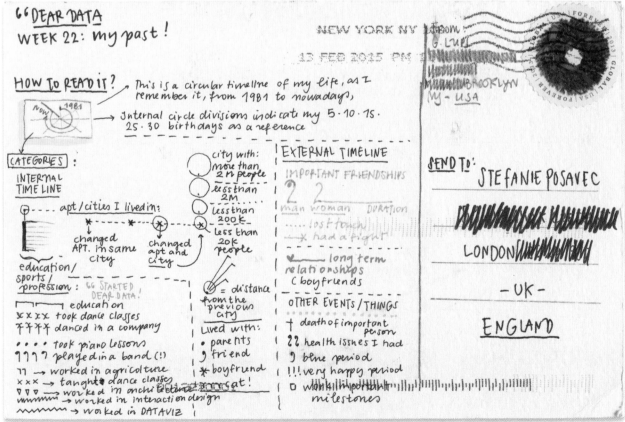

" DEAR DATA

WEEK 22 : my past !

HOW TO READ IT ? → This is a circular timeline of my life, as I
remember it, from 1981 to nowadays,

→ Internal circle divisions indicate my 5·10·15·
25·30 birthdays as a reference

NEW YORK NY 100 from
G. Lupi
13 FEB 2015 PM

Brooklyn
NY - USA

CATEGORIES :

INTERNAL
TIME LINE

⌐ ---- apt / cities I lived in:

* changed
APT. in same
city

✳ changed
apt and
city

education/
sports/
profession : " STARTED
DEAR DATA!

⌐_⌐ → education
x x x x → took dance classes
キキキキ → danced in a company
• • • • → took piano lessons
????? → played in a band (!)
刀 → worked in agriculture
x x x → taught dance classes
▽▽▽ → worked in architecture
wwww → worked in interaction design
∿∿∿ → worked in DATAVIZ

city with:
○ more than
2M people
○ less than
2M
○ less than
200 k
○ less than
20k people

= distance
from the
previous
city

lived with:
• parents
? friend
✳ boyfriend
⌐ cat!

EXTERNAL TIMELINE

IMPORTANT FRIENDSHIPS
? ?
man woman DURATION
------- lost touch
x had a fight

long term
relationships
(boyfriends

OTHER EVENTS / THINGS
† death of important
person
?? health issues I had
? blue period
!!! very happy period
▯ work / important
milestones

SEND TO: STEFANIE POSAVEC

LONDON

- UK -

ENGLAND

A postcard on Giorgia's past that led to a shameful revelation upon receival: Stefanie asked for more details, and
Giorgia had to text her a picture of when she used to play in a heavy metal band and only dressed in black.

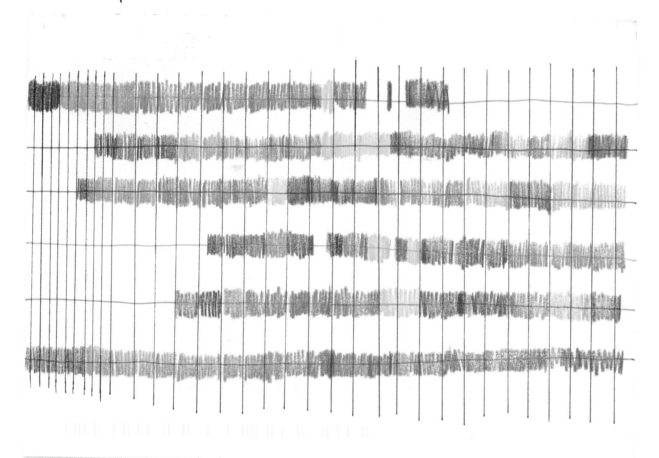

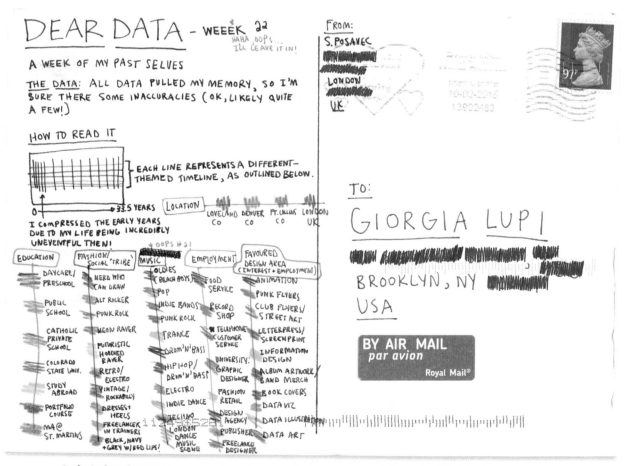

DEAR DATA - WEEEK 22
HAHA, OOPS...
I'LL LEAVE IT IN!

A WEEK OF MY PAST SELVES

THE DATA: ALL DATA PULLED MY MEMORY, SO I'M SURE THERE SOME INACCURACIES (OK, LIKELY QUITE A FEW!)

FROM:
S. POSAVEC
▓▓▓▓▓▓▓▓▓▓
LONDON
▓▓▓▓▓▓▓▓▓
UK

HOW TO READ IT

— EACH LINE REPRESENTS A DIFFERENT-
THEMED TIMELINE, AS OUTLINED BELOW.

0 ——————————→ 33.5 YEARS LOCATION LOVELAND DENVER FT. COLLINS LONDON
                                        CO   CO   CO   UK

I COMPRESSED THE EARLY YEARS
DUE TO MY LIFE BEING INCREDIBLY
UNEVENTFUL THEN!

TO:
GIORGIA LUPI
▓▓▓▓▓▓▓▓▓▓▓▓▓▓▓▓▓▓▓▓▓
BROOKLYN, NY
USA

BY AIR MAIL
par avion
Royal Mail®

OOPS #2!

EDUCATION	FASHION/ SOCIAL 'TRIBE'	MUSIC	EMPLOYMENT	FAVOURED DESIGN AREA (INTEREST + EMPLOYMENT)
DAYCARE/ PRESCHOOL	NERD WHO CAN DRAW	OLDIES (BEACH BOYS)	FOOD SERVICE	ANIMATION
		POP		PUNK FLYERS
PUBLIC SCHOOL	ALT ROCKER	INDIE BANDS	RECORD SHOP	CLUB FLYERS/ STREET ART
	PUNK ROCK	PUNK ROCK		
CATHOLIC PRIVATE SCHOOL	NEON RAVER	TRANCE	TELEPHONE CUSTOMER SERVICE	LETTERPRESS/ SCREENPRINT
	FUTURISTIC HOODIED RAVER	DRUM'N'BASS		INFORMATION DESIGN
COLORADO STATE UNIV.	RETRO/ ELECTRO	HIPHOP/ DRUM'N'BASS	UNIVERSITY: GRAPHIC DESIGNER	ALBUM ARTWORK/ BAND MERCH
STUDY ABROAD	VINTAGE/ ROCKABILLY	ELECTRO	FASHION RETAIL	BOOK COVERS
PORTFOLIO COURSE	DRESSES+ HEELS	INDIE DANCE		DATA VIZ
	FREELANCER IN TRAINERS	TECHNO	DESIGN AGENCY	DATA ILLUSTRATION
MA @ ST. MARTINS		LONDON DANCE MUSIC SCENE	PUBLISHER	DATA ART
	BLACK, NAVY +GREY W/RED LIPS!		FREELANCE DESIGNER	

Stefanie thought using the same colours for every single category would have simplified the data for Giorgia, `
but realized later that she may have made her drawing more complicated to read!

A MAP OF THE NEUROSES THAT UNFOLD
WHEN STEFANIE READS GIORGIA'S POSTCARD

1 GREAT! ANOTHER POSTCARD ARRIVED!

2 WOW, GIORGIA COLLECTS A LOT OF DATA.

3 SO. MUCH. DATA. HOW DOES SHE DO THIS?

4 WHAT?

EVEN MORE DATA?

HOW? HOW!

FROM:
GIORGIA

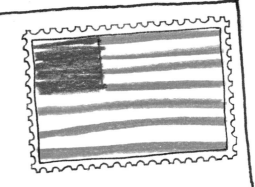

TO: STEFANIE

AND HER LEGEND IS ALWAYS
SO NEAT AND TIDY AND
MINE IS A MESS I MUST
TRY HARDER NEXT WEEK
AAARRGHHH

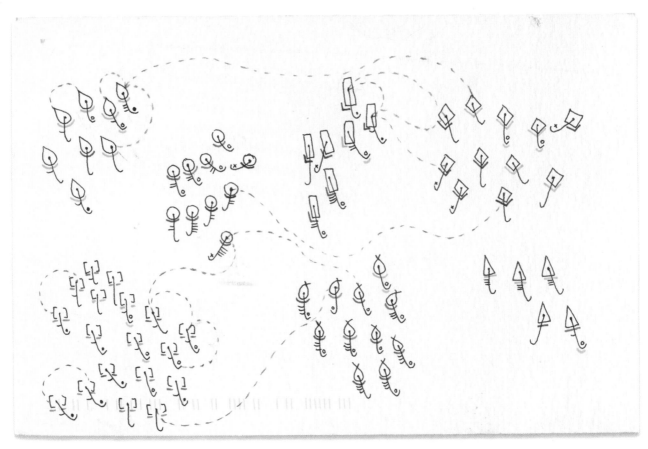

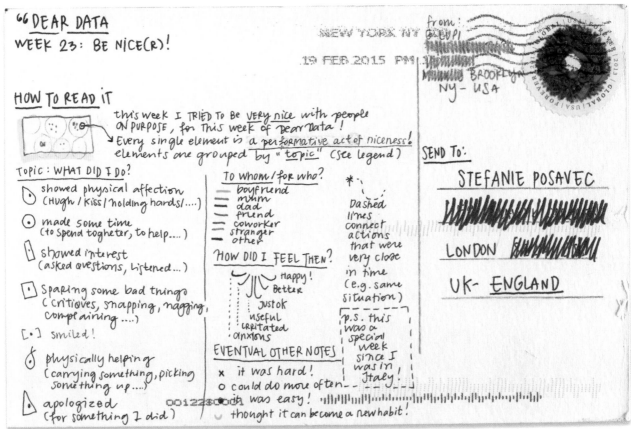

" DEAR DATA
WEEK 23: BE NICE(R)!

HOW TO READ IT

this week I TRIED to be VERY nice with people ON PURPOSE, for this week of Dear Data!
Every single element is a performative act of niceness!
elements are grouped by "topic" (see legend)

TOPIC: WHAT DID I DO?

- showed physical affection (HUGH / kiss / holding hands/....)
- made some time (to spend togheter, to help....)
- showed interest (asked questions, listened...)
- sparing some bad things (critiques, snapping, nagging, complaining ....)
- [•] smiled!
- physically helping (carrying something, picking something up....)
- apologized (for something I did)

To whom / for who?
— boyfriend
— mum
— dad
— friend
— coworker
— stranger
— other

HOW DID I FEEL THEN?
Happy!
Better
Just ok
useful
irritated
anxious

EVENTUAL OTHER NOTES
x it was hard!
o could do more often
• it was easy!
• thought it can become a new habit!

*
Dashed lines connect actions that were very close in time (e.g. same situation)

p.s. this was a special week since I was in Italy!

NEW YORK NY
19 FEB 2015 PM
BROOKLYN
NY — USA

from:
GIPPI

SEND TO:
STEFANIE POSAVEC
LONDON
UK — ENGLAND

On their journey, Giorgia and Stefanie tried to use data to become better human beings, at least for a week.
This week they performed nice acts on purpose, to be able to then report them. The hardest week ever.

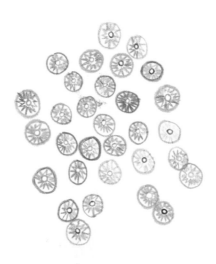

DEAR DATA - WEEK 23

A WEEK OF BEING NICE

(OTHERWISE ENTITLED "WHY I'M A TOTAL UNCARING ASSHOLE...") WITH PROOF! :)

ABOUT THE DATA: I ONLY TRACKED NICE ACTS THAT WERE TRULY HEARTFELT, SO NO 'COMMON COURTESY' ACTS WERE COUNTED (LIKE SAYING PLEASE + THANK YOU, ETC.) I DON'T THINK THE DATA-GATHERING MADE ME ANY NICER THAN NORMAL, ALAS.

HOW TO READ IT:

LOOK! CAN YOU SEE THOSE TINY SPECKS ON THE PAGE? BETTER USE A MAGNIFYING GLASS!

WOW... THERE AREN'T THAT MANY. EACH SPECK IS ONE NICE THING I DID THAT WEEK.

PERSON → NICE THING → LOCATION

HUSBAND, STUDIOMATE 1, FRIEND 1, STUDIOMATE 2, FRIEND 2, TWITTER FOLLOWER 1, FRIEND 3, TWITTER FOLLOWER 2, FRIEND 4, COLLEAGUE 1, COLLEAGUE 2, STRANGER 1, STRANGER 2

BOUGHT FOOD, BOUGHT GIFT, BOUGHT DRINK, GAVE COMPLIMENT, HELD DOOR OPEN, WENT OUT OF WAY TO MAKE THEM FEEL WELCOME, SENT ARTICLE THEY WOULD LIKE

ONLINE (DIGITAL COMMUNICATIONS), FRIEND'S HOUSE, HOME, PUB/RESTAURANT, STUDIO, SHOP/SHOPPING CENTRE

FROM: S. POSAVEC, LONDON, UK

TO: GIORGIA LUPI, BROOKLYN, NY USA

BY AIR MAIL
par avion
Royal Mail®

Stefanie drew the moments she was trying to be nicer very small, to highlight how she wasn't as kind as she would have liked to be this week.

week Twenty-four
a week of
DOORS

This week Giorgia and Stefanie were tracking the doors they passed through. As much as it sounds an unusual dataset, it was a pretext to show each other the pace of their days through their external and internal environments.

It is a reminder that you can still see the story of a life lived, even in the most uncommon types of data tracking, if you add the right details to your gathering.

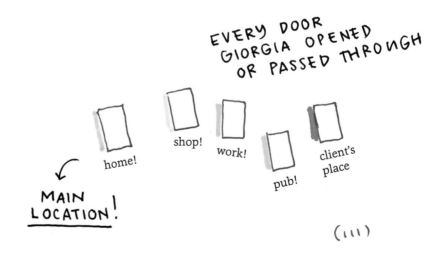

EVERY DOOR GIORGIA OPENED OR PASSED THROUGH

home!

shop!

work!

pub!

client's place

MAIN LOCATION!

(ııı)

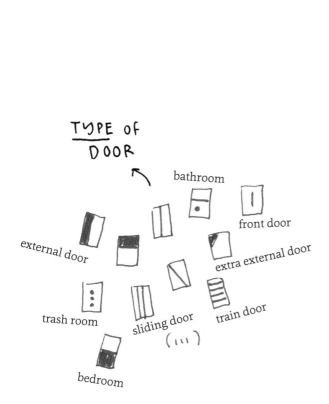

TYPE OF DOOR

external door

bathroom

front door

extra external door

trash room

sliding door (ııı)

train door

bedroom

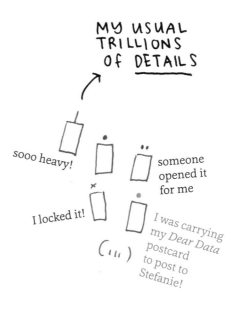

MY USUAL TRILLIONS OF DETAILS

sooo heavy!

someone opened it for me

I locked it!

I was carrying my *Dear Data* postcard to post to Stefanie!

(ııı)

Why can't I help oooooooooverdetailing my data collections???

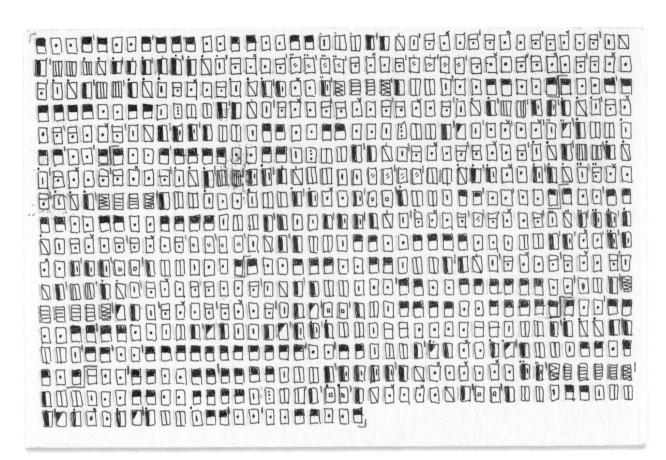

66 DEAR DATA
WEEK 24 : DOORS' PATTERNS

HOW TO READ IT:

Every little rectangle represents a door I opened and/or passed through, in chronological order, to enter a space. (P.S. closet doors and furniture doors are not included)

FROM:
G. LUPI

NEW YORK
24 FEB 2015 PM
BROOKLYN
NY- USA-

SEND TO:
STEFANIE POSAVEC

LONDON
- UK -
ENGLAND

→ TYPE OF DOOR :

MAIN LOCATION :

| my Building |
| Work (NEW. INC) |
| SHOP/STORE |
| CAFE/PUB RESTAURANT |
| CLIENT PLACE |
| TRANSPORTATION |

extra external door (iT's cold here ha!)

external door - entering the building

eventual MID DOOR

main space access (e.g. my APT)

when external door coincides to main space entrance

external sliding door

elevator automatic door 00123800

bathroom RESTROOM door

bathroom entry

the door between my bedroom and my living room

thrash room

glass door (e.g. meeting room)

turnstiles

train doors

cab door

ATTRIBUTES

so heavy !!

boy friend opened it for me

somebody opened it for me

I locked it!

I was carrying my Dear Data postcard to post it to you ☺

After spending more than six hours drawing this hyper-detailed card, Giorgia texted Stefanie as she posted it:
"You need to know that if this one doesn't get to you I won't redraw it. You'll see what I mean."

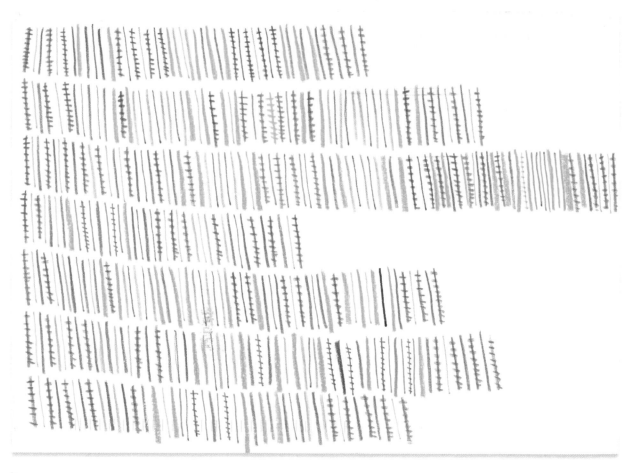

DEAR DATA — WEEK 24

SECOND POSTING ARGH!!

A WEEK OF DOORS/SPACES

ABOUT THE DATA: I GATHERED DATA ON ALL OF
THE SPACES I PASSED THROUGH IN THE WEEK,
BOTH INTERNAL + EXTERNAL. A SPACE IS
DEFINED BY WHETHER I HAD TO PASS THROUGH
A DOOR OR NOT.

HOW TO READ IT:
IN CHRONOLOGICAL ORDER

EACH SPACE IS REPRESENTED BY A
OR A | (CROSS-HATCHED LINES
CARRY NO IMPORTANCE,
MAINLY ONLY FOR
DIFFERENTIATION BETWEEN
SIMILAR COLOURS!) THIS

THE TYPES OF SPACES I PASSED WAS A LAST MINUTE SPONTANEOUS
THROUGH INCLUDE: DECISION ON THE 1st CARD TO MAKE THE
COLOURS CLEARER... Sooo ANNOYING I HAVE
TO REDRAW

LEFT HAND SMUDGE SIGH

IN THE HOME/
PERSONAL SPACE:
++++++ BEDROOM
—— SPARE BEDROOM
(1 OF 2)
—— GROUND FLOOR
(OPEN PLAN, INCLS.
KITCHEN + LOUNGE)
—— TOILET
—— BATHROOM

STUDIO:
—— STUDIO BLDG.
—— STUDIO SPACE

OUTSIDE:
—— IN THE
STREET

DOCTOR:
—— DOCTOR'S
OFFICE
—— WAITING
ROOM
UNIVERSITIES:
++++++ UNIV. BLDG.
—— CLASSROOM
—— TEAROOM

CULTURAL CENTRE:
++++++ MAIN BLDG.
—— GALLERY
TRANSPORT:
—— BUS
—— TUBE/TRAIN
—— TUBE/TRAIN STN
—— CAB

SHOPS/RESTAURANTS:
—— SHOP
—— BRIXTON MKT. BLDG.
—— PUB/RESTAURANT/
CAFE/BAR
FRIEND'S HOUSE:
—— MAIN HOUSE
—— BASEMENT
KITCHEN
—— LOUNGE

GYM:
—— MAIN BLDG.
++++++ CHANGING ROOM
—— EXERCISE ROOM
* CHANGING ROOMS +
TOILETS ARE FOUND
ACROSS DIFFERENT
SPACES

FROM:
S. POSAVEC
LONDON
UK

Royal Mail
Jubilee
Mail Centre
06-05-2015

£1.00

TO: GIORGIA LUPI

BROOKLYN, NY
USA

BY AIR MAIL
par avion
Royal Mail®

Unfortunately, while Giorgia's postcard arrived, Stefanie's postcard didn't, so she had to draw hers again
(luckily it wasn't as detailed, but it was still supremely annoying).

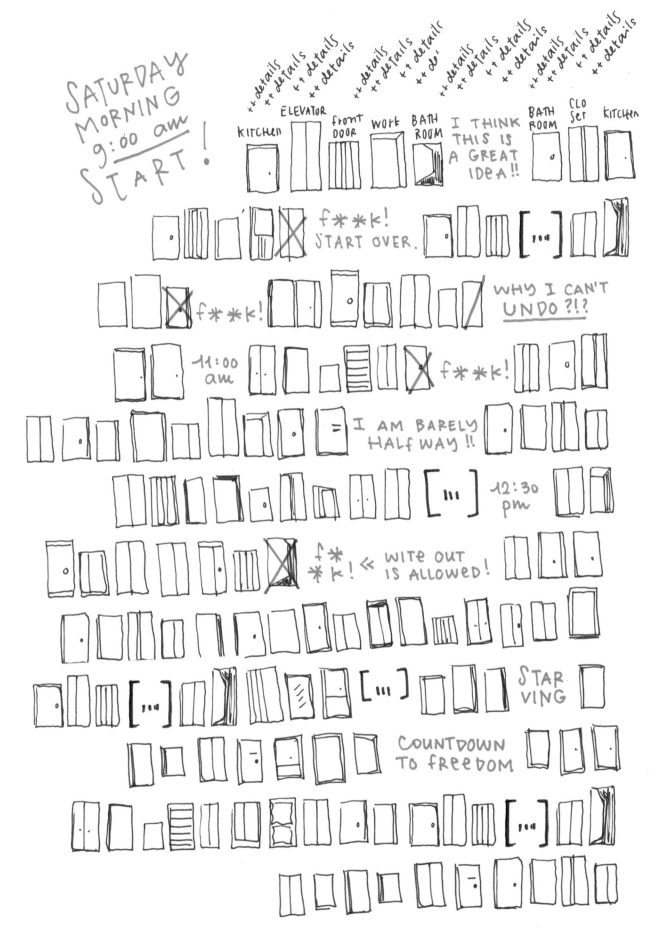

SATURDAY MORNING 9:00 am START!

++ details ++ details ++ details ++ details ++ details ++ de... ++ details ++ details ++ details ++ details ++ details ++ details ++ details

KITCHEN   ELEVATOR   FRONT DOOR   WORK   BATH ROOM   I THINK THIS IS A GREAT IDEA!!   BATH ROOM   CLOSET   KITCHEN

f**k! START OVER.

WHY I CAN'T UNDO?!?

11:00 am   f**k!

I AM BARELY HALF WAY!!

[III]   12:30 pm

f** k! « WITE OUT IS ALLOWED!

[...]   [III]   STAR VING

COUNTDOWN TO FREEDOM

[...]

126

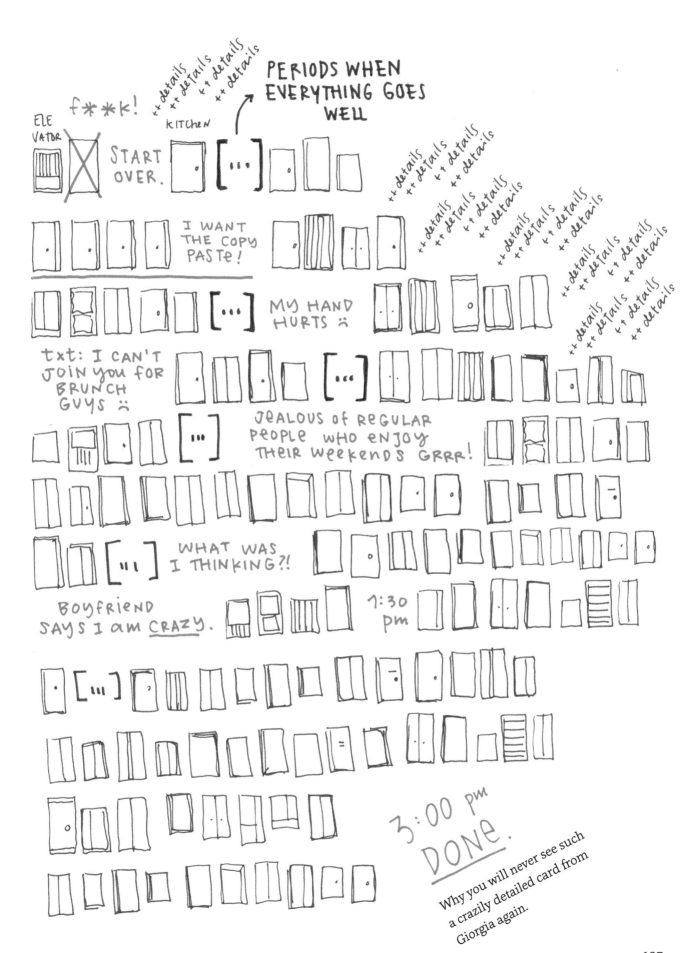

PERIODS WHEN EVERYTHING GOES WELL

ELE VATOR

f**k!

START OVER.

kitchen

++ details ++ details ++ details ++ details

I WANT THE COPY PASTE!

MY HAND HURTS

++ details ++ details ++ details ++ details ++ details ++ details ++ details ++ details ++ details ++ details ++ details ++ details ++ details ++ details ++ details ++ details ++ details ++ details ++ details ++ details

txt: I CAN'T JOIN YOU FOR BRUNCH GUYS

JEALOUS OF REGULAR PEOPLE WHO ENJOY THEIR WEEKENDS GRRR!

WHAT WAS I THINKING?!

BOYFRIEND SAYS I AM CRAZY.

1:30 pm

3:00 pm DONE.

Why you will never see such a crazily detailed card from Giorgia again.

127

SPENDING TIME
WITH YOUR DATA IS
SPENDING TIME
WITH YOURSELF.

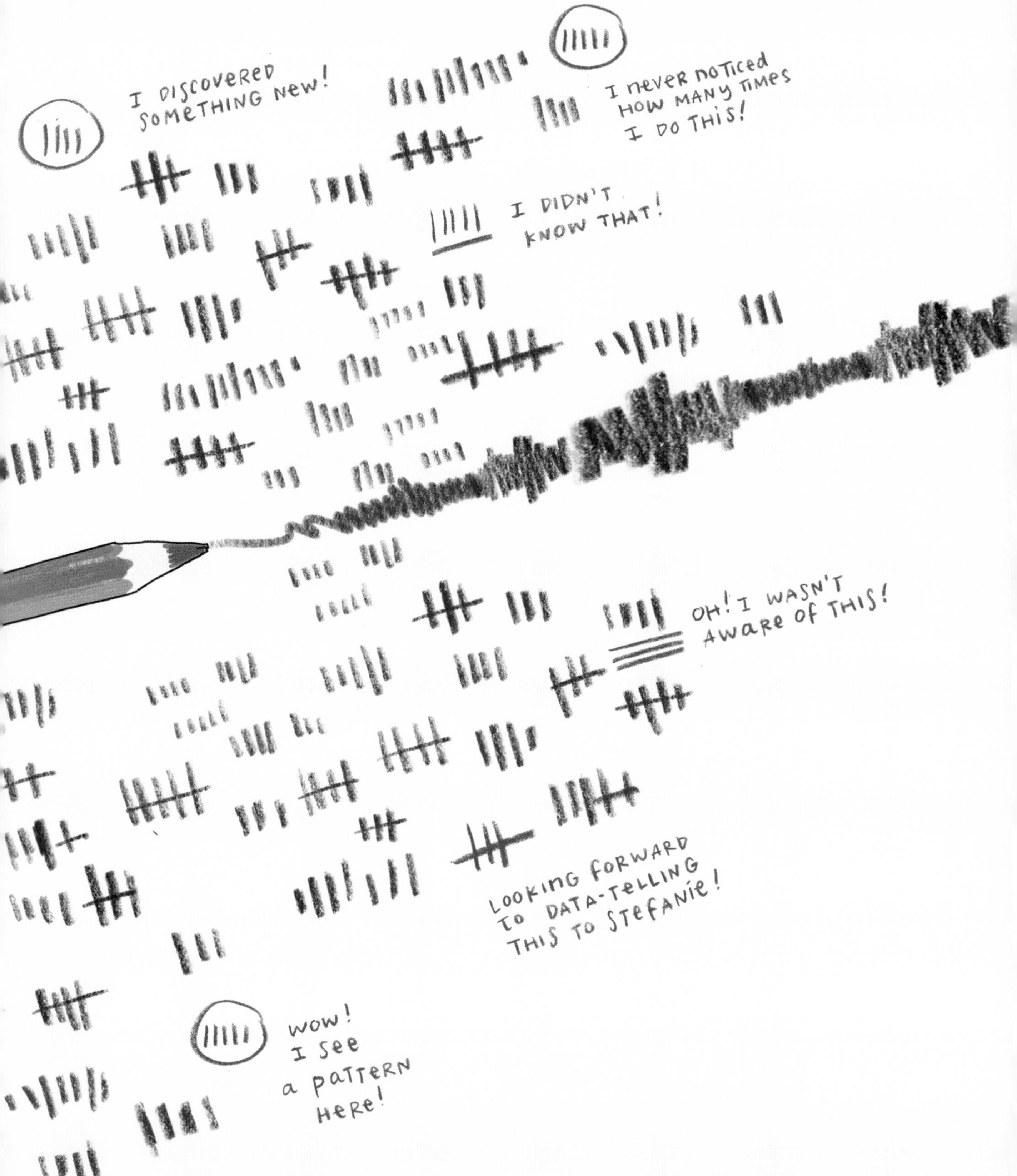
I DISCOVERED SOMETHING NEW!
I NEVER NOTICED HOW MANY TIMES I DO THIS!
I DIDN'T KNOW THAT!
OH! I WASN'T AWARE OF THIS!
LOOKING FORWARD TO DATA-TELLING THIS TO STEFANIE!
WOW! I SEE A PATTERN HERE!

week twenty-five
a week of

FRIENDS

At week twenty-five, Giorgia and Stefanie decided to share another important part of their lives: their friends. But how could they transform them into data?

Giorgia represented only her very close friends, who she feels are like family, while Stefanie included a broader range of pals and mapped out many details of their relationships.

NEW BIG FLOWER OF THE YEAR: Stefanie!!

In fifty-two weeks Stefanie and I became true friends. Before starting *Dear Data* I couldn't imagine we could become so close, sharing details of our lives that we wouldn't tell to almost any of our other close friends.

WHAT WE TALK ABOUT AND MY USUAL MILLIONS OF OTHER ATTRIBUTES ...

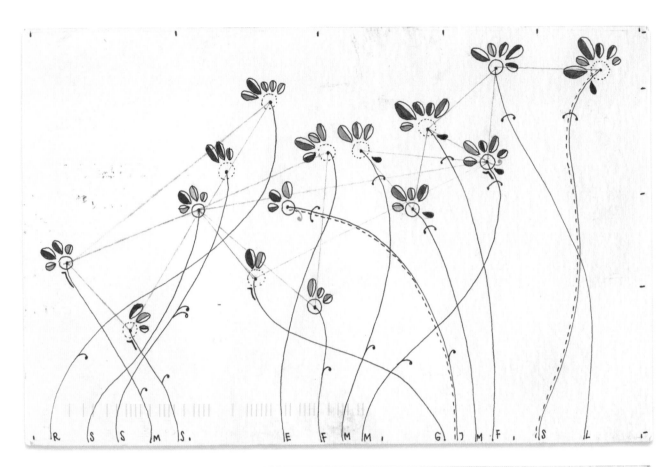

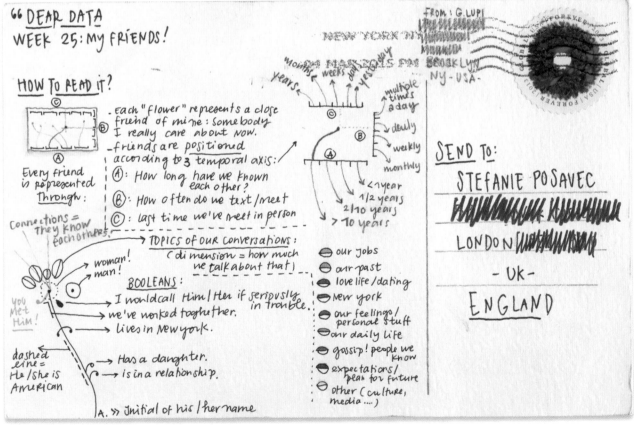

Giorgia's closest friends are her data flowers. She hopes they will read this book, figure out where they are on
her card, and accept her data-flowery homage to their friendship.

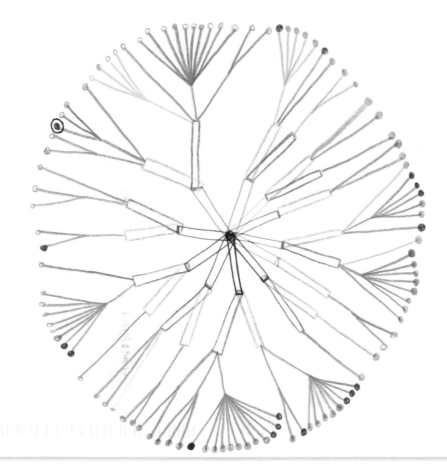

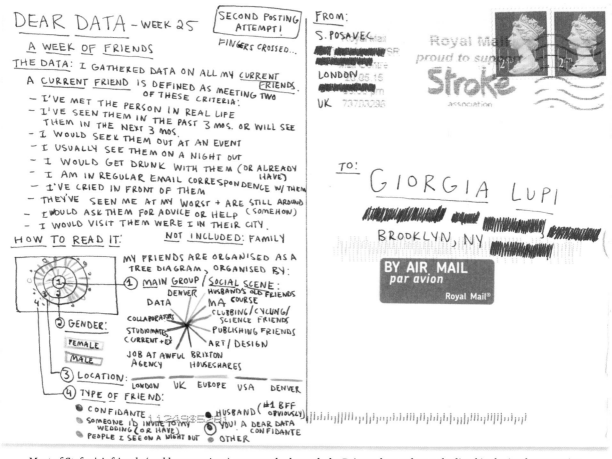

DEAR DATA - WEEK 25

SECOND POSTING ATTEMPT!
FINGERS CROSSED...

A WEEK OF FRIENDS

THE DATA: I GATHERED DATA ON ALL MY CURRENT FRIENDS.

A CURRENT FRIEND IS DEFINED AS MEETING TWO OF THESE CRITERIA:
- I'VE MET THE PERSON IN REAL LIFE
- I'VE SEEN THEM IN THE PAST 3 MOS. OR WILL SEE THEM IN THE NEXT 3 MOS.
- I WOULD SEEK THEM OUT AT AN EVENT
- I USUALLY SEE THEM ON A NIGHT OUT
- I WOULD GET DRUNK WITH THEM (OR ALREADY HAVE)
- I AM IN REGULAR EMAIL CORRESPONDENCE W/ THEM
- THEY'VE SEEN ME AT MY WORST + ARE STILL AROUND (SOMEHOW)
- I WOULD ASK THEM FOR ADVICE OR HELP
- I WOULD VISIT THEM WERE I IN THEIR CITY.

HOW TO READ IT: NOT INCLUDED: FAMILY

MY FRIENDS ARE ORGANISED AS A TREE DIAGRAM, ORGANISED BY:
① MAIN GROUP / SOCIAL SCENE:
   DENVER DATA, HUSBAND'S OLD FRIENDS, MA COURSE, COLLABORATORS, CLUBBING/CYCLING/SCIENCE FRIENDS, STUDIOMATES CURRENT + EX, PUBLISHING FRIENDS, ART/DESIGN, JOB AT AWFUL AGENCY, BRIXTON HOUSESHARES

② GENDER:
   FEMALE
   MALE

③ LOCATION: LONDON UK EUROPE USA DENVER

④ TYPE OF FRIEND:
   ● CONFIDANTE   ● HUSBAND (#1 BFF OBVIOUSLY)
   ● SOMEONE I'D INVITE TO MY WEDDING (OR HAVE) ● YOU! A DEAR DATA CONFIDANTE
   ● PEOPLE I SEE ON A NIGHT OUT   ● OTHER

FROM: S. POSAVEC, LONDON UK

TO: GIORGIA LUPI, BROOKLYN, NY

BY AIR MAIL par avion Royal Mail®

Most of Stefanie's friends (and her marriage) were made through the Brixton houseshares she lived in during her twenties.

133

How do I LOVE THEE? COUNTING SOMETHING means it matters.

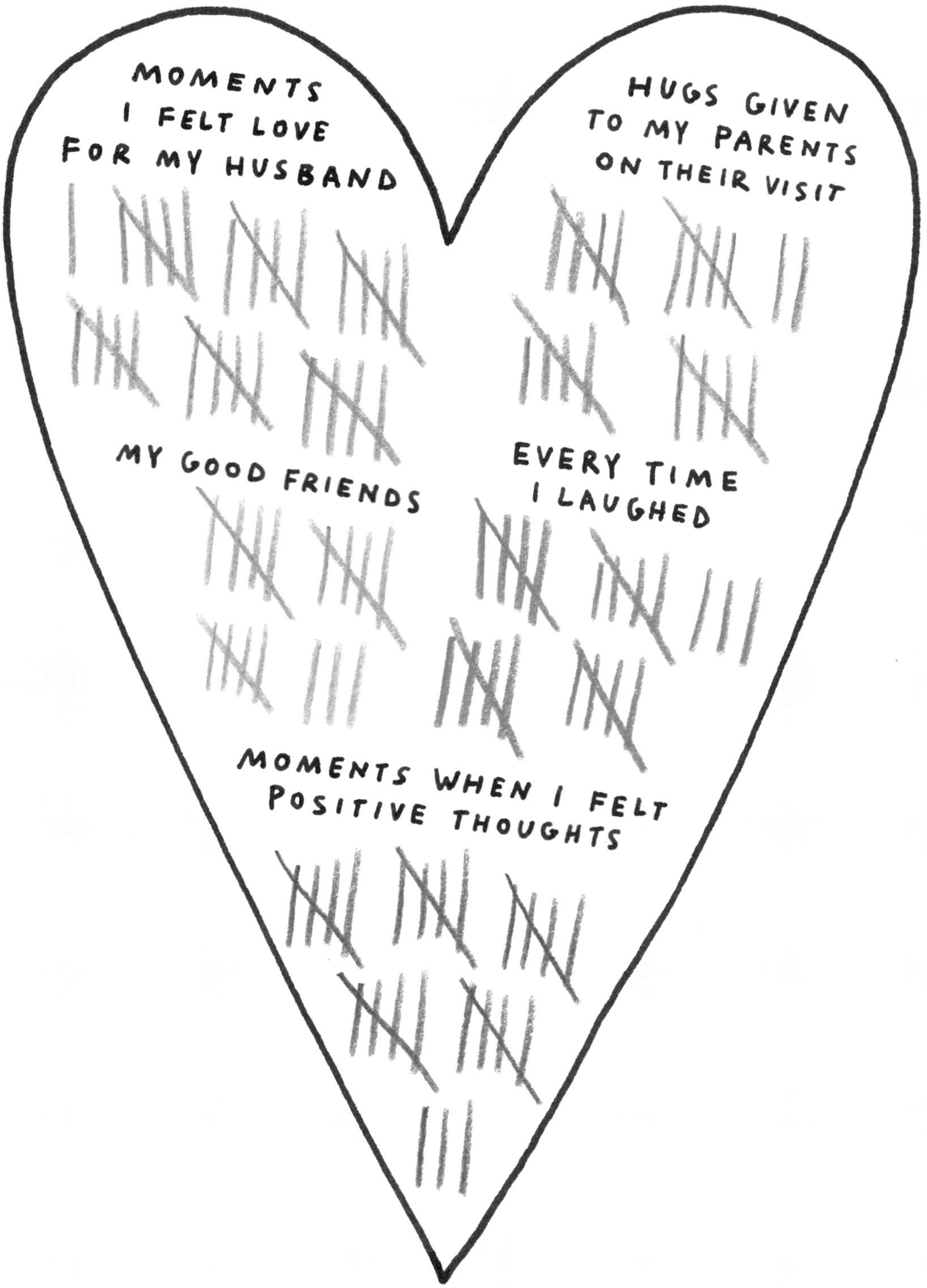

MOMENTS I FELT LOVE FOR MY HUSBAND

HUGS GIVEN TO MY PARENTS ON THEIR VISIT

MY GOOD FRIENDS

EVERY TIME I LAUGHED

MOMENTS WHEN I FELT POSITIVE THOUGHTS

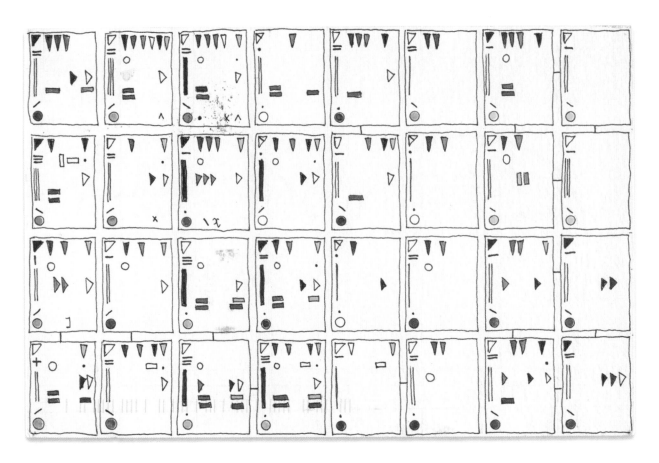

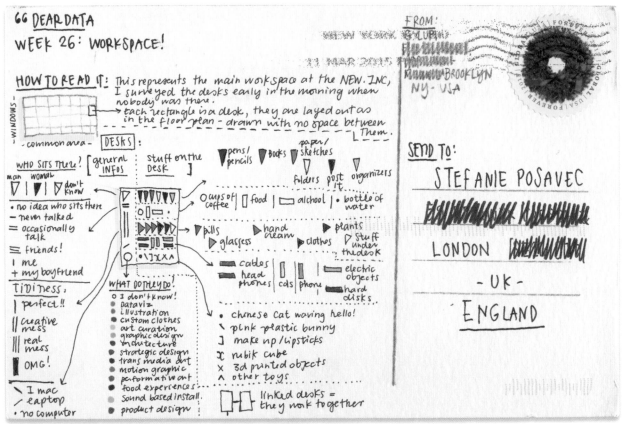

Giorgia surveyed her working space at 5:00 am, spying her coworkers' (messy) desks and finding the most unlikely objects.

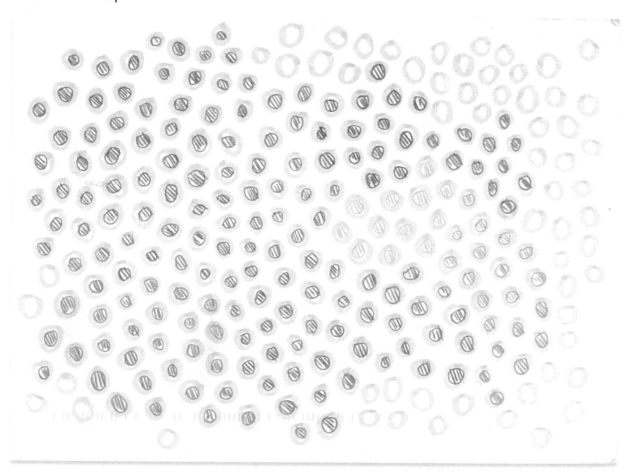

Stefanie rummaged through the detritus on her desktop in her shared studio and realized she doesn't have much of anything useful (well, "useful" in the professional sense).

Stefanie's

WORST DATA

MONDAY
MORNING

138

VOID / EVER.

I feel as though I'm forgetting something... oops.

SUNDAY EVENING

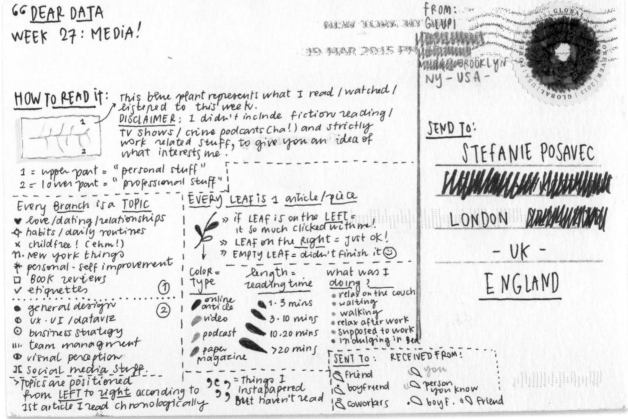

"DEAR DATA
WEEK 27: MEDIA!

HOW TO READ iT: This blue plant represents what I read / watched / listened to this week.
DISCLAIMER: I didn't include fiction reading / TV shows / crime podcasts (ha!) and strictly work related stuff, to give you an idea of what interests me.

1 = upper part = "personal stuff"
2 = lower part = "professional stuff"

Every Branch is a TOPIC
♥ love / dating / relationships
↶ habits / daily routines
✗ childfree! (ehm!)
⋔ new york things
✳ personal - self improvement
☐ Book reviews
✓ etiquettes   ①

● general design   ②
↺ ux · ui / dataviz
business strategy
ɪɪɪɪ team management
◉ visual perception
ⅠⅠ social media stuff

↳Topics are positioned from LEFT to right according to 1st article I read chronologically

EVERY LEAF is 1 article / piece

» if LEAF is on the LEFT = it so much clicked with me!
» LEAF on the Right = just ok!
» EMPTY LEAF = didn't finish it ☺

COLOR = TYPE
● online article
◗ video
⬎ podcast
⬎ paper magazine

length = reading time
⬤ 1 · 3 mins
⬤ 3 · 10 mins
⬤ 10 · 20 mins
⬤ >20 mins

what was I doing?
• relax on the couch
• waiting
• walking
• relax after work
• supposed to work
• indulging in bed

)))(= things I instapapered but haven't read

FROM: GIEUPI
BROOKLYN
NY - USA -

30 MAR 2015 PM

SEND TO:
STEFANIE POSAVEC
~~~~~~~~~~~~~
LONDON ~~~~~~~
- UK -
ENGLAND

SENT TO:	RECEIVED FROM:
friend	you
boyfriend	person you know
coworkers	boyf. · friend

Why does Giorgia always draw with a black pen to begin with? As an incredibly bold move, she used blue this time instead.

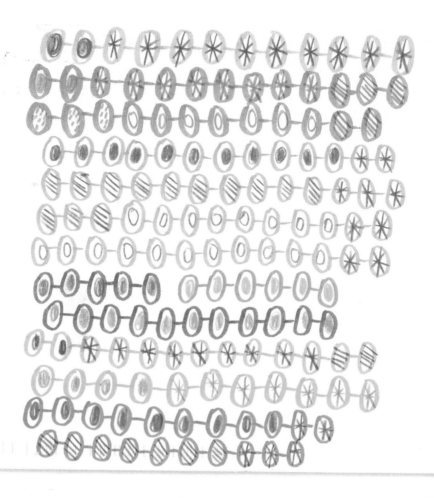

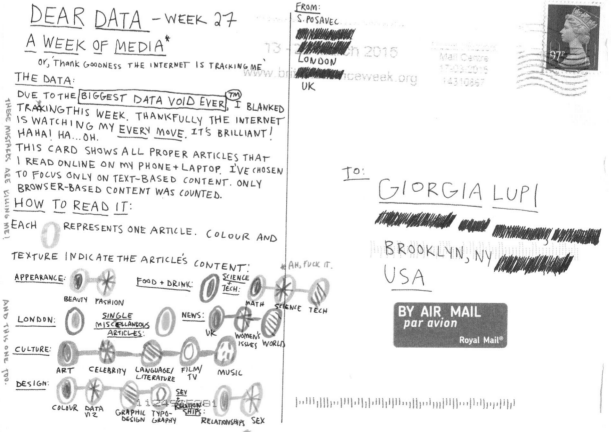

DEAR DATA – WEEK 27
A WEEK OF MEDIA*
or, Thank Goodness the internet is tracking me

THE DATA:

DUE TO THE BIGGEST DATA VOID EVER (TM), I BLANKED TRACKING THIS WEEK. THANKFULLY THE INTERNET IS WATCHING MY EVERY MOVE. IT'S BRILLIANT! HAHA! HA...OH.

THIS CARD SHOWS ALL PROPER ARTICLES THAT I READ ONLINE ON MY PHONE + LAPTOP. I'VE CHOSEN TO FOCUS ONLY ON TEXT-BASED CONTENT. ONLY BROWSER-BASED CONTENT WAS COUNTED.

HOW TO READ IT:

EACH ⬭ REPRESENTS ONE ARTICLE. COLOUR AND TEXTURE INDICATE THE ARTICLE'S CONTENT:

THESE MISTAKES ARE KILLING ME!
AND THIS ONE TOO.

APPEARANCE: BEAUTY   FASHION
FOOD + DRINK:
SCIENCE + TECH: MATH   SCIENCE   TECH
LONDON:
SINGLE MISCELLANEOUS ARTICLES:
NEWS: UK   WOMEN'S ISSUES   WORLD
CULTURE: ART   CELEBRITY   LANGUAGE/LITERATURE   FILM/TV   MUSIC
DESIGN: COLOUR   DATA VIZ   GRAPHIC DESIGN   TYPO-GRAPHY   SEX RELATIONSHIPS   RELATIONSHIPS   SEX

* AH, FUCK IT.

FROM:
S. POSAVEC
~~░░░░░░░~~
~~░░░░░░░~~
LONDON
~~░░░░░~~
UK

TO:
GIORGIA LUPI
~~░░░░░░░░░░░░░~~
BROOKLYN, NY ~~░░░~~
USA

BY AIR MAIL
par avion
Royal Mail®

Besides Week Two, this is the only week where Stefanie unintentionally relied on technology for her data-gathering (and thank goodness, otherwise she would have had to send an empty postcard to Giorgia).

MOMENTS YOU **DON'T** NOTICE ARE AS TELLING AS THOSE YOU **DO.**

A WEEK OF DATA VOIDS

MONDAY MEETING THEATRE

TUESDAY FIGHT WITH HUSBAND

WEDNESDAY WORK STRESS

THURSDAY BOOZY LUNCH CONCERT

FRIDAY PARTY!

SATURDAY HUNGOVER LATE FOR TRAIN

SUNDAY WEDDING

A week of SMILING at STRANGERS

This week, Giorgia thought it might be nice to use her and Stefanie's data-collecting as an opportunity to smile at more strangers than they usually did: a formidable challenge in two metropolises filled with busy, often unsmiling denizens.

"Performative" weeks such as these turn Stefanie into a sulky, petulant teenager being forced to do something she doesn't want to do, but she gritted her teeth and gave the challenge her best shot. Would she survive this week of trying to smile at strangers, or would this performative week be the straw that broke the camel's back?

STEFANIE
ON THE STREETS OF
LONDON DURING
PERFORMATIVE WEEKS

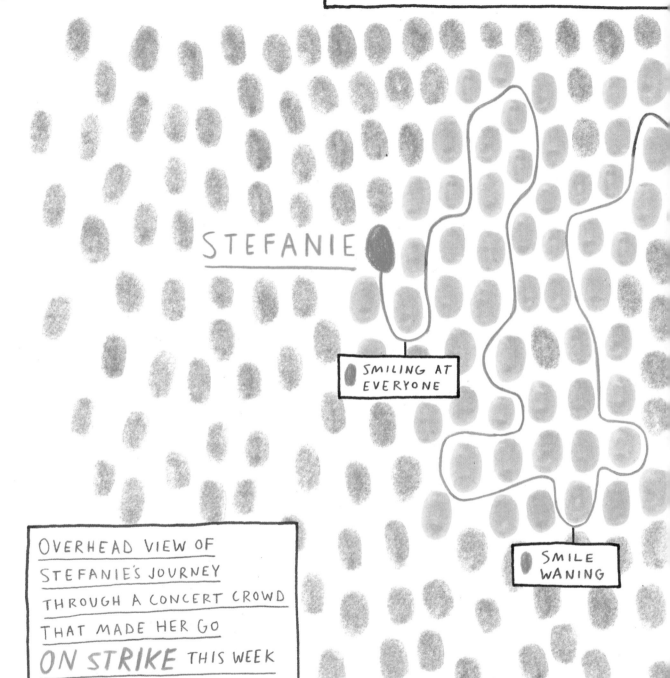

STEFANIE

SMILING AT
EVERYONE

SMILE
WANING

OVERHEAD VIEW OF
STEFANIE'S JOURNEY
THROUGH A CONCERT CROWD
THAT MADE HER GO
ON STRIKE THIS WEEK

HOW TO READ IT:

EACH ⬤ REPRESENTS A
CONCERTGOER

EACH ⬤ REPRESENTS AN
UNSMILING FACE

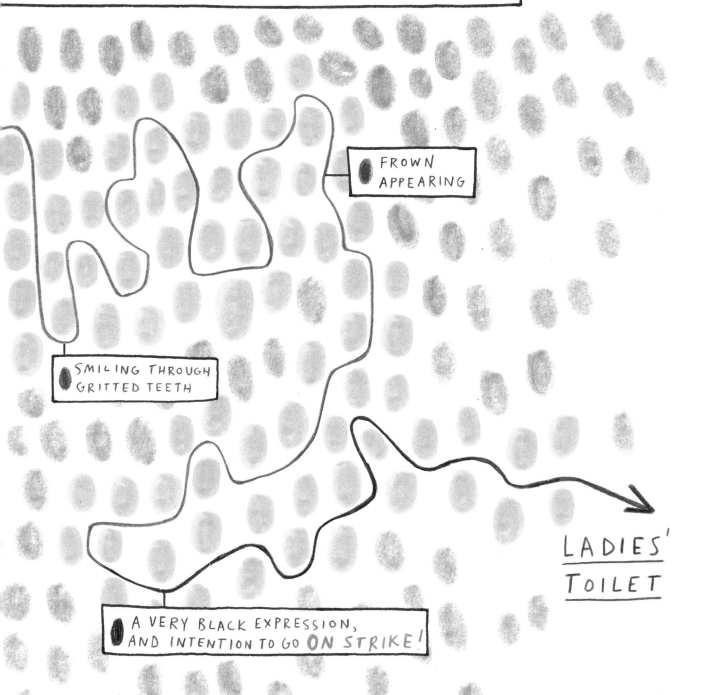

FROWN
APPEARING

SMILING THROUGH
GRITTED TEETH

A VERY BLACK EXPRESSION,
AND INTENTION TO GO **ON STRIKE!**

LADIES'
TOILET

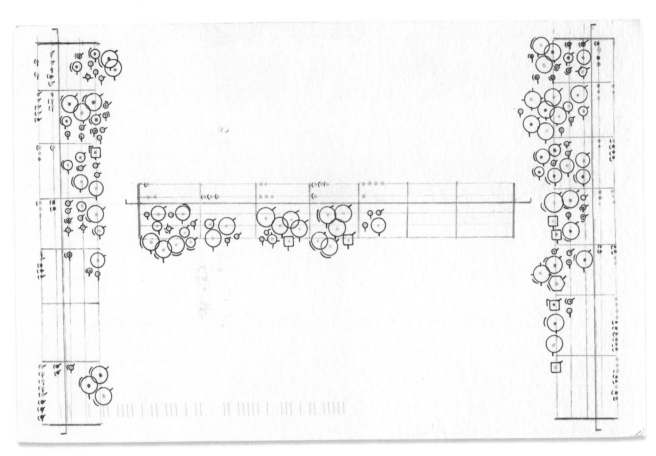

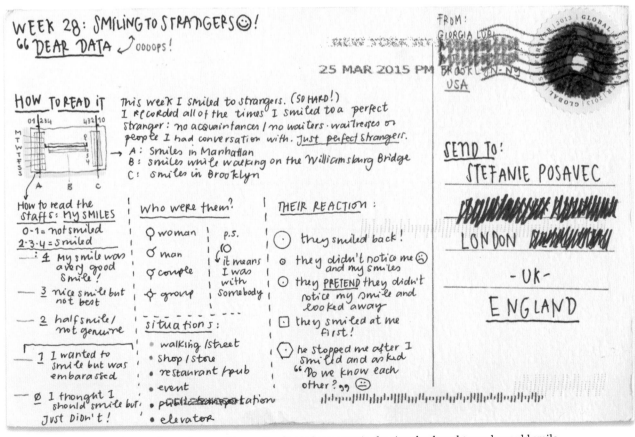

Giorgia drew a schematic map of her smiles divided per areas in the city: she thought people would smile
less in Manhattan than in Brooklyn, but it is not quite true!

DEAR DATA - WEEK 28

<u>A WEEK OF SMILES</u>

OR: "WHY I'M AN ASSHOLE (PART 2),
BUT SO IS <u>EVERYONE ELSE</u>!"

THE DATA: I TRIED TO GO OUT OF MY WAY TO
SMILE AT PEOPLE BUT ABSOLUTELY <u>HATED</u> IT.

LOCATION, TYPE OF PERSON (MAN/WOMAN/CHILD),
+ THEIR RESPONSE TO MY SMILE WERE ALL TRACKED
CULMINATING IN A MASSIVE DATA VOID
OF PROTEST AT THE END OF THE WEEK.

HOW TO READ IT:

BLANK DAY: ONLY
REALISED AFTER
I DIDN'T LEAVE
THE HOUSE <u>ALL DAY!</u>
BAD HABITS OF A
FREELANCER...

EACH <u>TRIANGLE</u> REPRESENTS
THE RESPONSE I RECEIVED TO
A SMILE:

SMILED BACK

<u>DIDN'T</u> SMILE BACK

<u>DIDN'T</u> NOTICE MY SMILE

TEXTURE = TYPE OF PERSON:

WOMAN MAN CHILD

LOCATION OF SMILE:
MY ESTATE
STREET
CAFE
TRANSPORT
SOMEONE'S OFFICE
CLUB/CONCERT
SHOP/MARKET

SPECIAL SYMBOLS:

MY NOTES SAY THIS REPRESENTS:
- the multitude of assholes
who wouldn't let me through
the crowd when I needed to get
STOPPED SMILING at the show &
IN PROTEST TO ASSHOLES (I WAS a little drunk)

FROM:
S POSAVEC
~~▓▓▓▓▓~~
~~▓▓▓▓▓~~
LONDON ~~▓▓▓~~
UK

Royal Mail
Mount Pleasant
Mail Centre
26-03-2015
44301575

TO:

GIORGIA LUPI

~~▓▓▓▓▓▓▓▓▓▓▓▓▓▓▓~~

BROOKLYN, NY ~~▓▓▓~~

USA

BY AIR MAIL
par avion
Royal Mail®

Stefanie drew right-side-up and upside-down triangles for this week as she thought they
looked visually similar to smiles and frowns.

GIORGIA'S
PATHS THROUGH
THE CITY TO CATCH
STRANGERS' ATTENTION
WITH HER SMILES

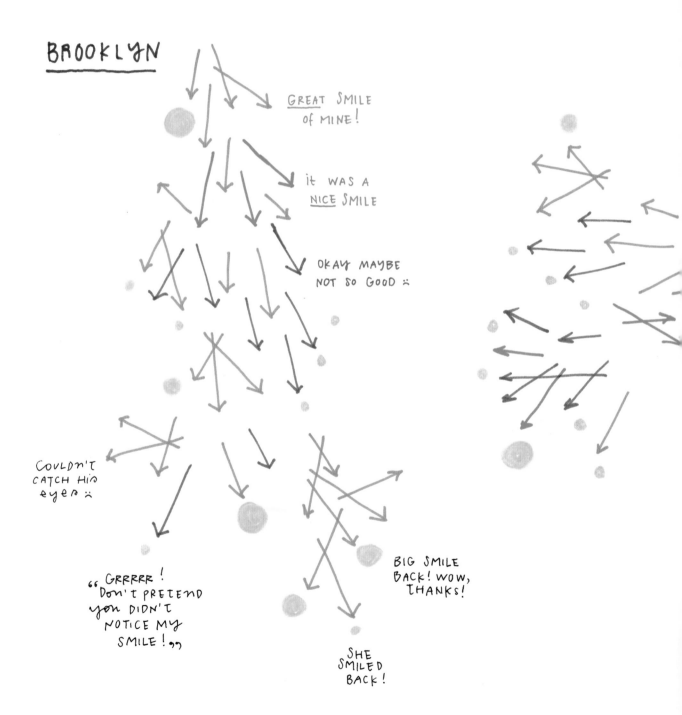

BROOKLYN

GREAT SMILE
of MINE!

it WAS A
NICE SMILE

OKAY MAYBE
NOT SO GOOD ∺

COULDN'T
CATCH HIS
eyes ∺

"GRRRRR!
Don't PRETEND
you DIDN'T
NOTICE MY
SMILE!"

BIG SMILE
BACK! WOW,
THANKS!

SHE
SMILED
BACK!

MANHATTAN

WALKING OVER THE BRIDGE

PEDESTRIAN REACTING TO MY BIG SMILE:

"EXCUSE ME, DO WE KNOW EACH OTHER?"

A week of a
BOYFRIEND / HUSBAND
(giorgia)   (Stefanie)

For many weeks now, Giorgia and Stefanie knew they wanted to spend time gathering data on their partners (the additional collaborators in this project, due to their patience with non-stop data-gathering!). However, as the pair didn't want their partners to influence the data-gathering process, they both agreed to gather this data secretly and only tell their partners about it afterwards (asking permission from them to use their data, of course).

Both Giorgia and Stefanie decided to track moments where their partners inspired positive or negative feelings in them, and had to change the subject when asked the usual question: "What are you tracking this week?"

However, as the week unfolded Stefanie felt a little uneasy: was it ok to secretly spy on your husband if you were doing it out of love? Or was it as questionable as secret data-gathering would be if a police force or a government was collecting data without permission?

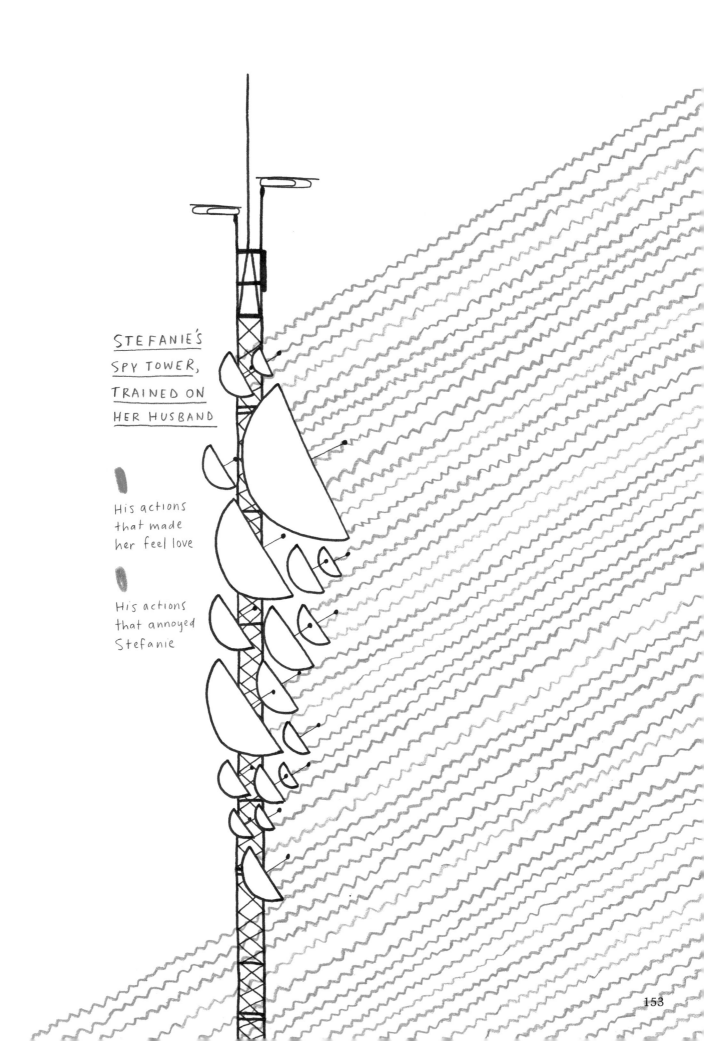

STEFANIE'S
SPY TOWER,
TRAINED ON
HER HUSBAND

His actions
that made
her feel love

His actions
that annoyed
Stefanie

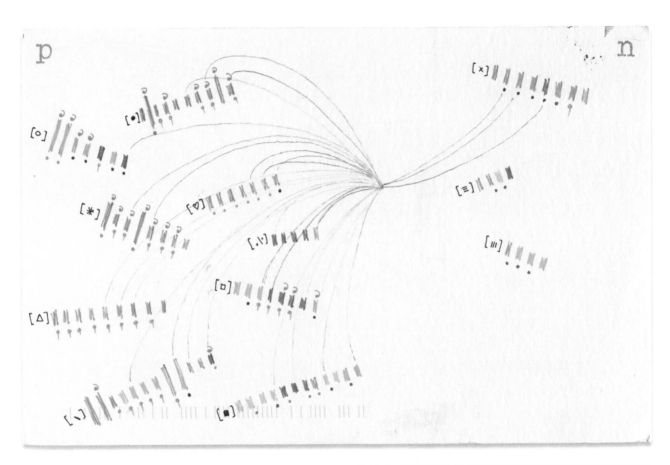

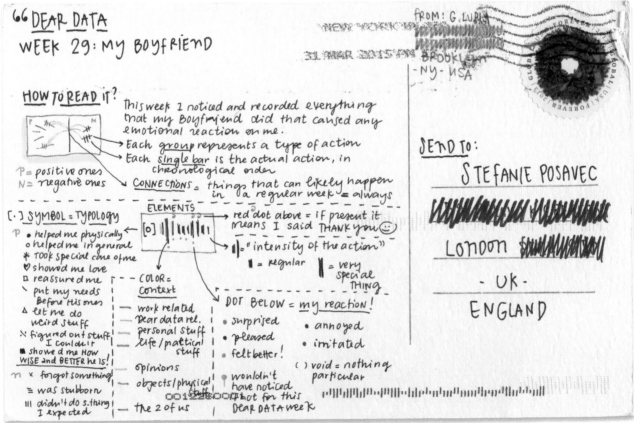

66 **DEAR DATA**
WEEK 29: MY BOYFRIEND

HOW TO READ IT?

This week I noticed and recorded everything that my Boyfriend did that caused any emotional reaction on me.

→ Each group represents a type of action
→ Each single bar is the actual action, in chronological order

P = positive ones
N = negative ones

CONNECTIONS = things that can likely happen in a regular week = always

[·] SYMBOL = TYPOLOGY

P
• helped me physically ←
o helped me in general
* took special care of me
♡ showed me love
▱ reassured me
↘ put my needs before His ones
△ let me do weird stuff
✕ figured out stuff I couldn'r
■ showed me How WISE and BETTER he is!

N
✕ forgot something
≡ was stubborn
ꟼꟼꟼ didn't do s.thing I expected

ELEMENTS
[o]

red dot above = if present it means I said THANK you ☺

∥ = "intensity of the action"
∣ = regular
∥ = very special THING

— COLOR = Context
— work related
— Dear data rel.
— personal stuff
— life / pratical stuff
— opinions
— objects / physical stuff
— the 2 of us

DOT BELOW = my reaction!
• surprised
• pleased
• felt better!
• wouldn't have noticed tho' not for this DEAR DATA week

• annoyed
• irritated

( ) void = nothing particular

FROM: G. LUPI
NEW YORK
31 MAR 2015
BROOKLYN
- NY - USA

SEND TO:

STEFANIE POSAVEC

LONDON

- UK -

ENGLAND

Giorgia found this an incredibly useful exercise for the week: it made her acknowledge the feelings her partner triggered, and counting and visualizing it made her see how she took his love and care for granted.

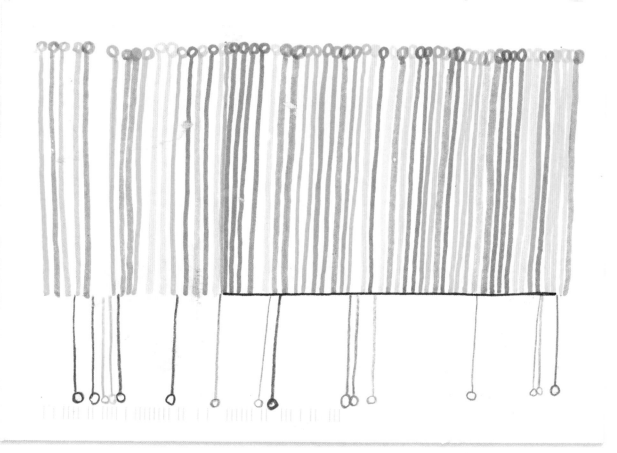

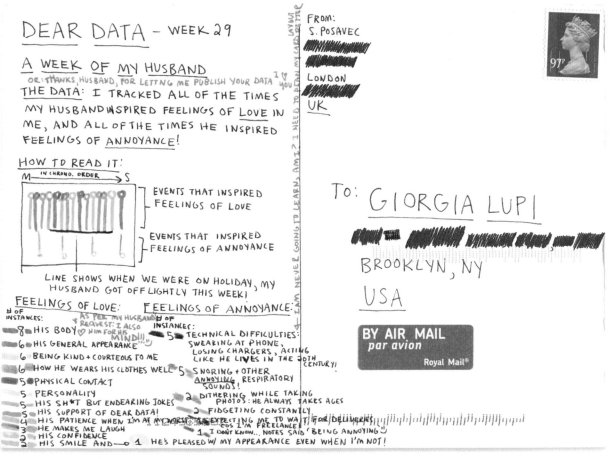

Since she was using his data, Stefanie asked her husband to approve the final postcard: due to "His Body" being the thing that most often inspired feelings of love, he asked her to add a caveat in red pen!

STEFANIE'S DATA-STALKING CONFESSION

LOVE

ANNOYANCE

SUNDAY EVENING, BEFORE BED

MONDAY, MAKING DINNER

I data you

BY COUNTING
ALL HER BOYFRIEND'S
POSITIVE ACTIONS,
GIORGIA REALIZED
HOW MANY THERE
ARE, AND HOW
LITTLE ATTENTION
SHE USUALLY
PAYS TO THEM.

*YOU SHOULD
ALL TRY THIS
AT HOME, AT
LEAST FOR A
WEEK.*

ALL of
THE TIMES
you

SHOWED
ME
YOUR
LOVE

'''

CARRIED
MY
BAGS

'''

HUGGED
ME
JUST
BECAUSE

'''

ORGANIZED
YOUR
TIME
AROUND
MY
NEEDS

'''

SOLVED
MY
TECHNOLOGICAL
PROBLEMS

'''

TOOK
SPECIAL
CARE
OF
ME

'''

LET
ME
EAT
FROM
YOUR
PLATE
(WITH
MY
HANDS)

'''

FIXED
A MESS
I MADE

'''

DIDN'T
GET
MAD
AT
ME
WHEN
YOU
SHOULD
TOTALLY
ABSOLUTELY
HAVE

'''

159

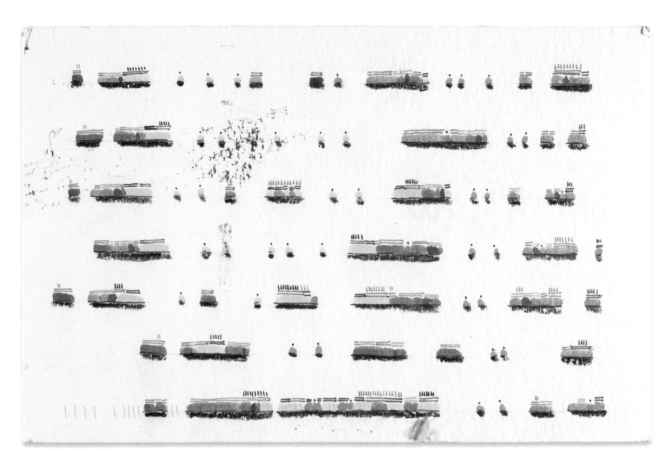

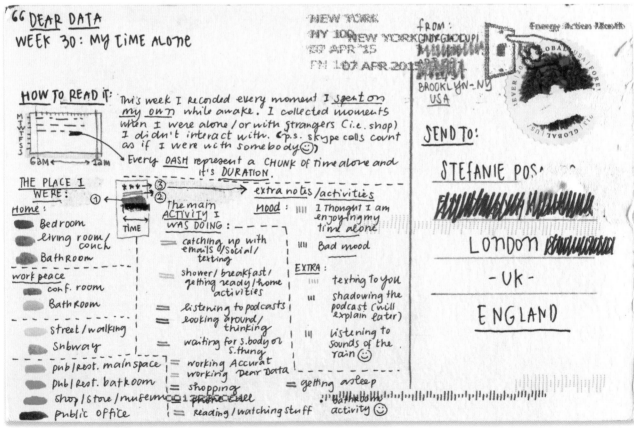

Giorgia's drawing of the negative space of her time alone during her days. It was a special week since
her boyfriend was away, and she happened to spend much more time on her own than usual.

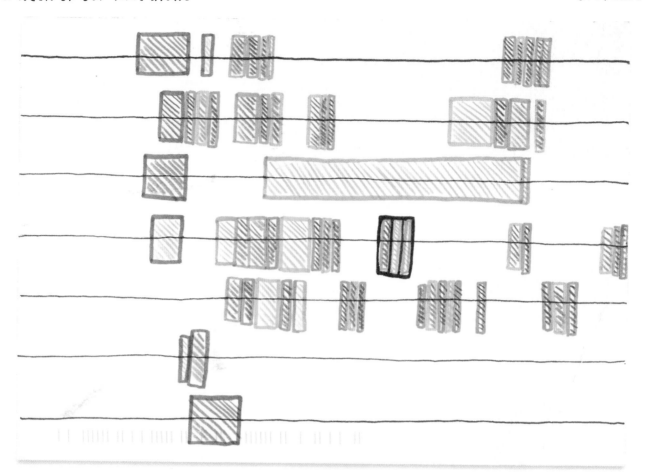

DEAR DATA - WEEK 30

A WEEK OF BEING ALONE

THE DATA: I COUNTED MOMENTS WHEN I WAS
ALONE, ALONE BEING THAT I WAS IN A PLACE
FILLED WITH STRANGERS OR IN A PLACE WHERE I
WAS PHYSICALLY ALONE. I'VE ALSO DIFFERENTIATED
BETWEEN BEING ALONE AND FEELING ALONE.

HOW TO READ IT:

0:00 ➡ 23:00

M
T
W
T
F
S
S

EACH ▨ REPRESENTS A TIME I WAS
ALONE.

THE WIDTH OF THE BAR INDICATES THE
LENGTH OF TIME I WAS ALONE IN THIS
PARTICULAR SITUATION, SCALED TO THE
WIDTH OF THE CARD (= 5 24 HOURS.)

WAYS I WAS
ALONE:

▯ IN HOUSE
WITH
HUSBAND
ASLEEP

▯ PHYSICALLY
ALONE IN
A SPACE

▯ ALONE IN
A SPACE
FILLED W/
STRANGERS

▯ ALONE IN
A CITY OF
STRANGERS
(OUTSIDE)

▯ THE ONLY
TIMES I FELT
EMOTIONALLY
ALONE

WHAT I
WAS DOING WHEN
I WAS ALONE:

//// EXERCISING
//// SHOPPING
//// WORKING
//// DEAR DATA!
//// WASTING TIME
ON INTERNET
//// MORNING/
EVENING ROUTINES
//// WALKING
//// TRAVELLING
(PUBLIC TRANSPORT)
//// BUYING/ PREPARING
FOOD, GETTING COFFEE

TOP 3 ACTIVITIES
I DID WHILE
ALONE THIS
WEEK:

① WORK - 17:11
(I WORK FROM HOME
WHEN I'M LAZY)

② DEAR DATA -
6:56
(I GET UP EARLY
TO DRAW)

③ WALKING -
5:46
(I WALK TO/FROM
MY STUDIO)

FROM:
S POSAVEC

LONDON
UK

Royal Mail
Mount Pleasant
Mail Centre
07-04-2015
44016000

97P

TO: GIORGIA LUPI

BROOKLYN, NY

USA

BY AIR MAIL
par avion
Royal Mail®

Stefanie is an early riser, evidenced by all her early-morning drawing: she works on *Dear Data*
in the mornings to keep her evenings free for spending time with her husband and friends.

A week of
POSITIVE
THOUGHTS

The flowers were blooming, the days were growing
longer, and Giorgia and Stefanie were filled with
the optimism that comes with warmer weather.
To commemorate this, they chose to spend a week
tracking the positive emotions they felt as they
walked through a week of springtime. When would
they feel positive thoughts, and to whom or what
would these positive thoughts be directed?

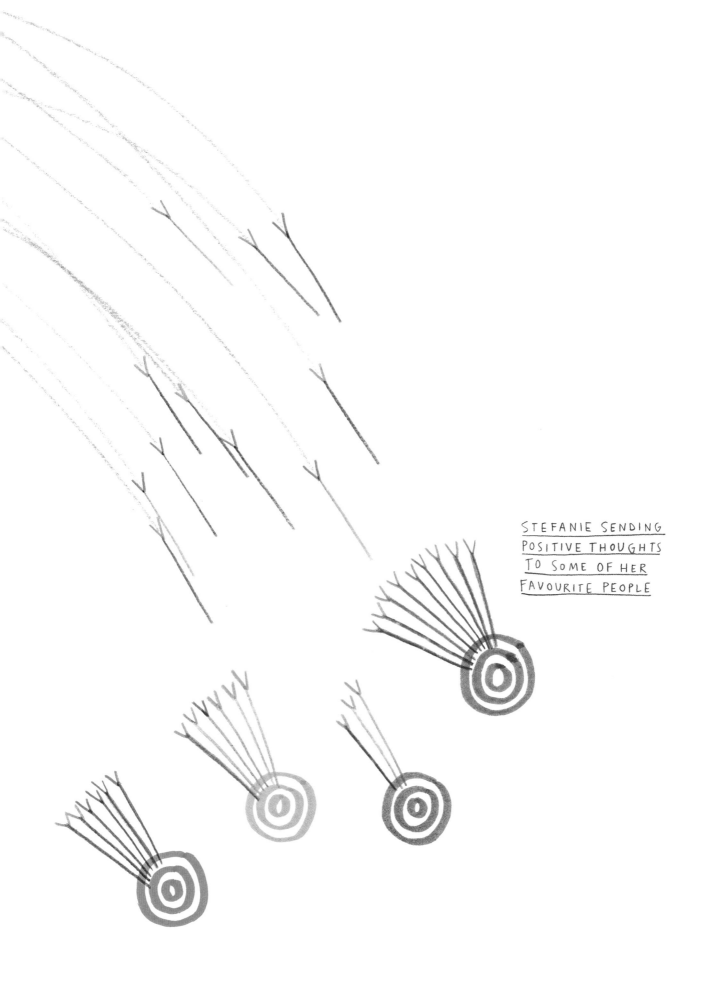

STEFANIE SENDING
POSITIVE THOUGHTS
TO SOME OF HER
FAVOURITE PEOPLE

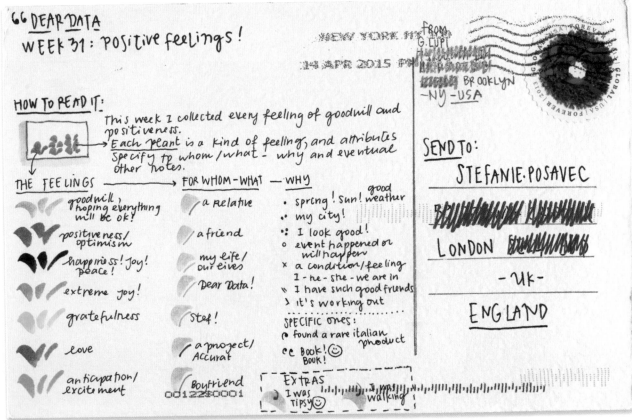

66 DEAR DATA
WEEK 31: Positive feelings!

NEW YORK NY
FROM
G. LUPI
14 APR 2015 PM
BROOKLYN
-NY-USA

HOW TO READ IT:

This week I collected every feeling of goodwill and
positiveness.
Each plant is a kind of feeling, and attributes
specify to whom/what - why and eventual
other notes.

THE FEELINGS   FOR WHOM-WHAT   WHY

goodwill,   a Relative   • spring! sun! good weather
hoping everything   •• my city!
will be ok!   a friend   •: I look good!
positiveness/   o event happened or
optimism   my life/   will happen
happiness! joy!   ourselves   × a condition/feeling
peace!   I - he - she - we are in
                                Dear Data!   ∾ I have such good friends
extreme joy!   ꒦ it's working out
                                Stef!
gratefulness   SPECIFIC ONES:
                                                     o found a rare italian
love   a project/   product
                                Accurat   cc Book! ☺
anticipation/   Boyfriend   Book!
excitement   0012230001

SEND TO:
STEFANIE·POSAVEC
~~~~~~~~~~~~~~~~
LONDON ~~~~~~
- UK -
ENGLAND

EXTRAS
I was
tipsy ☺   I was
               walking

What Giorgia took away from this week's data drawing: when you're tipsy and walking the streets
of New York, everything inspires joy and happiness. Argh!

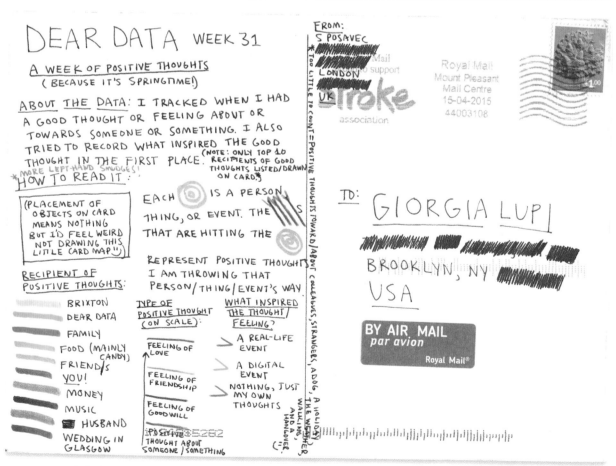

DEAR DATA WEEK 31

A WEEK OF POSITIVE THOUGHTS
(BECAUSE IT'S SPRINGTIME!)

ABOUT THE DATA: I TRACKED WHEN I HAD
A GOOD THOUGHT OR FEELING ABOUT OR
TOWARDS SOMEONE OR SOMETHING. I ALSO
TRIED TO RECORD WHAT INSPIRED THE GOOD
THOUGHT IN THE FIRST PLACE. (NOTE: ONLY TOP 10
RECIPIENTS OF GOOD
THOUGHTS LISTED/DRAWN
ON CARD.)
*MORE LEFT-HAND SMUDGES!
HOW TO READ IT:

(PLACEMENT OF
OBJECTS ON CARD
MEANS NOTHING
BUT I'D FEEL WEIRD
NOT DRAWING THIS
LITTLE CARD MAP!")

EACH ◎ IS A PERSON,
THING, OR EVENT. THE
THAT ARE HITTING THE

REPRESENT POSITIVE THOUGHTS
I AM THROWING THAT
PERSON/THING/EVENT'S WAY

RECIPIENT OF
POSITIVE THOUGHTS:

  ▬▬▬ BRIXTON
  ▬▬▬ DEAR DATA
  ▬▬▬ FAMILY
  ▬▬▬ FOOD (MAINLY
               CANDY)
  ▬▬▬ FRIEND/S
  ▬▬▬ YOU!
  ▬▬▬ MONEY
  ▬▬▬ MUSIC
  ▬▬ HUSBAND
  ▬▬▬ WEDDING IN
       GLASGOW

TYPE OF
POSITIVE THOUGHT
(ON SCALE):

  ⟶ FEELING OF
      LOVE

  ⟶ FEELING OF
      FRIENDSHIP

  ⟶ FEELING OF
      GOODWILL

  ⟶ POSITIVE
      THOUGHT ABOUT
      SOMEONE/SOMETHING

WHAT INSPIRED
THE THOUGHT/
FEELING?

  ⟶ A REAL-LIFE
      EVENT

  ⟶ A DIGITAL
      EVENT

  ⟶ NOTHING, JUST
      MY OWN
      THOUGHTS

FROM:
S POSAVEC
▬▬▬▬
LONDON
UK

Royal Mail
Mount Pleasant
Mail Centre
16-04-2015
44003108

$1.00

TO: GIORGIA LUPI
▬▬▬▬▬ ▬▬▬▬▬▬
BROOKLYN, NY
USA

BY AIR MAIL
par avion
Royal Mail®

Stefanie's vertical central tiny text reads: "too little to count: positive thoughts towards/about colleagues,
strangers, a dog, a holiday, the weather, walking, and a hangover."

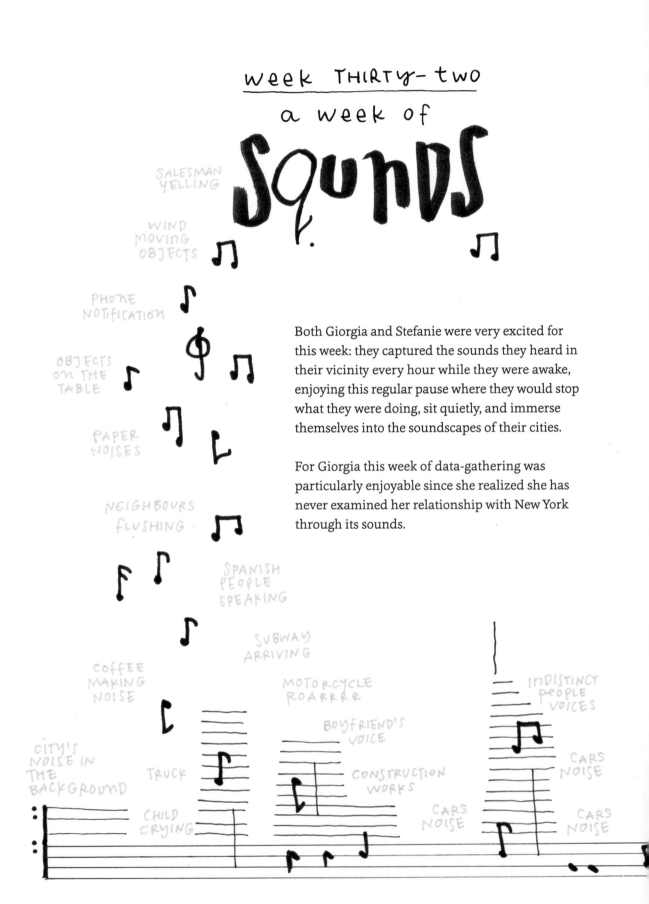

week THIRTY-two
a week of
SOUNDS

SALESMAN YELLING

WIND MOVING OBJECTS

PHONE NOTIFICATION

OBJECTS ON THE TABLE

PAPER NOISES

NEIGHBOURS FLUSHING

SPANISH PEOPLE SPEAKING

SUBWAY ARRIVING

COFFEE MAKING NOISE

MOTORCYCLE ROARRRR

BOYFRIEND'S VOICE

INDISTINCT PEOPLE VOICES

CITY'S NOISE IN THE BACKGROUND

TRUCK

CONSTRUCTION WORKS

CARS NOISE

CHILD CRYING

CARS NOISE

CARS NOISE

Both Giorgia and Stefanie were very excited for this week: they captured the sounds they heard in their vicinity every hour while they were awake, enjoying this regular pause where they would stop what they were doing, sit quietly, and immerse themselves into the soundscapes of their cities.

For Giorgia this week of data-gathering was particularly enjoyable since she realized she has never examined her relationship with New York through its sounds.

GIORGIA'S HOMAGE TO NEW YORK'S SOUNDSCAPE

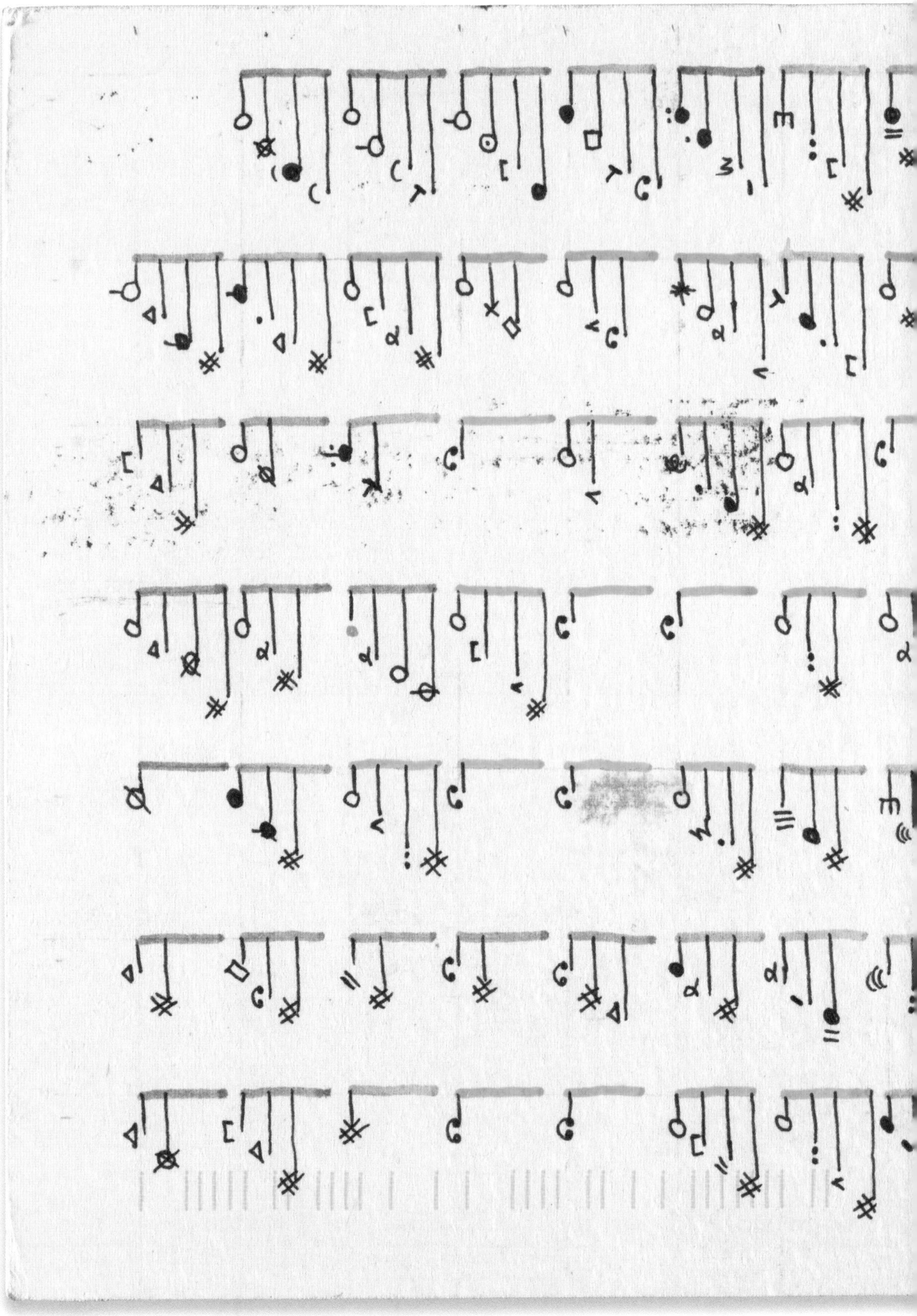

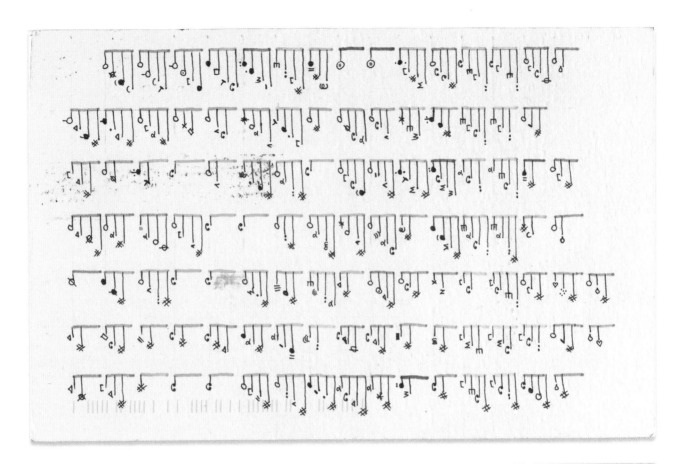

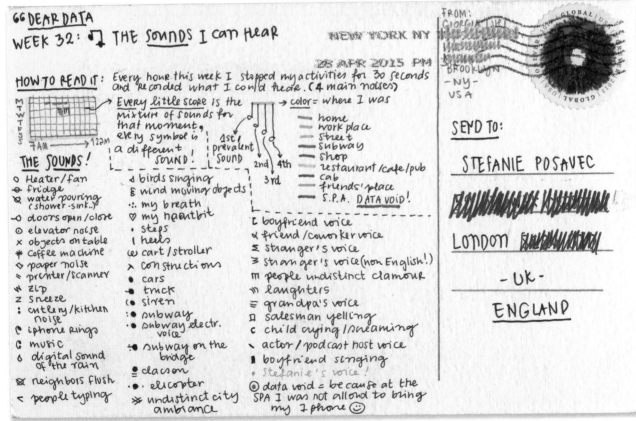

This week, while tracking at every clock of the hour, Giorgia sometimes closed her eyes to only listen and not see, imagining what was happening through the sounds of her surroundings.

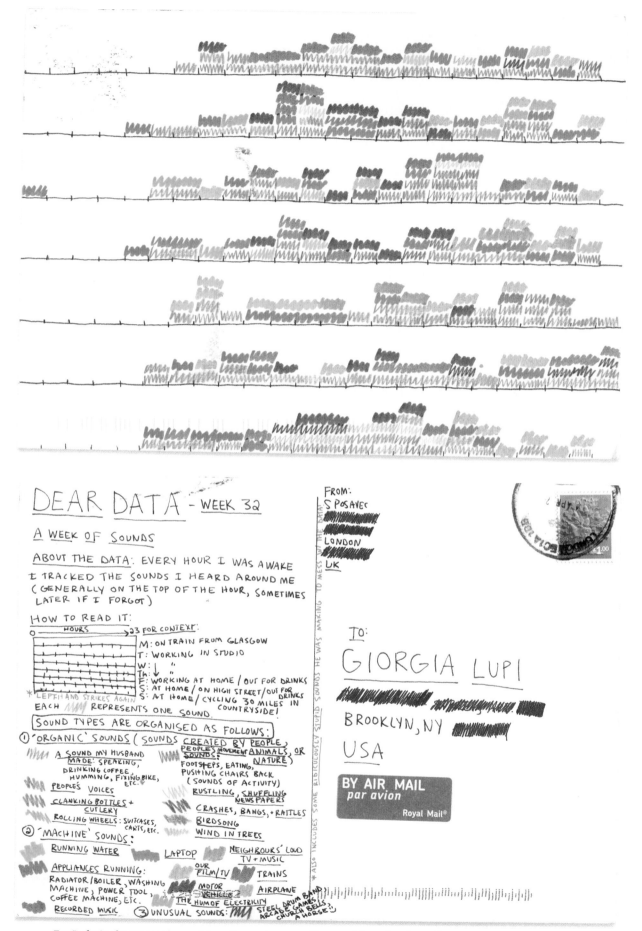

DEAR DATA - WEEK 32

A WEEK OF SOUNDS

ABOUT THE DATA: EVERY HOUR I WAS AWAKE
I TRACKED THE SOUNDS I HEARD AROUND ME
(GENERALLY ON THE TOP OF THE HOUR, SOMETIMES
LATER IF I FORGOT)

HOW TO READ IT:

0 ── HOURS ──→ 23 FOR CONTEXT:
M: ON TRAIN FROM GLASGOW
T: WORKING IN STUDIO
W: ↓ "
Th: ↓ "
F: WORKING AT HOME / OUT FOR DRINKS
S: AT HOME / ON HIGH STREET / OUT FOR DRINKS
S: AT HOME / CYCLING 30 MILES IN COUNTRYSIDE!

*LEFTH AND STRIKES AGAIN

EACH ʍ REPRESENTS ONE SOUND.

SOUND TYPES ARE ORGANISED AS FOLLOWS:
① 'ORGANIC' SOUNDS (SOUNDS CREATED BY PEOPLE,
PEOPLE'S MOVEMENT, ANIMALS, OR
SOUNDS: NATURE)

A SOUND MY HUSBAND
MADE: SPEAKING,
DRINKING COFFEE,
HUMMING, FIXING BIKE,
ETC.
PEOPLE'S VOICES
CLANKING BOTTLES +
CUTLERY
ROLLING WHEELS: SUITCASES,
CARTS, ETC.
② 'MACHINE' SOUNDS:
RUNNING WATER
APPLIANCES RUNNING:
RADIATOR/BOILER, WASHING
MACHINE, POWER TOOL,
COFFEE MACHINE, ETC.
RECORDED MUSIC

FOOTSTEPS, EATING,
PUSHING CHAIRS BACK
(SOUNDS OF ACTIVITY)
RUSTLING, SHUFFLING
NEWSPAPERS
CRASHES, BANGS, + RATTLES
BIRDSONG
WIND IN TREES

LAPTOP   NEIGHBOURS' LOUD
                TV + MUSIC
OUR
FILM/TV   TRAINS
MOTOR
VEHICLE   AIRPLANE
THE HUM OF ELECTRICITY
③ UNUSUAL SOUNDS: STEEL DRUM BAND
                   ARCADE GAMES,
                   CHURCH BELLS,
                   A HORSE!

*ALSO INCLUDES SOME RIDICULOUSLY STUPID SOUNDS HE WAS MAKING TO MESS UP THE DATA

FROM:
S POSAVEC
▓▓▓▓▓▓▓▓▓
LONDON
UK   £1.00

TO:
GIORGIA LUPI
▓▓▓▓▓▓▓▓▓▓▓▓
BROOKLYN, NY
USA

BY AIR MAIL
par avion
Royal Mail®

For Stefanie, the "unusual sounds" are the most memorable: a steel drum band outside Brixton tube station, playing
arcade games in a bar, cycling out of London on a sunny Sunday afternoon and hearing a horse and church bells!

A WEEK OF ENVY

A year of gathering personal data wouldn't be complete without an interrogation of the worst parts of the self, and envy is one of the worst, and one of the most revealing.

What personal insecurities and vulnerabilities are revealed to each other when Giorgia and Stefanie capture these dark thoughts on paper?

envious of their SUCCESS

envious of their
APPEARANCE

STEFANIE RUINING

NICE MEMORIES WITH ENVY

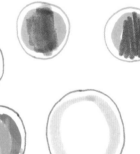

envious of their LIFE EXPERIENCES

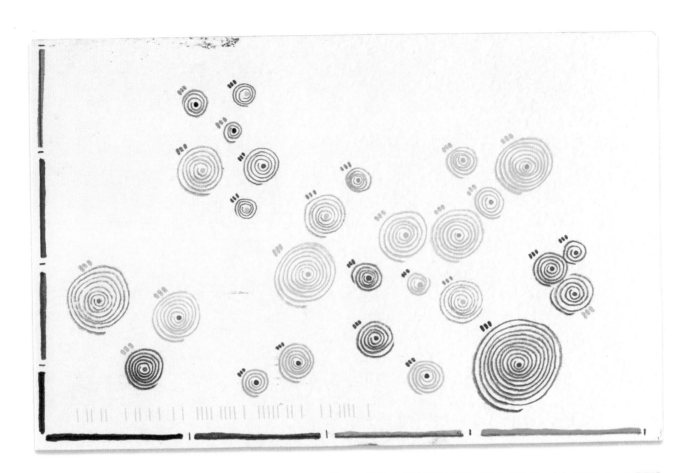

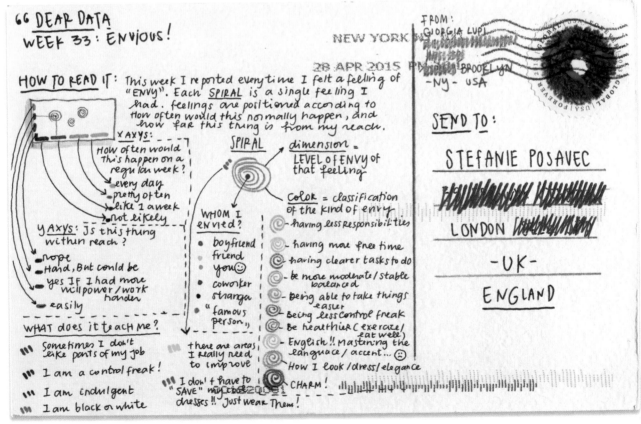

Giorgia: "I am so envious of all of you charming native English speakers with no accent! Grrrr!"

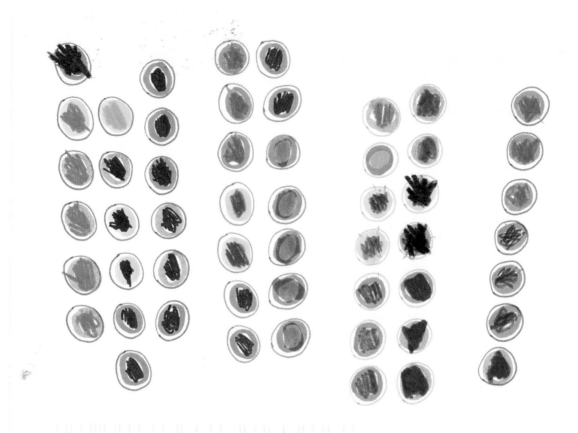

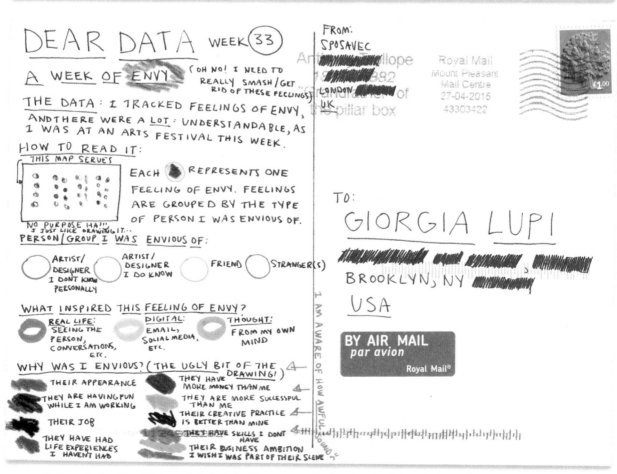

DEAR DATA   WEEK ③③

A WEEK OF ENVY (OH NO! I NEED TO REALLY SMASH/GET RID OF THESE FEELINGS)

THE DATA: I TRACKED FEELINGS OF ENVY, AND THERE WERE A LOT: UNDERSTANDABLE, AS I WAS AT AN ARTS FESTIVAL THIS WEEK.

HOW TO READ IT:
THIS MAP SERVES
NO PURPOSE HA!! I JUST LIKE DRAWING IT...

EACH ⬤ REPRESENTS ONE FEELING OF ENVY. FEELINGS ARE GROUPED BY THE TYPE OF PERSON I WAS ENVIOUS OF.

PERSON/GROUP I WAS ENVIOUS OF:
○ ARTIST/DESIGNER I DONT KNOW PERSONALLY   ○ ARTIST/DESIGNER I DO KNOW   ○ FRIEND   ○ STRANGER(S)

WHAT INSPIRED THIS FEELING OF ENVY?
⬤ REAL LIFE: SEEING THE PERSON, CONVERSATIONS, ETC.   ○ DIGITAL: EMAIL, SOCIAL MEDIA, ETC.   ⬤ THOUGHT: FROM MY OWN MIND

WHY WAS I ENVIOUS? (THE UGLY BIT OF THE DRAWING!)
THEIR APPEARANCE
THEY ARE HAVING FUN WHILE I AM WORKING
THEIR JOB
THEY HAVE HAD LIFE EXPERIENCES I HAVENT HAD
THEY HAVE MORE MONEY THAN ME
THEY ARE MORE SUCCESSFUL THAN ME
THEIR CREATIVE PRACTICE IS BETTER THAN MINE
THEY HAVE SKILLS I DONT HAVE
THEIR BUSINESS AMBITION I WISH I WAS PART OF THEIR SCENE

I AM AWARE OF HOW AWFUL I SOUND

FROM: SPOSAVEC
London UK
Royal Mail Mount Pleasant Mail Centre 27-04-2015

TO: GIORGIA LUPI
BROOKLYN, NY
USA
BY AIR MAIL par avion Royal Mail®

By the end of writing this legend, Stefanie had begun to realize how irrational these feelings of envy sounded, because she was often envious of things that she couldn't change about herself.

175

SHARE YOUR ~~BEST~~ VULNERABLE
SELF TO MAKE THE BEST ~~Y~~ AND MORE REAL
CONNECTIONS

⑦ MY UN·NECESSARY COMPLAINTS

㉗ MY DIS·INTEREST for POLITICS and news

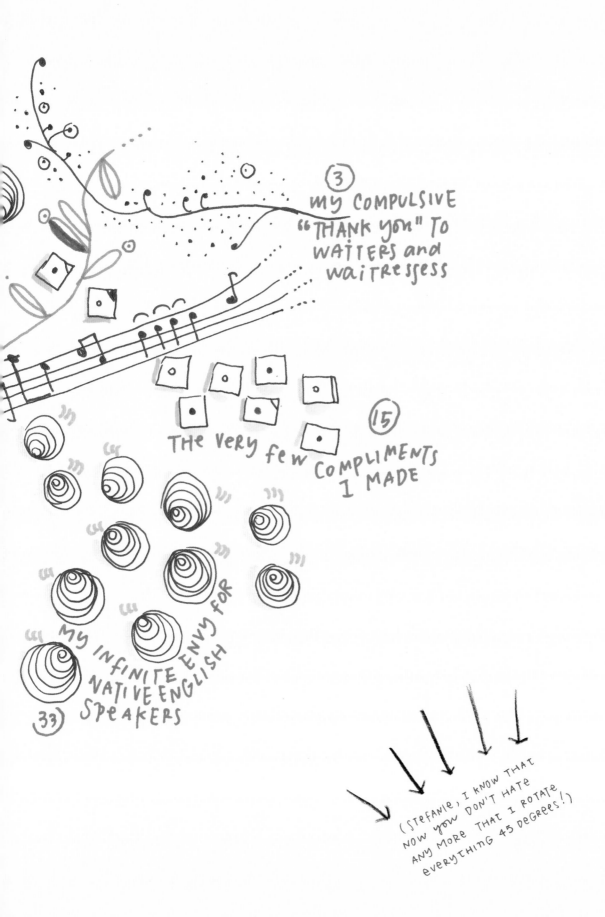

③ MY COMPULSIVE "THANK YOU" TO WATTERS and WAITRESSESS

⑮ THE VERY FEW COMPLIMENTS I MADE

MY INFINITE ENVY FOR NATIVE ENGLISH 33) SPEAKERS

(STEFANIE, I KNOW THAT NOW YOU DON'T HATE ANY MORE THAT I ROTATE EVERYTHING 45 DEGREES!)

WEEK THIRTY-FOUR

A WEEK OF

Urban wildlife

Stefanie eagerly anticipated this week of data-gathering, as she was looking forward to gathering data on all of the cats she regularly petted and said hello to on her London housing estate, while Giorgia's favourite friends were all the dogs she saw on the streets of New York.

As the week commenced both Giorgia and Stefanie kept their eagle eyes on all the animals (and with any luck, eagles) they spotted in their urban environments.

A blurred flock of
SOUTH LONDON PARAKEETS*
as they fly from treetop
to treetop in Stefanie's
local park

* Captive mating parakeets were released or escaped into the wild in the 1990s,
and now flocks of these alien birds can be seen across South London!

179

STEFANIE'S STRATEGY TO REMEMBER

ANIMALS WHILE CYCLING

(whispered over and over to herself)

POINT
Ⓐ

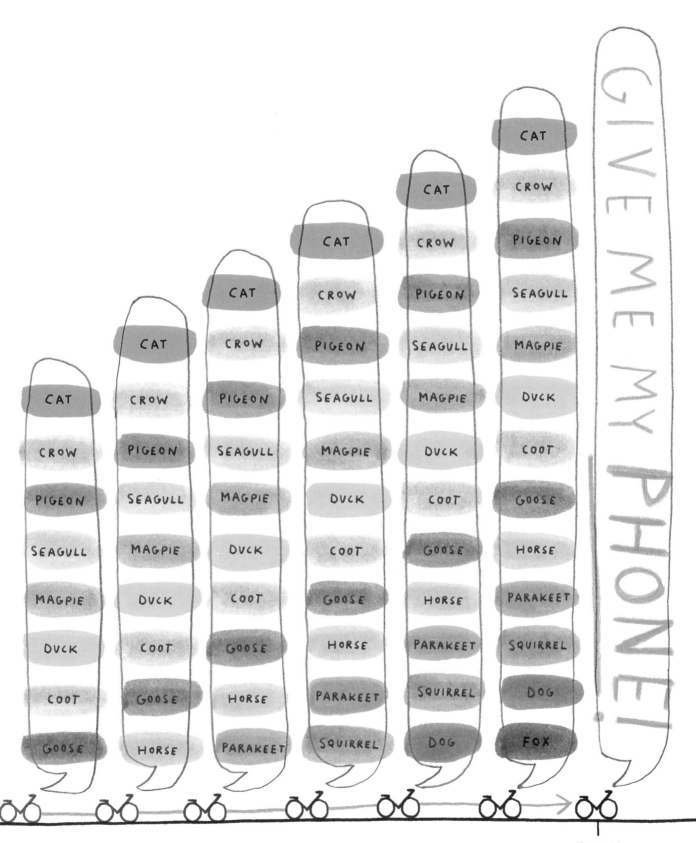

181

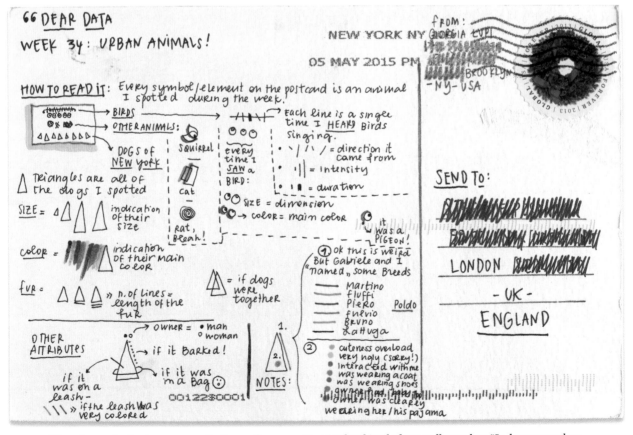

When data gathering becomes a collective performance: Giorgia's boyfriend after a walk together: "So, how many dogs have you spotted? I had eight!" He was counting as well without telling her!

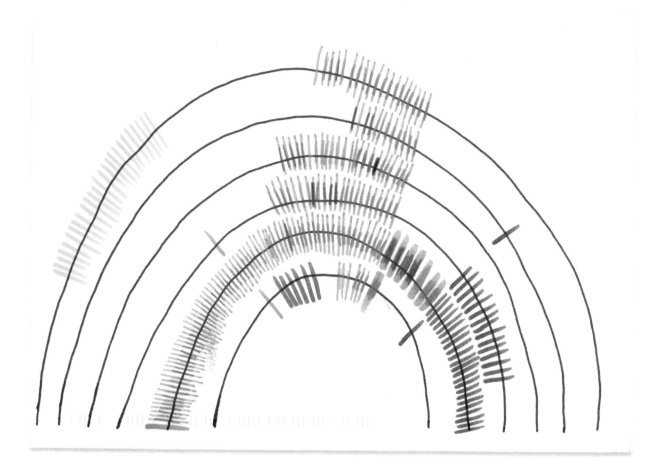

DEAR DATA - WEEK 34

A WEEK OF URBAN WILDLIFE

ABOUT THE DATA: I TRACKED EVERY TIME
I NOTICED AN ANIMAL IN MY VICINITY. 'NOTICE'
BEING THE OPERATIVE WORD HERE... SOMETIMES
I WAS CYCLING OR DAYDREAMING AND FORGOT
TO KEEP WATCH FOR WILDLIFE. NOTE: URBAN
WILDLIFE INCLUDES <u>ALL</u> ANIMALS, WILD OR
DOMESTICATED (HEY, IN A CITY I TAKE WHAT I CAN
                                                    GET)

HOW TO READ IT:

HOME

EACH ▬▬ REPRESENTS AN ANIMAL.
EACH ARC REPRESENTS <u>A PART</u>
<u>OF LONDON</u> WHERE I SAW AN
ANIMAL, STARTING WHERE I LIVE
AND RADIATING OUTWARD:

1. MY ESTATE
2. CENTRAL LONDON: STREET
3. CENTRAL LONDON: PARK
4. SUBURBAN LDN: STREET
5. SUBURBAN LDN: PARK
6. COUNTRYSIDE (LDN'S EDGE)

ANIMALS SPOTTED:

<u>BIRDS</u> ▬▬
SINGLE   FLOCK OF BIRDS
UNIDENTIFIED
MAGPIE
PIGEON
WOOD PIGEON
COOT (I ♡ THESE!)
PARAKEET!! ('FERAL' PET PARAKEETS
HEN! (WE HAVE A HEN   RELEASED + POPULATING
COOP ON OUR ESTATE)   S. LDN ☺)
SEAGULL
GOOSE
BLACKBIRD
DUCK   1 1 2 4 9 8 5 2 8 2
CROW
KESTREL! (A BIRD OF PREY!)

DOG
SQUIRREL
(INCLUDING THE
ONE I HEARD
UP IN OUR ROOF)
HORSE
CATS OF THE ESTATE
FOX
(MY HUSBAND SAW
THIS BUT SINCE I WAS
WITH HIM I'M TAKING IT!)

FROM:
SPOSAVEC
▬▬▬
LONDON
UK

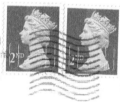
Royal Mail
Mount Pleasant
Mail Centre
08-05-2015
44015407

TO: GIORGIA LUPI
▬▬▬▬ , ▬▬▬
BROOKLYN, NY ▬▬▬
USA

BY AIR MAIL
par avion
Royal Mail®

This postcard was drawn as rings radiating out from Stefanie's home to highlight how the variety of animals
changed as she travelled further away from London's centre.

GIORGIA wants to see a RAT

GIORGIA wants to see a RAT

GIORGIA wants to see a RAT

GIORGIA wants to see a RAT

GIORGIA wants to see a RAT

GIORGIA wants to see a RAT

GIORGIA wants to see a RAT

GIORGIA wants to see a RAT

GIORGIA wants to see a RAT

GIORGIA wants to see a RAT

GIORGIA wants to see a RAT

GIORGIA wants to see a RAT

GIORGIA wants to see a RAT

GIORGIA wants to see a RAT

GIORGIA wants to see a RAT

GIORGIA wants to see a RAT

GIORGIA wants to see a RAT

GIORGIA wants to see a RAT

GIORGIA wants to see a RAT

GIORGIA wants to see a RAT

GIORGIA wants to see a RAT

GIORGIA wants to see a RAT

GIORGIA wants to see a RAT

GIORGIA wants to see a RAT

GIORGIA wants to see a RAT

GIORGIA wants to see a RAT

GIORGIA wants to see a RAT

GIORGIA wants to see a RAT

GIORGIA wants to see a RAT

GIORGIA wants to see a RAT

GIORGIA wants to see a RAT

GIORGIA wants to see a RAT

GIORGIA wants to see a RAT

GIORGIA wants to see a RAT

GIORGIA wants to see a RAT

GIORGIA wants to see a RAT

GIORGIA wants to see a RAT

GIORGIA wants to see a RAT

GIORGIA wants to see a RAT

GIORGIA wants to see a RAT

GIORGIA wants to see a RAT

GIORGIA wants to see a RAT

GIORGIA
wants to
see a Rat

GIORGIA
wants to
see a Rat

GIORGIA
wants to
see a Rat

GIORGIA
wants to
see a Rat

GIORGIA
wants to
see a Rat

GIORGIA
wants to
see a Rat

GIORGIA
wants to
see a Rat

GIORGIA
wants to
see a Rat

GIORGIA
wants to
see a Rat

GIORGIA
wants to
see a Rat

GIORGIA
wants to
see a Rat

GIORGIA
wants to
see a Rat

GIORGIA
wants to
see a Rat

GIORGIA
wants to
see a Rat

GIORGIA
wants to
see a Rat

GIORGIA
wants to
see a Rat

GIORGIA
wants to
see a Rat

GIORGIA
wants to
see a Rat

GIORGIA
wants to
see a Rat

GIORGIA
wants to
see a Rat

GIORGIA
wants to
see a Rat

yay!

✓ on my
POSTCARD!

GIORGIA
wants to
see a Rat

GIORGIA
wants to
see a Rat

GIORGIA
wants to
see a Rat

GIORGIA
wants to
see a Rat

GIORGIA
wants to
see a Rat

GIORGIA
wants to
see a Rat

The only, unique, sole, unrepeated, once-in-a-life-time
moment when you're happy to see a rat in New York.

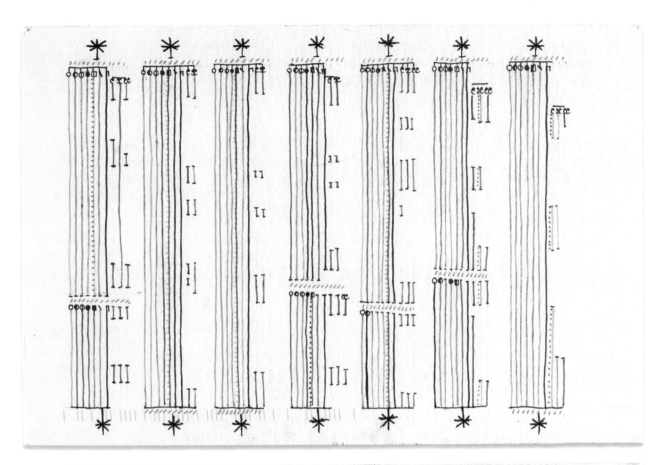

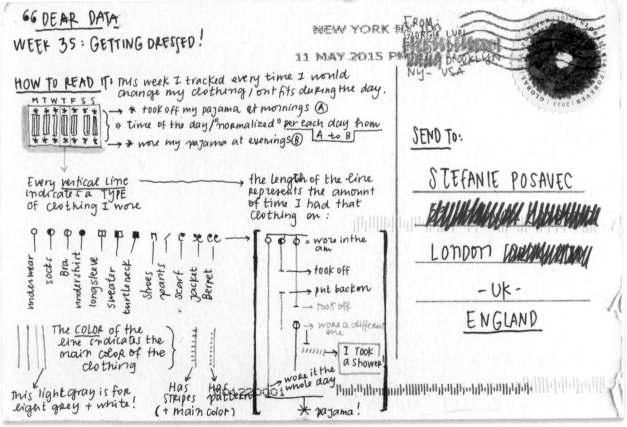

Giorgia noted how similar hers and Stefanie's drawings were, again.

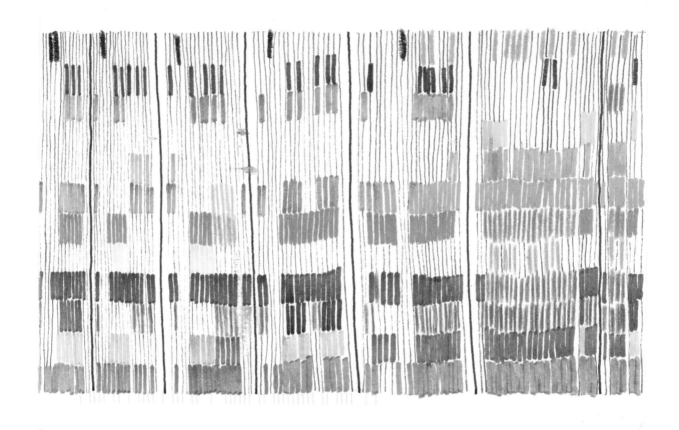

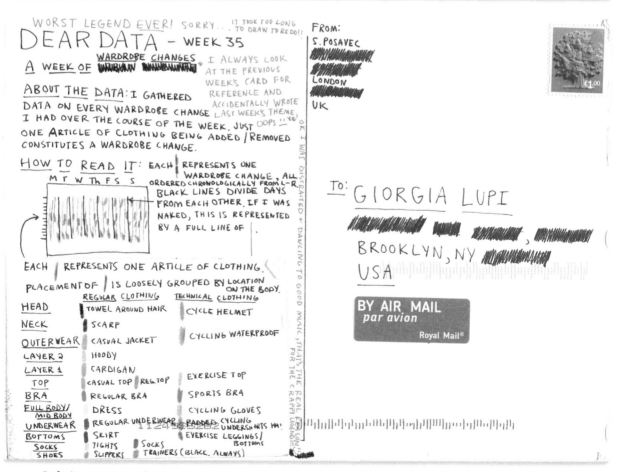

DEAR DATA - WEEK 35

A WEEK OF ~~URBAN~~ ~~MINIMALISM~~ **WARDROBE CHANGES** * I ALWAYS LOOK AT THE PREVIOUS WEEK'S CARD FOR REFERENCE AND ACCIDENTALLY WROTE LAST WEEK'S THEME, OOPS !! ♥

ABOUT THE DATA: I GATHERED DATA ON EVERY WARDROBE CHANGE I HAD OVER THE COURSE OF THE WEEK. JUST ONE ARTICLE OF CLOTHING BEING ADDED/REMOVED CONSTITUTES A WARDROBE CHANGE.

HOW TO READ IT: EACH | REPRESENTS ONE
M T W Th F S S   WARDROBE CHANGE, ALL ORDERED CHRONOLOGICALLY FROM L-R. BLACK LINES DIVIDE DAYS FROM EACH OTHER. IF I WAS NAKED, THIS IS REPRESENTED BY A FULL LINE OF |.

EACH | REPRESENTS ONE ARTICLE OF CLOTHING.

PLACEMENT OF | IS LOOSELY GROUPED BY LOCATION ON THE BODY.

	REGULAR CLOTHING	TECHNICAL CLOTHING
HEAD	TOWEL AROUND HAIR	CYCLE HELMET
NECK	SCARF	
OUTERWEAR	CASUAL JACKET	CYCLING WATERPROOF
LAYER 2	HOODY	
LAYER 1	CARDIGAN	
TOP	CASUAL TOP REG. TOP	EXERCISE TOP
BRA	REGULAR BRA	SPORTS BRA
FULL BODY/ MID BODY	DRESS	CYCLING GLOVES
UNDERWEAR	REGULAR UNDERWEAR	PADDED CYCLING UNDERSHORTS HA!
BOTTOMS	SKIRT	EXERCISE LEGGINGS/ BOTTOMS
SOCKS	TIGHTS SOCKS	
SHOES	SLIPPERS	TRAINERS (BLACK, ALWAYS)

FROM:
S. POSAVEC
~~████████████~~
LONDON
~~████████~~
UK

TO: GIORGIA LUPI
~~█████████ ████ ████████, ████████~~
BROOKLYN, NY ~~████████~~
USA

BY AIR MAIL
par avion
Royal Mail®

Stefanie went on a weekend cycling holiday from Friday onward, and this can be seen in how her wardrobe changed.

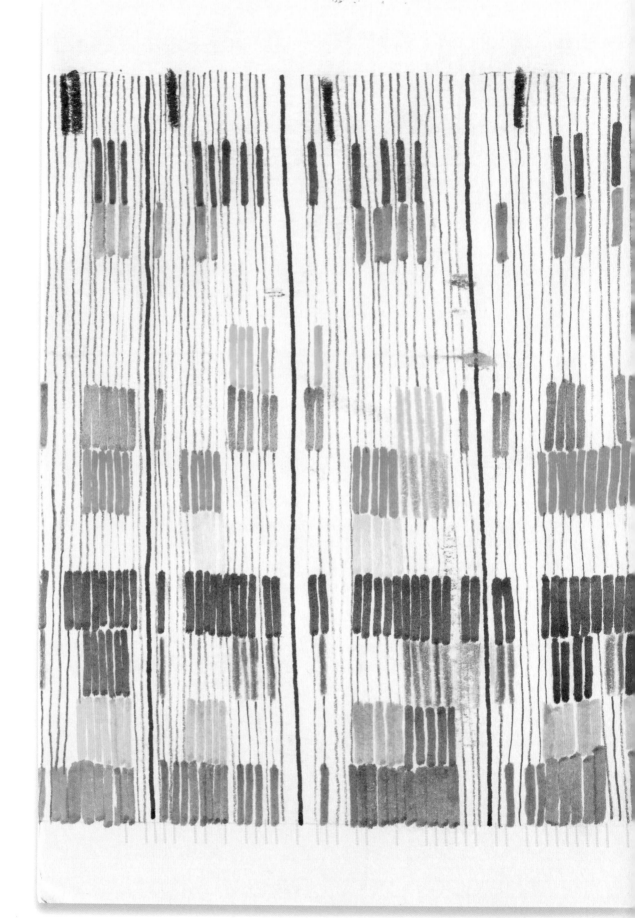

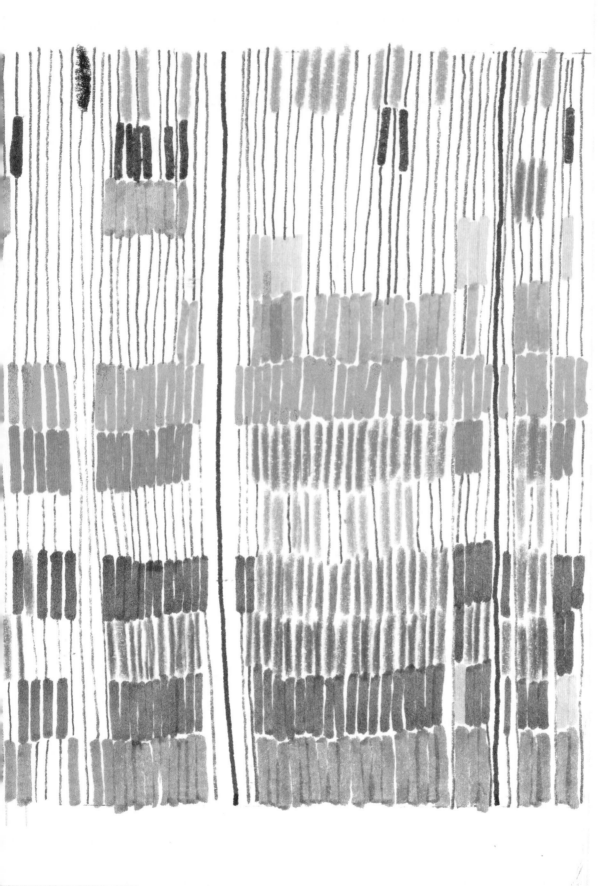

week THIRTY-six
a week of

?nDEC?S?On?

At week thirty-six, Giorgia and Stefanie decided to
show each other how indecisive they are, counting
and drawing all of their hesitations for seven days
and recording specific details about their doubts to
better understand what caused them to waver.

MAYBE I COULD...   ...BUT THEN WHAT IF...

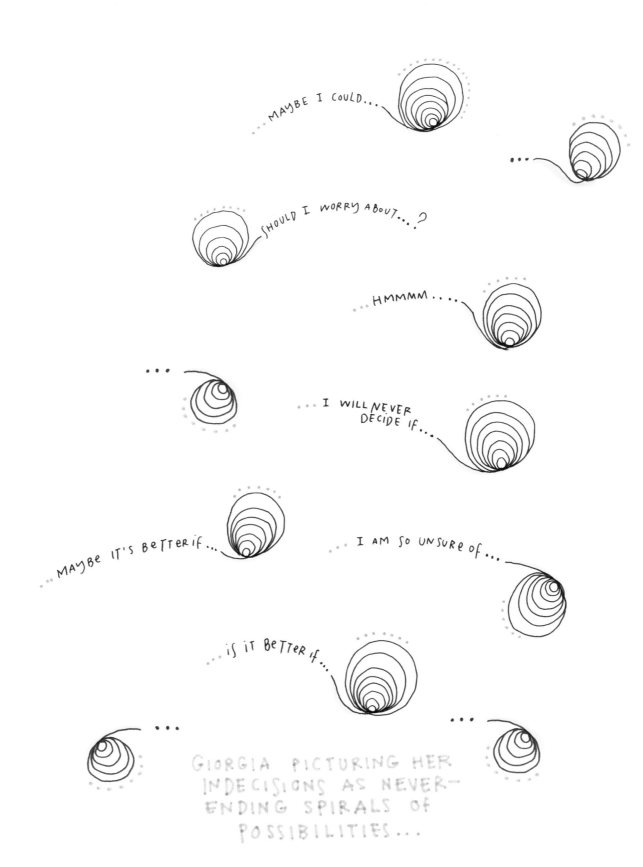

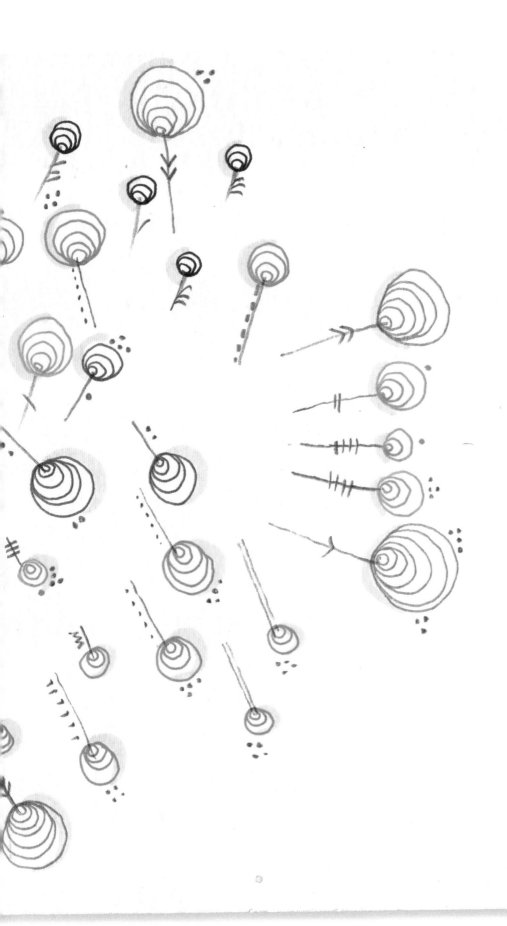

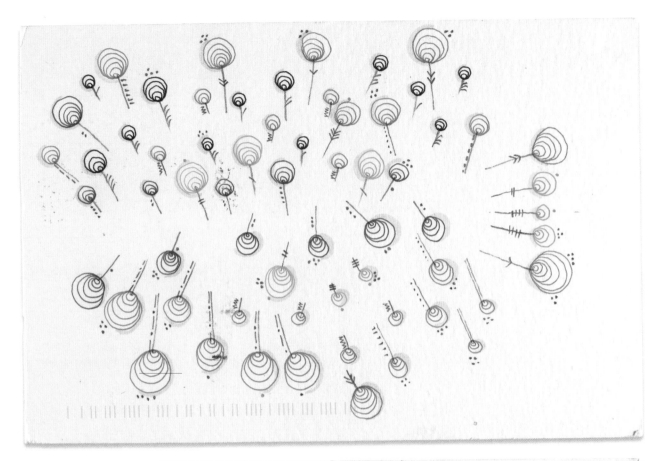

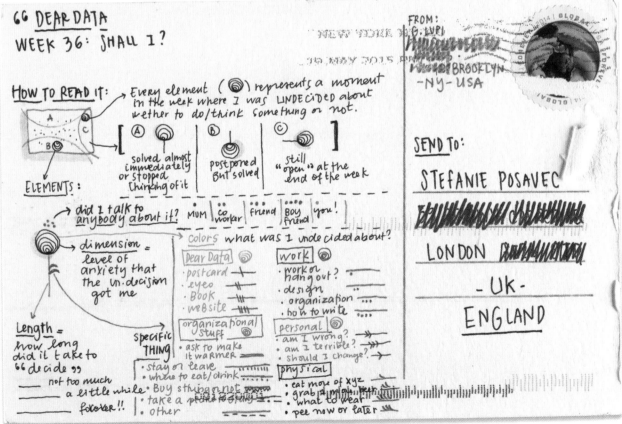

Giorgia realized that when she was undecided she felt better if she told someone. So she added that data as further information.

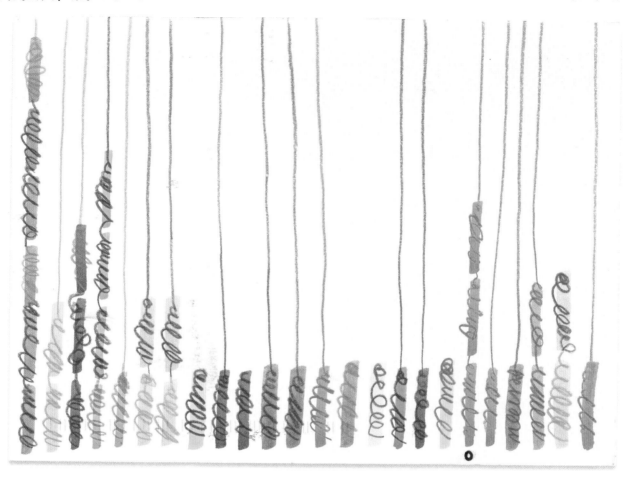

DEAR DATA - WEEK 36

A WEEK OF INDECISION

(ANOTHER COMPLEX LEGEND! SO SORRY :'( )

ABOUT THE DATA: I TRACKED MOMENTS OF INDECISION, WHICH ARE DEFINED AS MOMENTS WHERE I COULDN'T DECIDE/CHOOSE + IT MADE ME SLIGHTLY STRESSED (A HEALTHY WEIGHING-UP OF MY OPTIONS BEFORE DECIDING DOESN'T COUNT AS INDECISION)

HOW TO READ IT:

① DECISIONS ARE ORGANISED IN CHRONOLOGICAL ORDER BY 1st MOMENT OF INDECISION.

② EACH DECISION IS REPRESENTED BY ONE VERTICAL LINE. ALL INSTANCES OF INDECISION RELATED TO THE DECISION ARE INDICATED BY NUMBER OF LINE SEGMENTS.

③ DECISION-MAKING PROCESS STARTS AT BOTTOM AND MOVES UPWARD AS FOLLOWS:

← LINE TO TOP OF PAGE IF DECISION REACHED

← LINE ENDS IF NO DECISION MADE

2ND INSTANCE OF INDECISION

○ = IF I REGRETTED MY DECISION

1st INSTANCE OF INDECISION

DECISION 1   DECISION 2

TYPES OF DECISIONS:
- FRIENDS
- SOCIAL CALENDAR/ ETIQUETTE
- WORK
- SOCIAL MEDIA (EX: SHOULD I ACCEPT FRIEND REQUEST?)
- LIFE DECISIONS
- BEAUTY/APPEARANCE
- EXERCISE
- FOOD/DRINK
- PARTY-RELATED (A RESTRAINED EVENING? OR STAY OUT LATE + GO CRAZY)

TYPE OF INCIDENT THAT SPURRED INDECISIVENESS:
- DIGITAL   - THOUGHT   - REAL LIFE

FROM:
S. POSAVEC
LONDON
UK

TO: GIORGIA LUPI

BROOKLYN, NY
USA

BY AIR MAIL
par avion
Royal Mail®

Stefanie drew indecision as a twisting, ruminating line. The only decision she regretted this week: her poor selection off the menu while eating at a restaurant.

DESPITE MY IDEA of
MYSELF AS A DECISIVE
HUMAN BEING, IT TURNED
OUT SOMETIMES I AM
NOT SO DETERMINED.

THIS WEEK MY GRANDFATHER
PASSED AWAY. HE HAS BEEN
ILL FOR A LONG TIME, BUT
IN THE LAST DAYS, AS HIS
CONDITION WENT DOWN HILL
I HAVE BEEN INCREDIBLY
UNDECIDED WETHER TO TAKE A
LAST MINUTE FLIGHT TO ITALY.

BUT I DIDN'T.

THIS WEEK HAS BEEN
THE MOST INTRUSIVE SINCE
WE STARTED <u>DEAR DATA</u>. I WAS
DEALING WITH MY LIFE
HESITANCIES and
BY HAVING TO TRACK THEM
I FELT OVERWHELMED.

MY INDECISION, AND OUR MISSED GOODBYE.

NOW THOUGH, LOOKING
AT THIS POSTCARD WARMS
MY HEART. I SEE IT AS
A HOMAGE TO HIS MEMORY
and TO MY PARTICULAR
STRUGGLE in DEALING
WITH OUR DISTANCE, and
TO OUR MISSED GOODBYE.

A WEEK OF ~~F---ING~~ SWEARING

TOO RUDE!

Stefanie loves swearing, but was worried that she might swear too much, having even been told off in public for using too many rude words (yes, really), and she wanted to be more aware of her swearing... did she really leave a trail of blue words in her wake?

This week, Giorgia and Stefanie asked themselves: how often do they use swear words, which do they use most often, and in front of whom? Are some types of swearing (such as swearing without intent to insult) more socially acceptable than others?

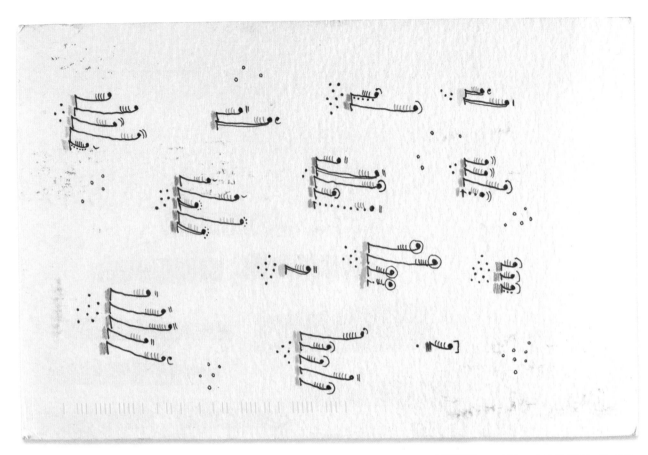

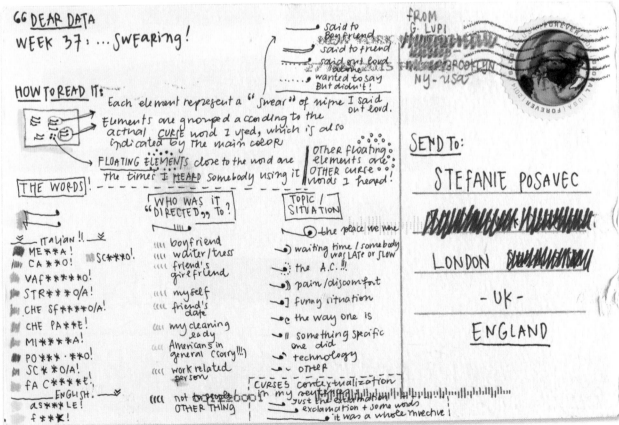

Stefanie: "Why don't you swear in English?" Giorgia: " I am afraid I don't know how to!"

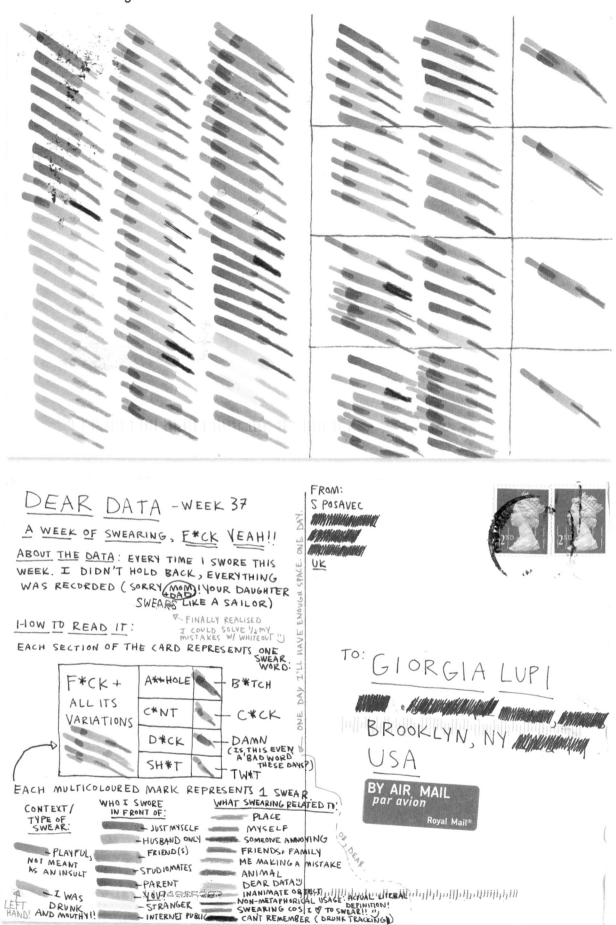

DEAR DATA - WEEK 37

A WEEK OF SWEARING, F*CK YEAH!!

ABOUT THE DATA: EVERY TIME I SWORE THIS
WEEK, I DIDN'T HOLD BACK, EVERYTHING
WAS RECORDED (SORRY (MOM +DAD)! YOUR DAUGHTER
            SWEARS LIKE A SAILOR)

HOW TO READ IT:

EACH SECTION OF THE CARD REPRESENTS ONE
                                    SWEAR
                                    WORD:

▷ FINALLY REALISED
I COULD SOLVE ½ MY
MISTAKES W/ WHITEOUT "

F*CK + ALL ITS VARIATIONS	A**HOLE	→ B*TCH
	C*NT	→ C*CK
	D*CK	→ DAMN (IS THIS EVEN A 'BAD WORD THESE DAYS?)
	SH*T	→ TW*T

EACH MULTICOLOURED MARK REPRESENTS 1 SWEAR

CONTEXT/
TYPE OF
SWEAR:

WHO I SWORE
IN FRONT OF:
- JUST MYSELF
- HUSBAND ONLY
- FRIEND(S)
- STUDIOMATES
- PARENT
- YOU?
- STRANGER
- INTERNET PUBLIC

- PLAYFUL,
NOT MEANT
AS AN INSULT

I WAS
DRUNK
AND MOUTHY!
↑
LEFT
HAND!

WHAT SWEARING RELATED TO:
- PLACE
- MYSELF
- SOMEONE ANNOYING
- FRIENDS + FAMILY
- ME MAKING A MISTAKE
- ANIMAL
- DEAR DATA :)
- INANIMATE OBJECT
- NON-METAPHORICAL USAGE: ACTUAL LITERAL DEFINITION!
- SWEARING COS I ♥ TO SWEAR!! ")
- CAN'T REMEMBER (DRUNK TRACKING)

FROM:
S POSAVEC
▨▨▨▨▨▨
▨▨▨▨▨▨
▨▨▨▨▨▨
UK

ONE DAY I'LL HAVE ENOUGH SPACE. ONE DAY.

TO: GIORGIA LUPI
▨▨▨▨▨ ▨▨▨▨▨▨▨
BROOKLYN, NY ▨▨▨▨▨
USA

BY AIR MAIL
par avion
                Royal Mail®

OH DEAR.

Stefanie highlighted when she was swearing in a playful, joking way, to show how she often doesn't swear to offend.

EXCUSES, EXCUSES...

AMOUNT STEFANIE
NORMALLY SWEARS
EACH WEEK

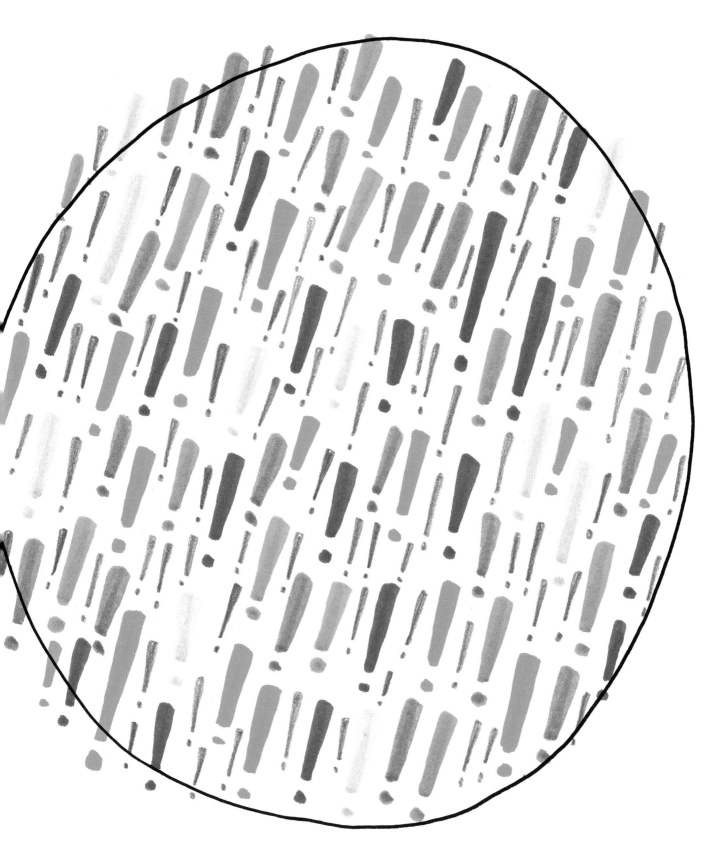

AMOUNT STEFANIE SWORE
DURING A WEEK OF SWEARING

A WEEK OF NEGATIVE THOUGHTS

I DON'T LIKE THIS

THIS COULD BE BETTER

I WILL FAIL AT THIS

THIS WILL NEVER WORK

THIS IS BORING

THEY DON'T LIKE ME

THIS IS THE WORST DAY EVER

I CAN'T DO THIS

WE DID AN AWFUL JOB

I HATE MY BODY

MY DRAWINGS ARE RUBBISH

I LOOK TERRIBLE

Stefanie is the first to say she is a grumbling, pessimistic person, but she still doesn't like days where her negative thoughts outweigh the good: what if they become a habit, and take over every day?

Following on from their week of positive thoughts, Giorgia and Stefanie decided to gather data on their opposing, negative thoughts, tracking who and what they direct their negative thoughts towards in the hopes they can better understand this side of themselves.

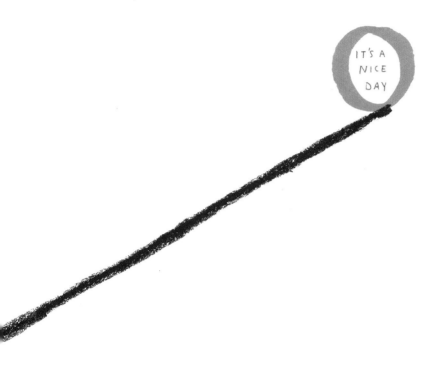

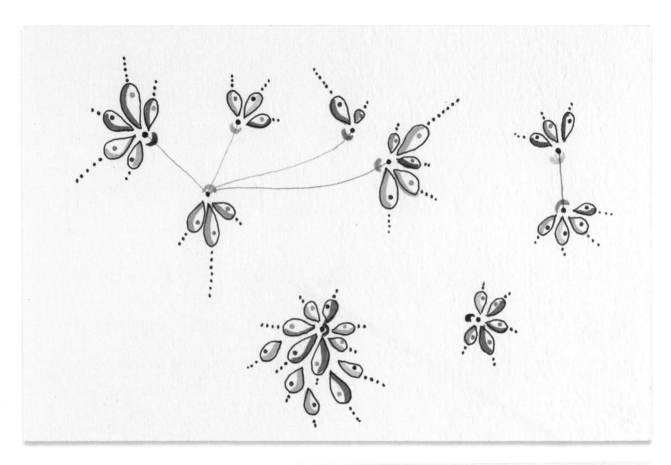

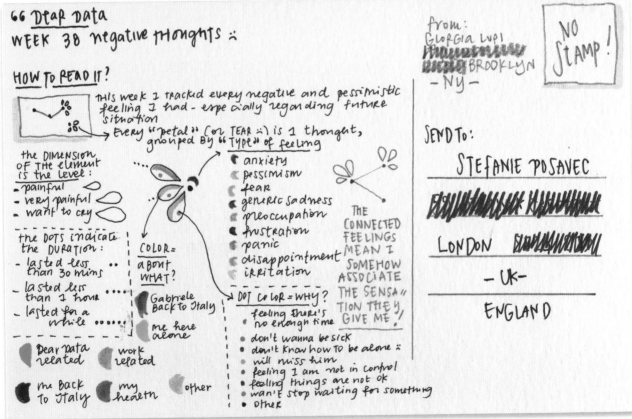

While trying to classify her negative feelings as they showed up, Giorgia found it incredibly hard to grasp them and discern the very reason she was feeling blue. This was the most insightful revelation of the week.

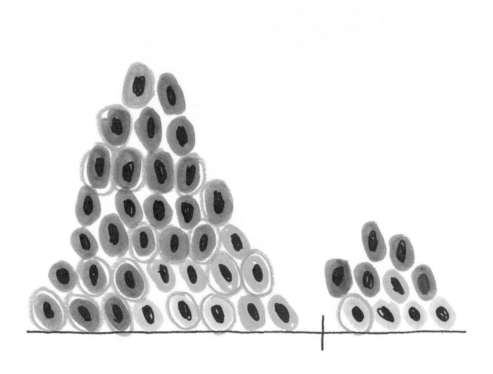

DEAR DATA - WEEK 38

A WEEK OF NEGATIVE THOUGHTS / PESSIMISM

ABOUT THE DATA: I TRACKED EVERY TIME
I FELT NEGATIVE. TO COMBAT THE NEGATIVE
FEELINGS I ALSO TRIED TO MAKE NOTE OF
A MORE POSITIVE, MEASURED VIEW OF THE
SITUATION THOUGH THIS WASN'T ALWAYS SUCCESSFUL!

HOW TO READ IT:

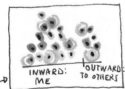

INWARD: OUTWARD:
ME   TO OTHERS

THOUGHTS ARE
DIVIDED INTO
INWARD / OUTWARD.

IF I TRIED TO
COMBAT THE NEGATIVE
THOUGHT WITH A
POSITIVE / MEASURED
THOUGHT IT'S CIRCLED
LIKE THIS:

IF I WAS
NEGATIVE IN
FRONT OF YOU:

EACH IS A NEGATIVE
THOUGHT.

COLOURS REPRESENT A NEGATIVE
THOUGHT ABOUT:

DEAR DATA: NO ONE WILL
LIKE THE PROJECT, MY
DRAWING IS BAD, ETC.

INTERACTIONS WITH
OTHER PEOPLE

MY BODY, MY APPEARANCE

MY CREATIVE WORK /
MY PROFESSIONAL
PRACTICE

ME AS A PERSON

PUBLIC TRANSPORT
(OUT OF ALL THE NEGATIVE
THOUGHTS, SURELY THIS
ONE IS TOTALLY ALLOWED / VALID? ☺)

FROM:
S. POSAVEC
~~~~~~~~~~~
~~~~~~~~~~~
~~~~~~~~~~~
LONDON
UK

MINNEAPOLIS

TO: GIORGIA LUPI
~~~~~~~~~~~~~~~~~~~~~~~~~~~~~~~
BROOKLYN, NY ~~~~~~~~
USA

SPECIAL IN-PERSON
DELIVERY !!!!!

Stefanie created her drawing as a scale, to show whether her negative thoughts were weighed mainly
towards herself, or towards others.

GIORGIA'S CLEARLY IDENTIFIABLE TYPES of NEGATIVE FEELINGS

anxiety,
fear,
preoccupation,
frustration,
disappointment,
panic,
generic sadness,
pessimism.

theres's something wrong
theres's something wrong
theres's something wrong
theres's something wrong
theres's something wrong
theres's something wrong
theres's something wrong
theres's something wrong
theres's something wrong
theres's something wrong
theres's something wrong
theres's something wrong
theres's something wrong
theres's something wrong
theres's something wrong
theres's something wrong
theres's something wrong
theres's something wrong
theres's something wrong
theres's something wrong
theres's something wrong
theres's something wrong
theres's something wrong
theres's something wrong
theres's something wrong
theres's something wrong
theres's something wrong
theres's something wrong
theres's something wrong
theres's something wrong
theres's something wrong
theres's something wrong
theres's something wrong
theres's something wrong
theres's something wrong

REST of THE week ⤵

week THIRTY-NINE
a week of
Beauty

By living your routines and patterns, have you ever wondered just how much beauty you fail to notice on a daily basis?

This week Giorgia and Stefanie stopped to perceive and record the beauty all around them, asking themselves the question: "what is it that we find beautiful?"

They wanted to use this exercise not only to pay more attention to the tiny pleasant things of their everyday life, but also to investigate their concept of "beauty".

GIORGIA TRYING TO EXPERIMENT MORE WITH RADIAL SHAPES TO PLEASE STEFANIE

finding
something
Beautiful
while I was
tipsy !

Boyfriend when he saw my card:
"Nice to know you find me handsome
only when you are tipsy."
"You're lucky I don't dislike drinking!"

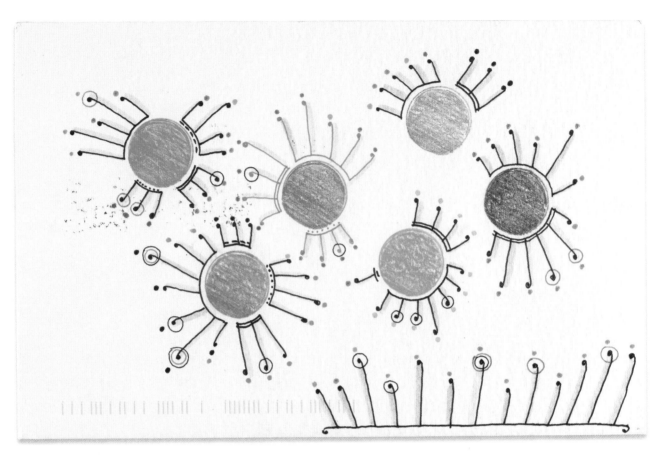

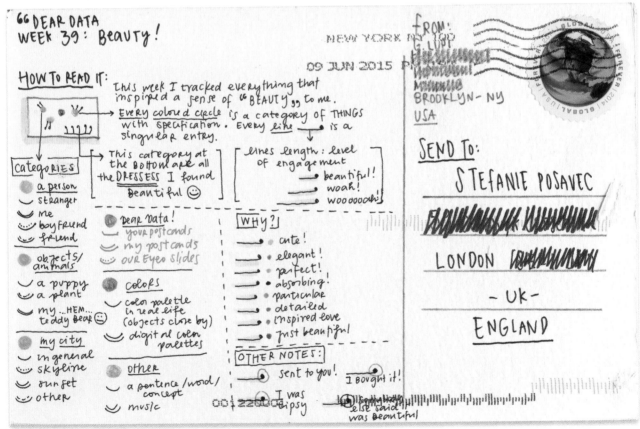

Visually, Giorgia tried to experiment. She had quite a hard time conceiving her data as radial shapes,
but she tried to force herself. Stefanie told Giorgia she liked this postcard particularly!

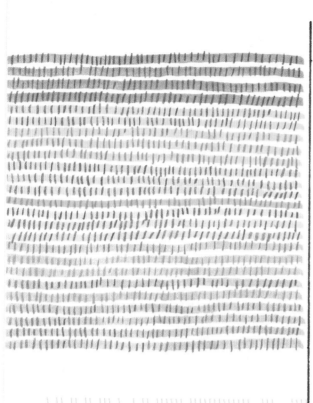

DEAR DATA— WEEK 39

A WEEK OF BEAUTY

ABOUT THE DATA: I GATHERED DATA ON ALL
TIMES SOMETHING BEAUTIFUL STRUCK ME
ENOUGH TO MAKE ME TAKE A SECOND LOOK, OR
COMMENT ABOUT IT, OR MADE ME FEEL
EXCITEMENT OR JOY.

HOW TO READ IT:

FROM:
S. POSAVEC N IL 60M
~~...~~
~~...~~ 2015 PM 9 L

EACH ~~▨▨▨▨~~ IS ONE INSTANCE
OF A MOMENT I FOUND BEAUTY
IN SOMETHING.
MOMENTS ARE DIVIDED INTO
BEAUTY MADE BY NATURE, AND
BEAUTY THAT IS MAN-MADE.

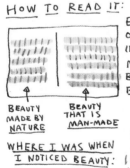

BEAUTY
MADE BY
NATURE

BEAUTY
THAT IS
MAN-MADE

TO:

GIORGIA LUPI

~~▨▨▨▨▨~~ ~~▨▨▨~~ ~~▨▨▨▨~~, ~~▨▨▨▨~~

BROOKLYN, NY ~~▨▨▨▨~~

WHERE I WAS WHEN
I NOTICED BEAUTY:

- HOME
- PARK
- SHOP/MARKET
- STREET
- MY ESTATE
- MY STUDIO
- AIRPORT
  (HEATHROW)

BEAUTY
MADE BY
NATURE:

|||||||||
MY HUSBAND'S
SMILE/BODY ")

|||||||||
RED HAIR
(INCL MY HUSBAND'S
ONE TIME!)

||||||| |||||||
ANIMAL BIRDSONG
||||||||
GARDEN/PLANT/FLOWERS
|||||| — SUNSET
||||||| - SOMEONE'S
APPEARANCE/FEATURES

BEAUTY THAT IS
MAN-MADE:
||||||||| WALL
MURALS:
GRAFFITI + TRADITIONAL
|||||| MY LOVELY NEW
DINING TABLE ☺
|||||| LONDON
ARCHITECTURE
|||||| MY LOVELY HOUSE
|||||| GRAPHIC
PATTERNING
|||| A CHIMING
SOUND IN SONG
|||||| LONDON
NEIGHBOURHOOD
|||| OUR GREAT
DATA DRAWINGS "
||||||| MY FAVOURITE
COLOURS (MELON
OR INDIGO BLUE)

"My lovely new dining table": Can a woman be faulted for spending a little too much time finding
beauty in the new piece of furniture in her house?

COLLECTING
DATA IS
A FORM of
MEDITATION

"...I SHOULD
REMEMBER TO..."

"...I AM
WORRIED
ABOUT..."

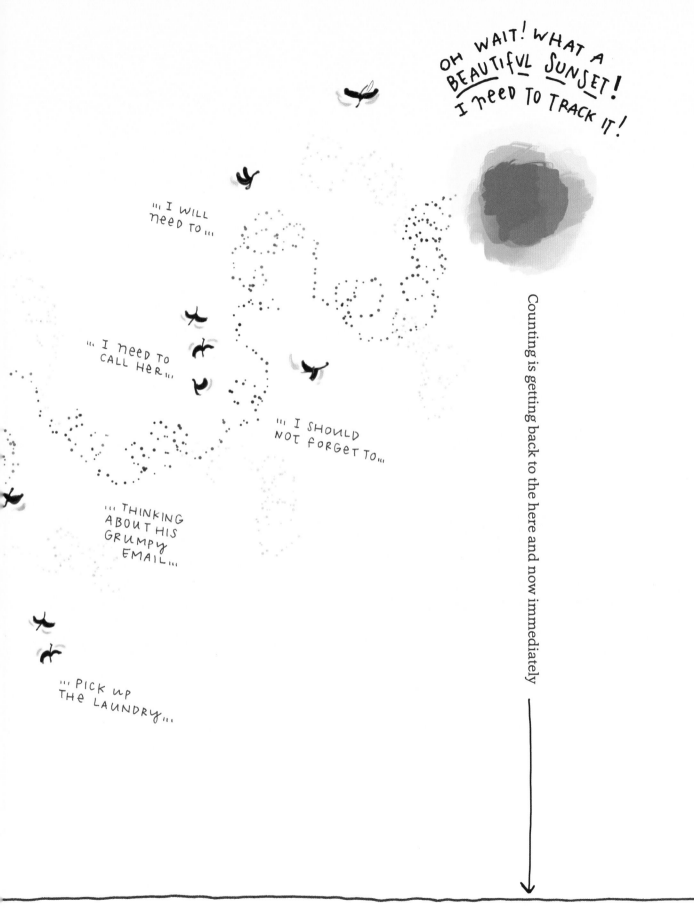

215

week forty
a week of
meeting new
people

This week Stefanie and Giorgia met for the fourth time in their lives at the festival where they first met in Minneapolis. They couldn't be more excited: what better way to celebrate their time there than opening the festival with a duo-keynote talk about *Dear Data*?

They decided that since they would be meeting so many people they would gather data on their new encounters.

However, they may have made things slightly difficult for themselves when, at the end of the talk, they told the entire festival population that they were tracking all the people they met for that week.

" COME AND SAY
HELLO "

(Giorgia realizing they've just ruined
their next days at the festival.)

"HI! I WANT TO BE IN YOUR POSTCARD!"

(AND THEN THEY DECIDED THAT AFTER FOUR DRINKS THEY WERE ALLOWED TO STOP TRACKING)

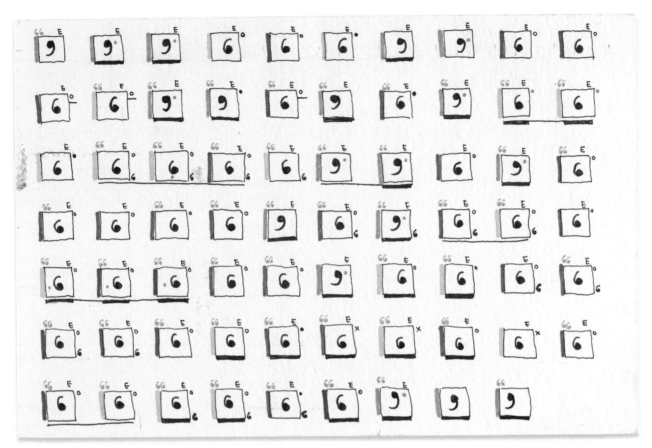

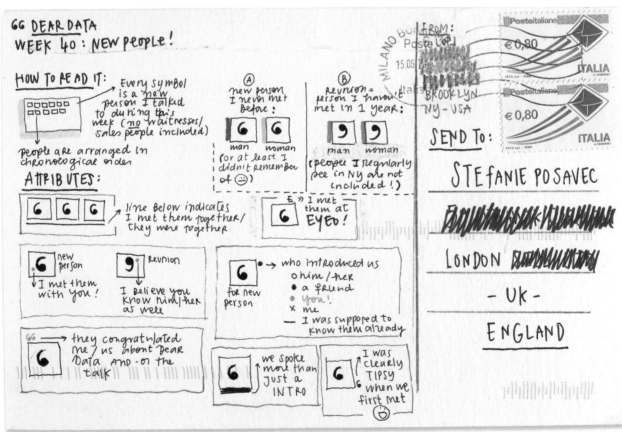

This week Stefanie and Giorgia met in person. It was only the fourth time in their lives, but it felt like they'd spent the last forty weeks together.

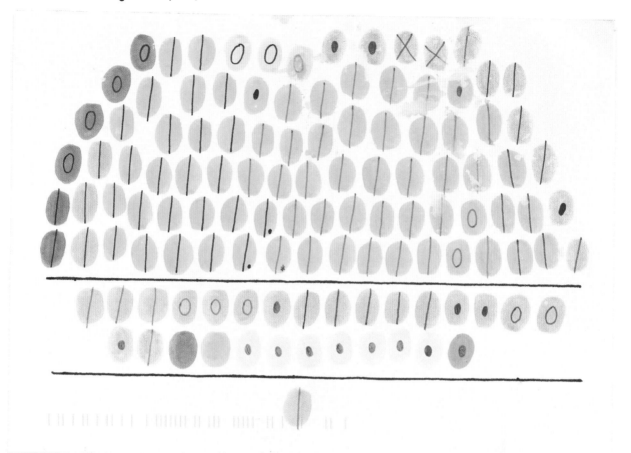

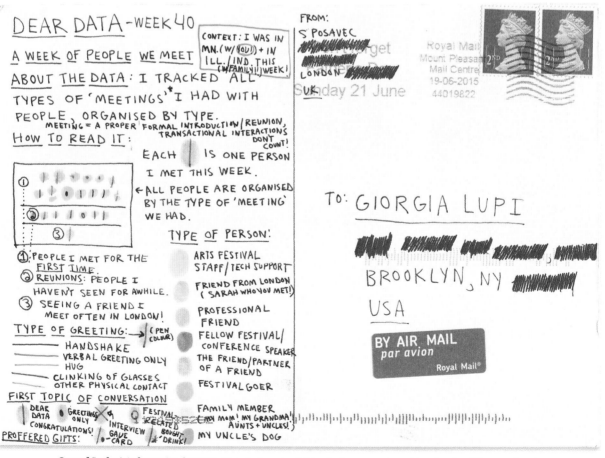

DEAR DATA - WEEK 40

A WEEK OF PEOPLE WE MEET

ABOUT THE DATA: I TRACKED ALL
TYPES OF 'MEETINGS'* I HAD WITH
PEOPLE, ORGANISED BY TYPE.
MEETING = A PROPER FORMAL INTRODUCTION/REUNION,
TRANSACTIONAL INTERACTIONS DON'T COUNT!

CONTEXT: I WAS IN
MN. (W/ YOU!) + IN
ILL. IND. THIS
(W/FAMILY!) WEEK!

HOW TO READ IT:

EACH | IS ONE PERSON
I MET THIS WEEK.

←ALL PEOPLE ARE ORGANISED
BY THE TYPE OF 'MEETING'
WE HAD.

① PEOPLE I MET FOR THE
FIRST TIME.
② REUNIONS: PEOPLE I
HAVEN'T SEEN FOR AWHILE.
③ SEEING A FRIEND I
MEET OFTEN IN LONDON!

TYPE OF GREETING: → (PEN COLOUR)
——— HANDSHAKE
——— VERBAL GREETING ONLY
——— HUG
——— CLINKING OF GLASSES
OTHER PHYSICAL CONTACT
FIRST TOPIC OF CONVERSATION
DEAR   GREETINGS   FESTIVAL
DATA   ONLY   RELATED
CONGRATULATIONS! INTERVIEW
PROFFERED GIFTS: • GAVE   BOUGHT
              • CARD   # DRINK!

TYPE OF PERSON:
ARTS FESTIVAL
STAFF / TECH SUPPORT
FRIEND FROM LONDON
(SARAH WHO YOU MET!)
PROFESSIONAL
FRIEND
FELLOW FESTIVAL/
CONFERENCE SPEAKER
THE FRIEND/PARTNER
OF A FRIEND
FESTIVAL GOER
FAMILY MEMBER
(MY MOM! MY GRANDMA!
MY AUNTS + UNCLES!)
MY UNCLE'S DOG

FROM:
S POSAVEC
LONDON
UK

TO: GIORGIA LUPI

BROOKLYN, NY

USA

BY AIR MAIL
par avion
Royal Mail®

One of Stefanie's favourite datasets: Giorgia, her good friends, her parents, and her family all in one place!

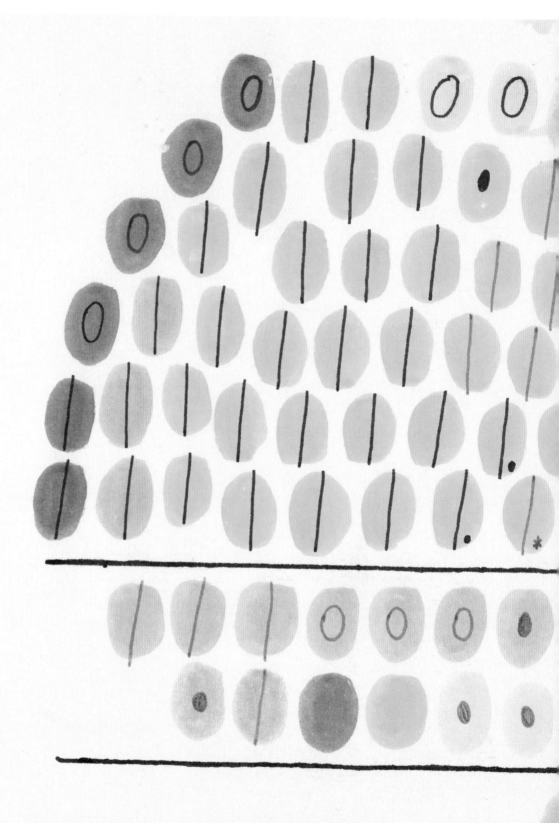

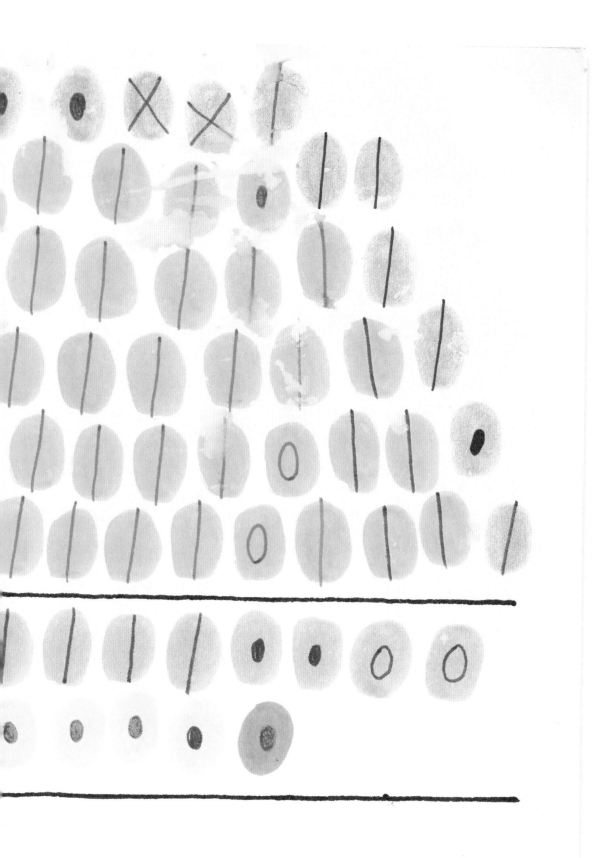

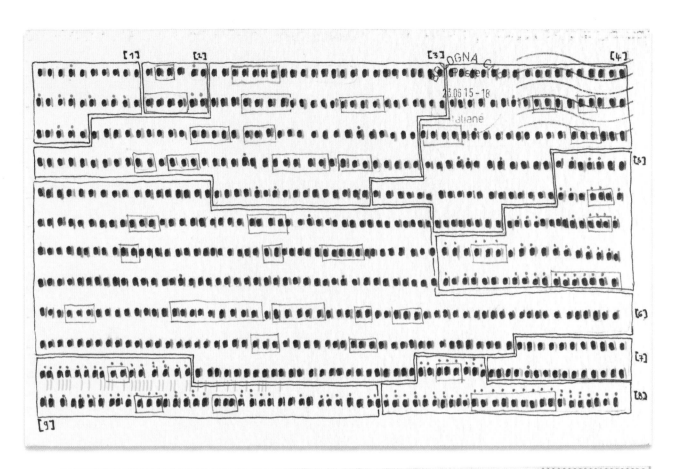

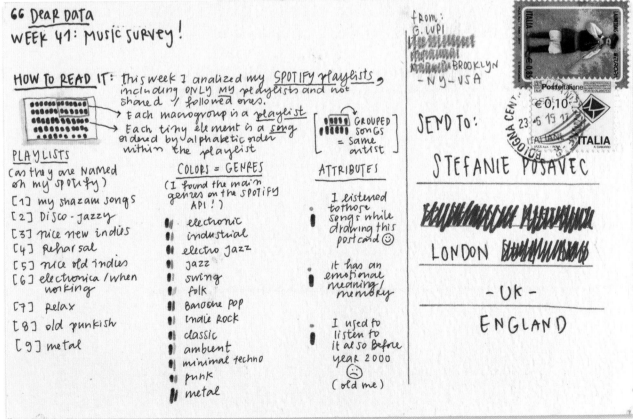

66 DEAR DATA
WEEK 41: MUSIC SURVEY!

HOW TO READ IT: This week I analized my SPOTIFY playlists, including ONLY MY playlists and not shared / followed ones.
→ Each macrogroup is a playlist
→ Each tiny element is a song ordered by alphabetic order within the playlist

[▪▪▪] GROUPED SONGS = same artist

PLAYLISTS
(as they are Named on my spotify)
[1] my shazam songs
[2] Disco-jazzy
[3] nice new indies
[4] Rehearsal
[5] nice old indies
[6] electronica /when working
[7] relax
[8] old punkish
[9] metal

COLORS = GENRES
(I found the main genres on the SPOTIFY API!)
▪ electronic
▪ industrial
▪ electro jazz
▪ jazz
▪ swing
▪ folk
▪ Baroque pop
▪ indie ROCK
▪ classic
▪ ambient
▪ minimal techno
▪ punk
▪ metal

ATTRIBUTES
▪ I listened to those songs while drawing this postcard ☺
▪ it has an emotional meaning/ memory
▪ I used to listen to it also Before year 2000 ☹ (old me)

FROM:
G. LUPI
~~~~~~~
~~~~~ BROOKLYN
~ N Y ~ USA

SEND TO:

STEFANIE POSAVEC

~~~~~~~~~~~~~~~~

LONDON ~~~~~~

- UK -

ENGLAND

Growing up, Giorgia made fun of her parents for listening only to songs that were popular when they were teenagers.
Guess what. Now she's listening to twenty-year-old songs. *facepalm*

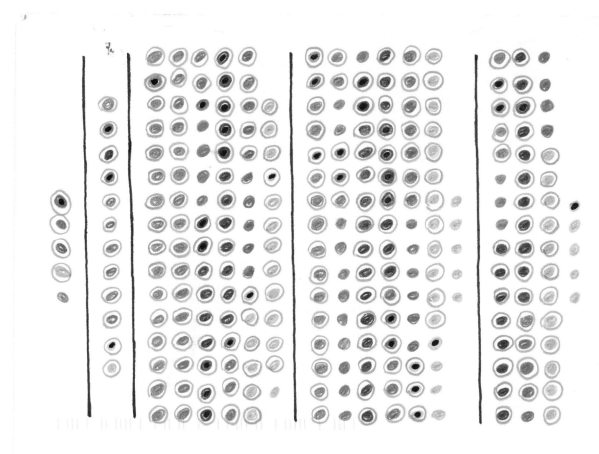

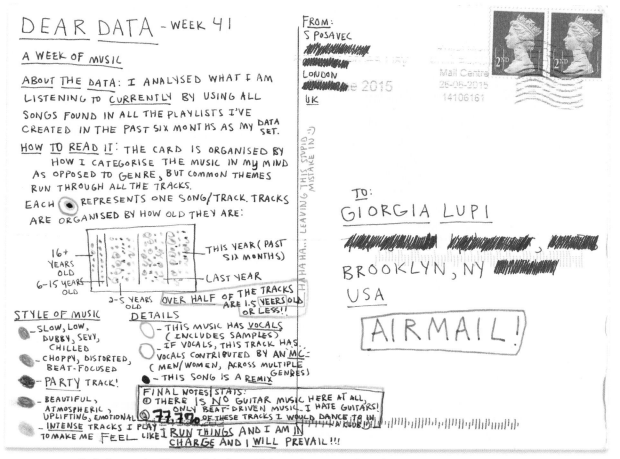

DEAR DATA - WEEK 41

A WEEK OF MUSIC

ABOUT THE DATA: I ANALYSED WHAT I AM
LISTENING TO CURRENTLY BY USING ALL
SONGS FOUND IN ALL THE PLAYLISTS I'VE
CREATED IN THE PAST SIX MONTHS AS MY DATA SET.

HOW TO READ IT: THE CARD IS ORGANISED BY
HOW I CATEGORISE THE MUSIC IN MY MIND
AS OPPOSED TO GENRE, BUT COMMON THEMES
RUN THROUGH ALL THE TRACKS.

EACH ⦿ REPRESENTS ONE SONG/TRACK. TRACKS
ARE ORGANISED BY HOW OLD THEY ARE:

16+ YEARS OLD
6-15 YEARS OLD
2-5 YEARS OLD
THIS YEAR (PAST SIX MONTHS)
LAST YEAR

OVER HALF OF THE TRACKS
ARE 1.5 YEARS OLD
OR LESS!!

STYLE OF MUSIC
- SLOW, LOW, DUBBY, SEXY, CHILLED
- CHOPPY, DISTORTED, BEAT-FOCUSED
- PARTY TRACK!
- BEAUTIFUL, ATMOSPHERIC, UPLIFTING, EMOTIONAL
- INTENSE TRACKS I PLAY TO MAKE ME FEEL LIKE I RUN THINGS AND I AM IN CHARGE AND I WILL PREVAIL!!!

DETAILS
○ - THIS MUSIC HAS VOCALS (INCLUDES SAMPLES)
○ - IF VOCALS, THIS TRACK HAS VOCALS CONTRIBUTED BY AN MC (MEN/WOMEN, ACROSS MULTIPLE GENRES)
● - THIS SONG IS A REMIX

FINAL NOTES/STATS:
① THERE IS NO GUITAR MUSIC HERE AT ALL, ONLY BEAT-DRIVEN MUSIC. I HATE GUITARS!
② 77.3% OF THESE TRACKS I WOULD DANCE TO IN A CLUB!

FROM:
S POSAVEC
~~XXXXXXXXX~~
~~XXXXXXXXX~~
LONDON
~~XXXXXXXXX~~
UK

HA HA HA... LEAVING THIS STUPID MISTAKE IN :)

Mail Centre
26-06-2015
14106161

June 2015

TO:
GIORGIA LUPI
~~XXXXXXXXXX~~ ~~XXXXXXXX~~, ~~XXXXXX~~
BROOKLYN, NY ~~XXXXXX~~
USA

AIRMAIL!

Stefanie organized her music by how old the tracks were, as she is the opposite of Giorgia: she prefers
to mainly listen to music of-the-moment.

223

You can PAINT a PORTRAIT with DATA

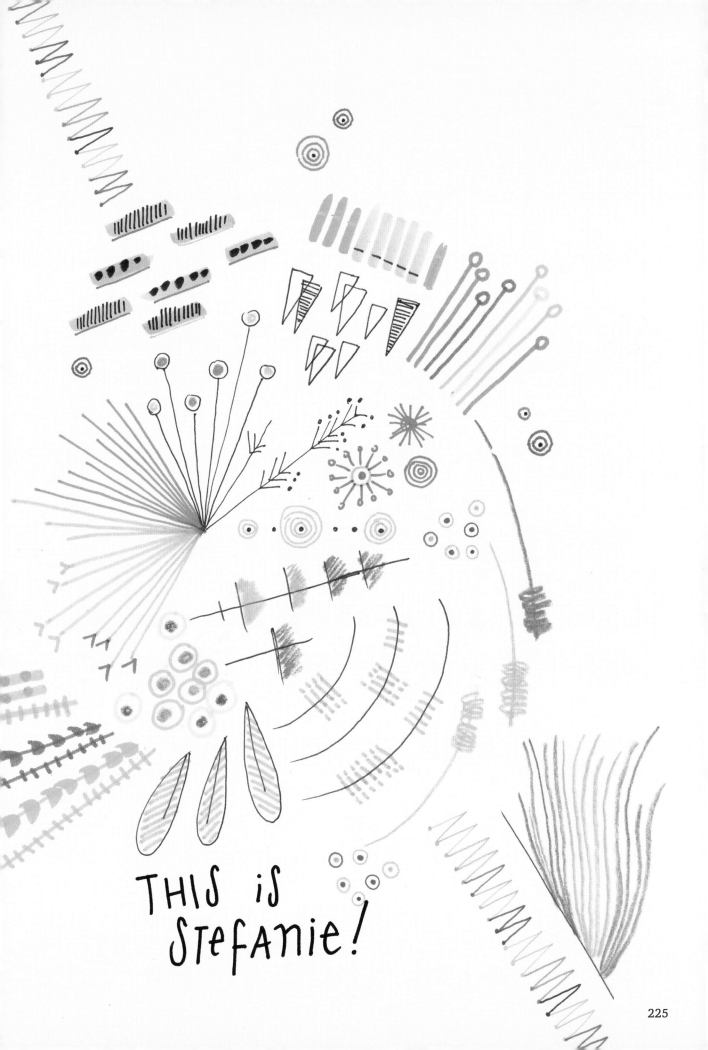

THIS iS
STEFANiE!

week forty-two
a week of

laughters

For both Giorgia and Stefanie this was a good week to capture laughters: Giorgia was paying a short visit to her family and Stefanie had a birthday and nice summer weather in London.

Over the course of the project they realized how focusing on positive feelings and moments, such as when you laugh, brings joy and cheerfulness to the week.

MUM

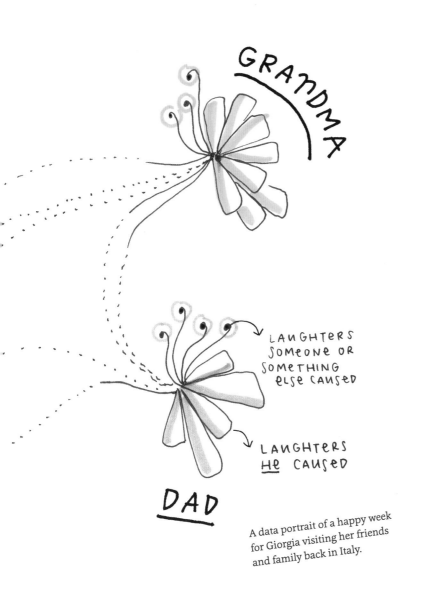

GRANDMA

LAUGHTERS
SOMEONE OR
SOMETHING
ELSE CAUSED

LAUGHTERS
HE CAUSED

DAD

A data portrait of a happy week
for Giorgia visiting her friends
and family back in Italy.

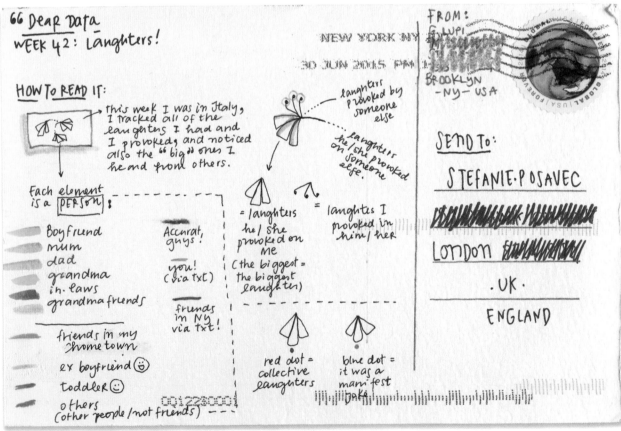

When data-gathering gets in the way: Giorgia laughs and then has to report it. So, is she fully enjoying her cheerful moments as they pop up?

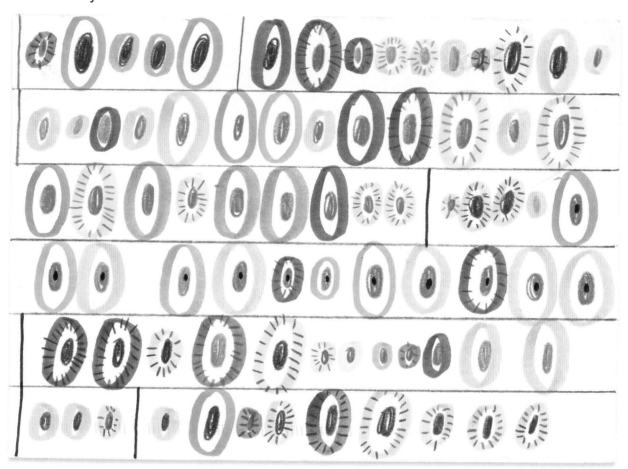

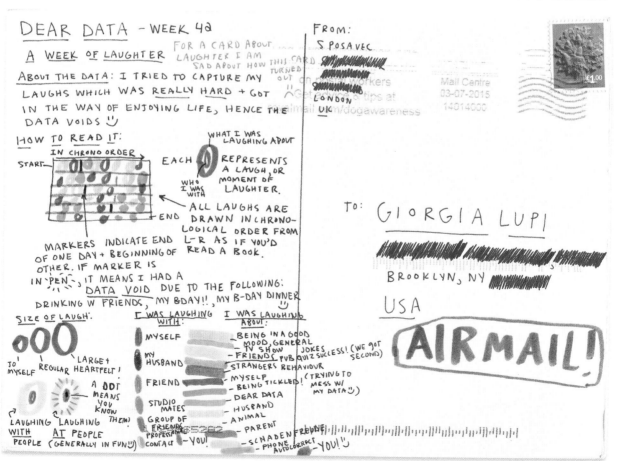

Stefanie was banned by her husband from gathering data at her birthday dinner in a posh restaurant
(for obvious reasons). Hence the "data void".

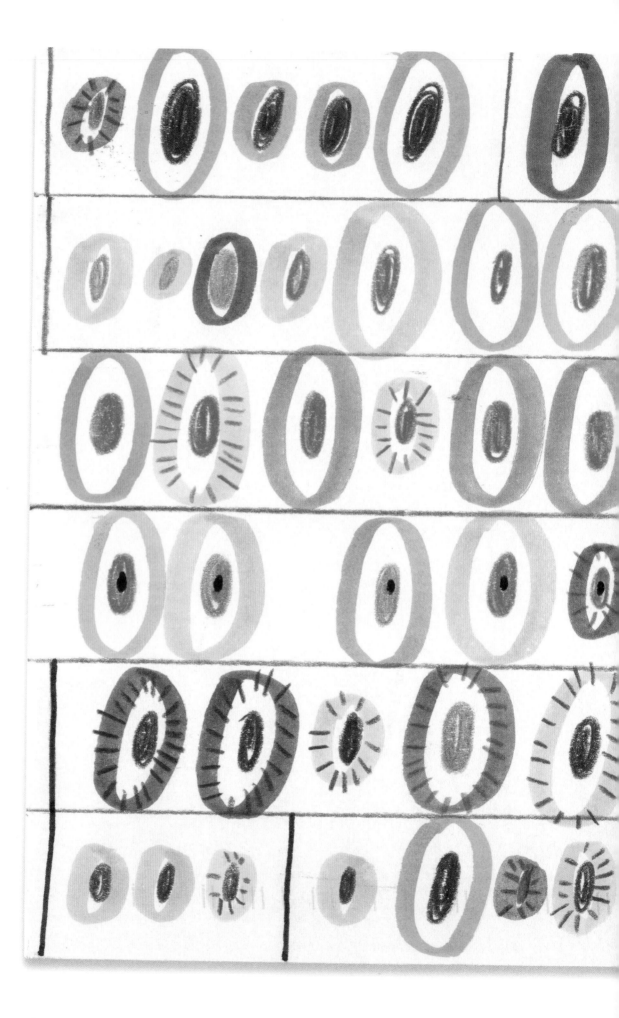

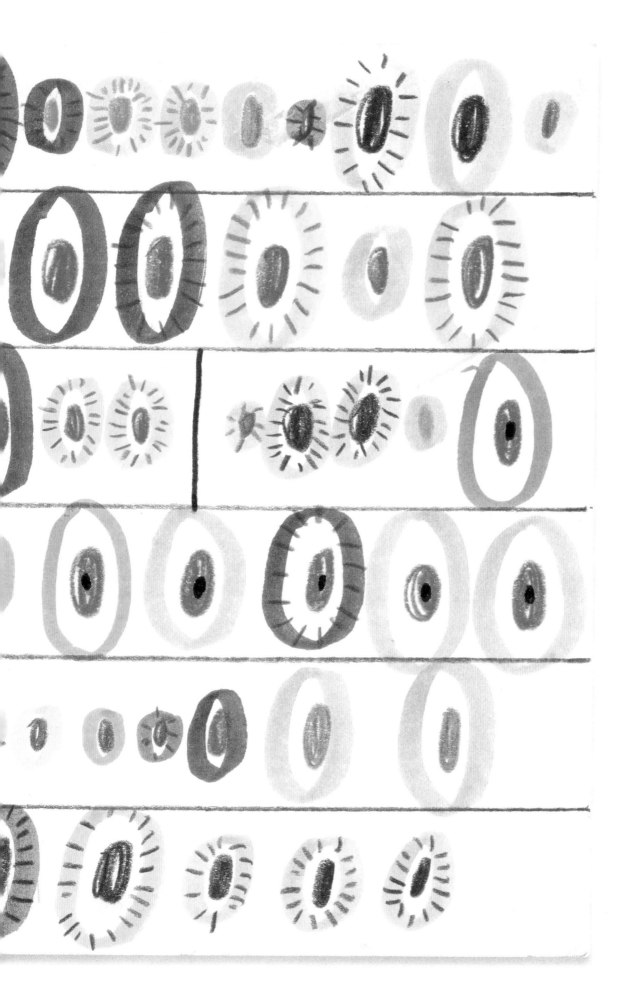

forty-three: week of week of week

Oh, no, it's another performative week, which Giorgia enjoys the challenge of and Stefanie always grumbles about.

The pair decided to use data-gathering to inspire them to try new things in different parts of their lives this week.

Will a concerted week of data-collection make them be bold and leap out of their routines, or will they only tiptoe towards new experiences, and be afraid of change?

trying something new.

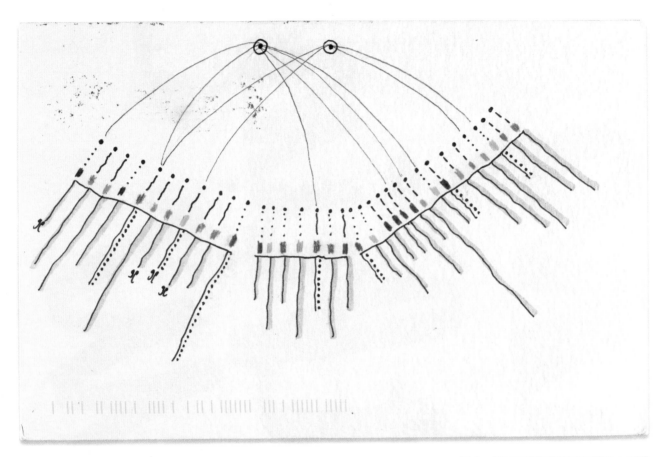

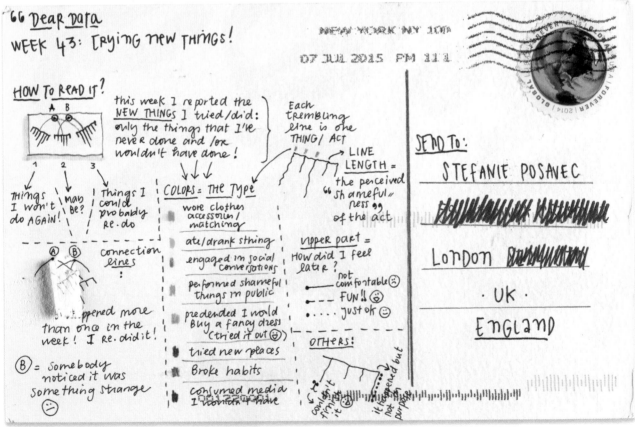

Giorgia's efforts to fight her routines span from eating a portion of vegetables to entering an extra fancy shop and trying on a dress she could never ever buy, and singing a song out loud while walking (fun!).

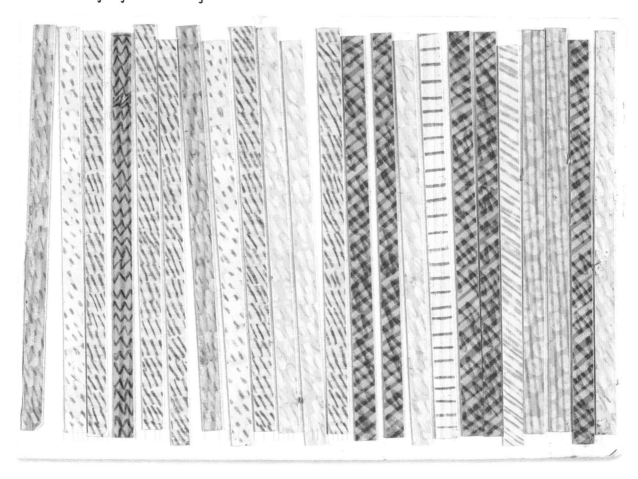

DEAR DATA - WEEK 43 (2nd time lucky... I hope this gets to you in one piece!)

A WEEK OF NEW THINGS (PERFORMATIVE)

ABOUT THE DATA: I EXPANDED THE DEFINITION OF 'TRYING NEW THINGS' TO INCLUDE ANYTHING THAT BROKE MY USUAL ROUTINE. THE CONCLUSION:
- I AM REALLY BORING !! - (AND SET IN MY WAYS!!)

HOW TO READ IT: TO DEFLECT FROM HOW DIFFICULT IT WAS FOR ME TO TRY NEW THINGS THIS WEEK I ALSO TRIED NEW APPROACHES AND MATERIALS ON MY POSTCARD!

EACH STRIP OF PAPER = ONE INSTANCE OF ME TRYING SOMETHING NEW/ BREAKING MY ROUTINE! (ALL ORDERED CHRONOLOGICALLY)

M ——→ S

LEFT HAND!

EACH TEXTURE IS ONE WAY I TRIED SOMETHING NEW: MY FAVE WAS EATING ICE CREAM FOR BREAKFAST!!

GOING SOMEWHERE/ DOING SOMETHING NEW FOR A MEAL

EATING/DRINKING SOMETHING NEW

CHANGED GYM ROUTINE (I SOUND SO BORING!)

VISITED NEW PLACE (OXFORD UNIV.)

WALKED NEW ROUTE TO WORK

CHANGED MY 'GETTING-READY' ROUTINE (AND YES I SOUND BORING HERE TOO!)

CHANGED WORK ROUTINE

WORKED IN DIFFERENT CAFES THAN MY USUAL

☆TRIED NEW ACTIVITY! (PUNTING)

FROM:
S. POSAVEC
~~~~~~~~~~~~
~~~~~~~~~~~~
~~~~~~~~~~~~
LONDON
UK

TO:
GIORGIA LUPI
~~~~~~~~~~~~~~~, ~~~~
BROOKLYN, ~~~~~~~~~~
USA

AIRMAIL

The first version that Stefanie sent of this postcard looked like it went through a paper shredder, as half of the collaged strips were torn off the card … luckily Giorgia allowed her to send another card made with super-strong glue!

GIORGIA TRYING TO DRAW SOMETHING ORIGINAL in a week of TRYING SOMETHING NEW

>> LINKING SIMILAR ENTRIES?

NO! I HAVE ALREADY DONE THAT!

>> COLOUR = TYPE OF ACTION

DIMENSION = FEELING AFTERWARDS?

BOOOOOOORING!

MY LOGS PLACED ONE AFTER THE OTHER? ← IT DOESN'T REALLY SHOW MY DATA COLLECTION!

>> FLOWERS WITH LINES SHOWING THE LEVEL OF SHAME? TOO ILLUSTRATIVE!!

pelikan AL 20

>> SOMETHING TRI-DIMENSIONAL? IT DOESN'T WORK WITH MY DATA!

>> SMALL SYMBOLS? BOOOOORING! I ALWAYS DO THAT!

>> SOMETHING "RADIAL" AS STEFANIE WOULD DO? BUT IT'S NOT MY THING!

>> LEAVES AGGREGATING MY DATA? NO!! THE POSTCARD LOOKS EMPTY!!

WHATEVER!!

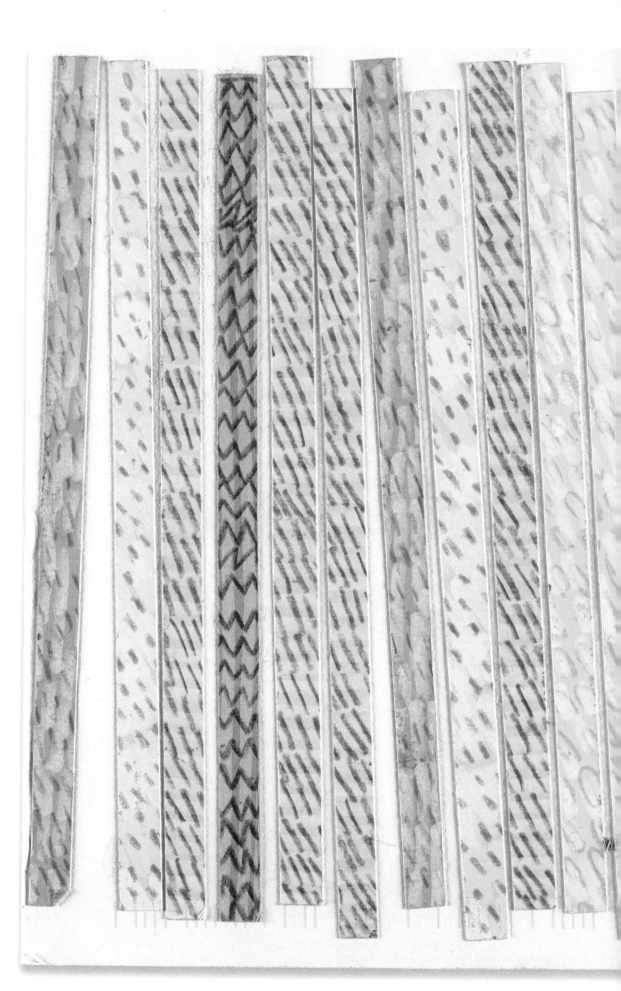

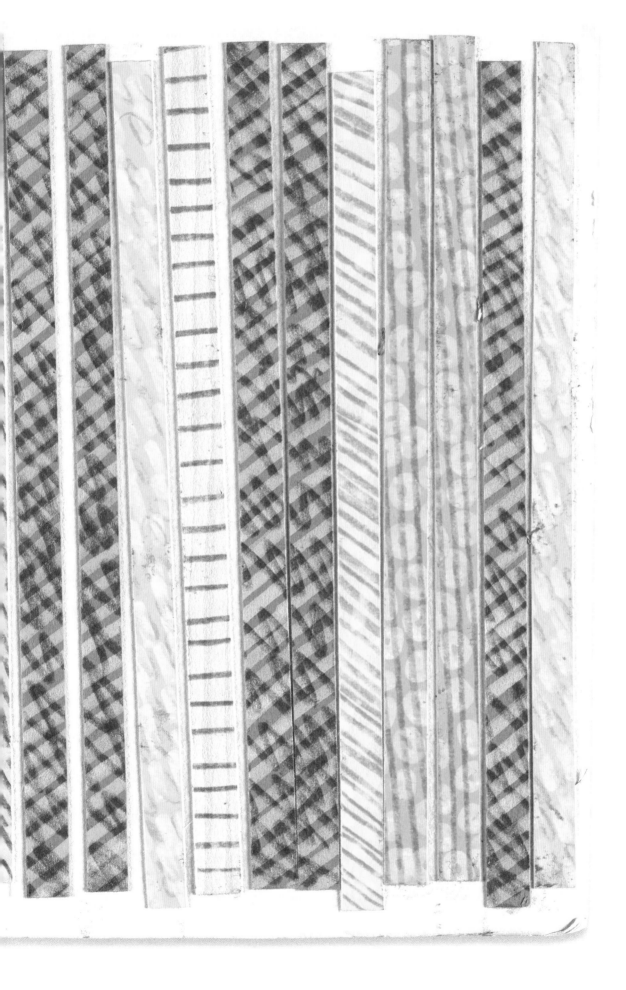

Week Forty-four:
A week of
distract**IONS**

With a limitless stream of new content online
and our continual connection to the digital world
through our phones and laptops, it's becoming
more and more difficult to stay focused.

Giorgia and Stefanie were curious to understand
which distractions were keeping them from being
productive at work, so they made sure they were
in the office all week so they could discover how
often they were distracted, and by what. And, does
Dear Data count as a distraction (they hope not)?

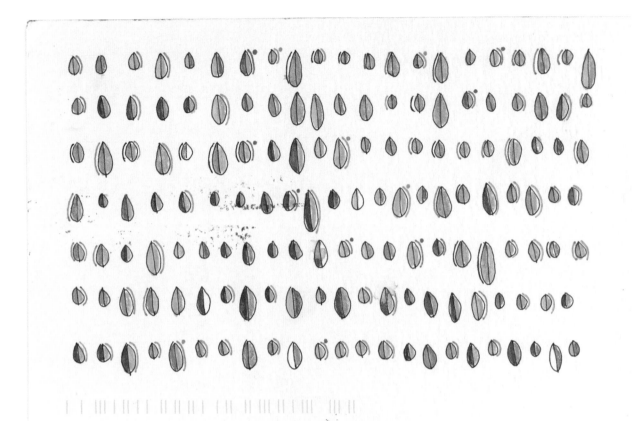

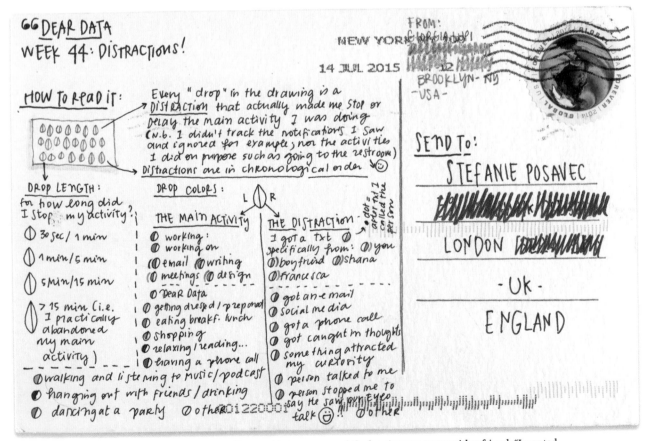

66 DEAR DATA
WEEK 44: DISTRACTIONS!

FROM:
NEW YORK GIORGIA LUPI
14 JUL 2015
BROOKLYN - NY
- USA -

HOW TO READ IT:

Every "drop" in the drawing is a
DISTRACTION that actually made me stop or
delay the main activity I was doing
(N.b. I didn't track the notifications I saw
and ignored for example; nor the activities
I did on purpose such as going to the restroom) :)
Distractions are in chronological order

DROP LENGTH:
for how long did
I stop my activity?

○ 30 sec / 1 min
◐ 1 min / 5 min
◑ 5 min / 15 min
◗ > 15 min (i.e.
I practically
abandoned
my main
activity)

DROP COLORS:
        L   R

THE MAIN ACTIVITY
○ working:
○ working on
○ email ○ writing
○ meetings ○ design

○ DEAR DATA
○ getting dressed / prepared
○ eating breakf. lunch
○ shopping
○ relaxing / reading...
○ having a phone call
○ walking and listening to music / podcast
○ hanging out with friends / drinking
○ dancing at a party   ○ other

THE DISTRACTION
• dot = after txt I
  called the
  person
I got a txt ○
specifically from: ○ you
○ boyfriend ○ shana
○ francesca

○ got an e-mail
○ social media
○ got a phone call
○ got caught in thoughts
○ something attracted
  my curiosity
○ person talked to me
○ person stopped me to
  say he saw my eyes
  talk :)!!   ○ other

SEND TO:
STEFANIE POSAVEC
LONDON
- UK -
ENGLAND

What are the odds! Giorgia got distracted by a stranger while dancing at a party with a friend: "I wanted
to tell you how much I loved your *Dear Data* talk!" :) a fun *Dear Data* recursion!

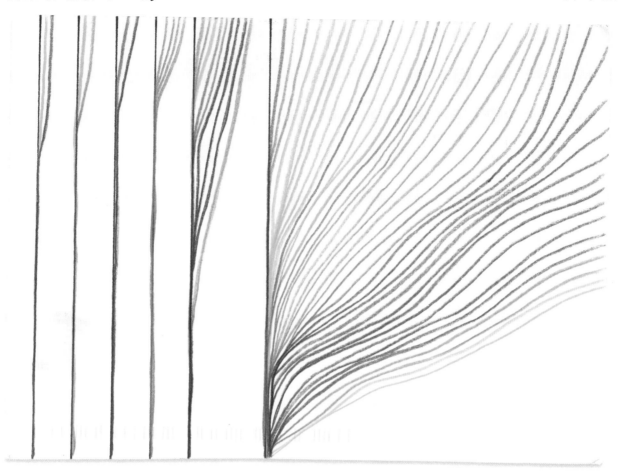

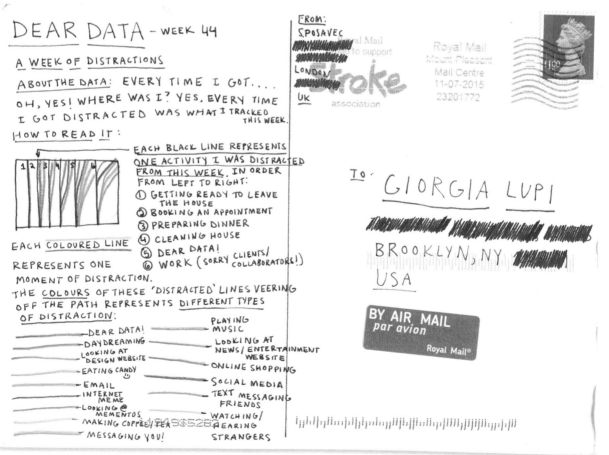

DEAR DATA - WEEK 44

A WEEK OF DISTRACTIONS

ABOUT THE DATA: EVERY TIME I GOT....
OH, YES! WHERE WAS I? YES. EVERY TIME
I GOT DISTRACTED WAS WHAT I TRACKED
THIS WEEK.

HOW TO READ IT:

EACH BLACK LINE REPRESENTS
ONE ACTIVITY I WAS DISTRACTED
FROM THIS WEEK, IN ORDER
FROM LEFT TO RIGHT:
1. GETTING READY TO LEAVE THE HOUSE
2. BOOKING AN APPOINTMENT
3. PREPARING DINNER
4. CLEANING HOUSE
5. DEAR DATA!
6. WORK (SORRY CLIENTS/ COLLABORATORS!)

EACH COLOURED LINE
REPRESENTS ONE
MOMENT OF DISTRACTION.
THE COLOURS OF THESE 'DISTRACTED' LINES VEERING
OFF THE PATH REPRESENTS DIFFERENT TYPES
OF DISTRACTION:

- DEAR DATA!
- DAYDREAMING
- LOOKING AT DESIGN WEBSITE
- EATING CANDY
- EMAIL
- INTERNET MEME
- LOOKING @ MEMENTOS
- MAKING COFFEE/TEA
- MESSAGING YOU!

- PLAYING MUSIC
- LOOKING AT NEWS/ENTERTAINMENT WEBSITE
- ONLINE SHOPPING
- SOCIAL MEDIA
- TEXT MESSAGING FRIENDS
- WATCHING/ HEARING STRANGERS

FROM:
S.POSAVEC
LONDON
UK

Royal Mail
Mount Pleasant
Mail Centre
11-07-2015
23201772

TO GIORGIA LUPI

BROOKLYN, NY

USA

BY AIR MAIL
par avion
Royal Mail®

Stefanie's drawing was created from "distracted" lines veering off a path.

WEEK FORTY-FIVE

A WEEK OF
APOLOGIES

This week's topic was suggested by Stefanie's mother, who thought that perhaps the pair ought to track what is often a bad habit for many people: apologising for everything they do, regardless of whether the apology was necessary or not.

As Stefanie apologises to Giorgia in red pen for every mistake she makes on a postcard, she thought this might be a bad habit that it would be interesting to keep track of, and agreed to her mother's suggestion.

Giorgia and Stefanie kept their ears open, trying to see how often they apologise and for what reasons. Which "sorrys" are allowed, and which should they be more aware of?

Stefanie's
apologetic annotations
taking over the postcard

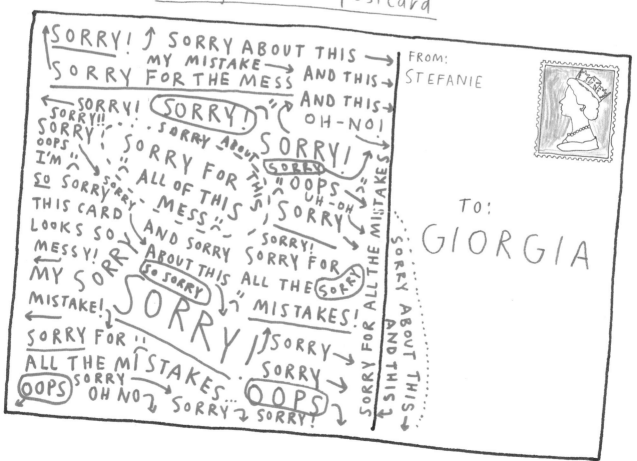

247

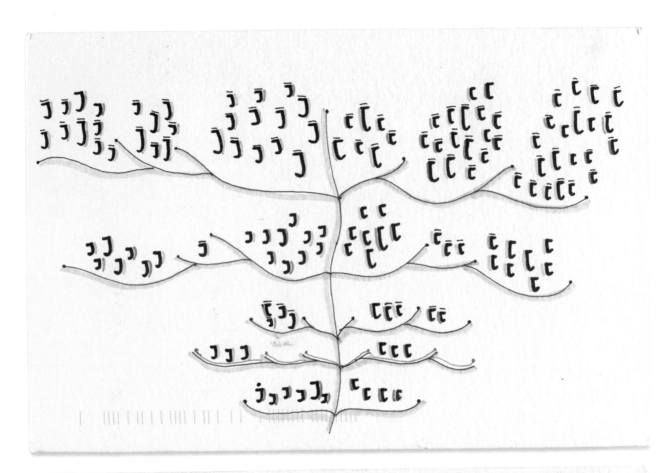

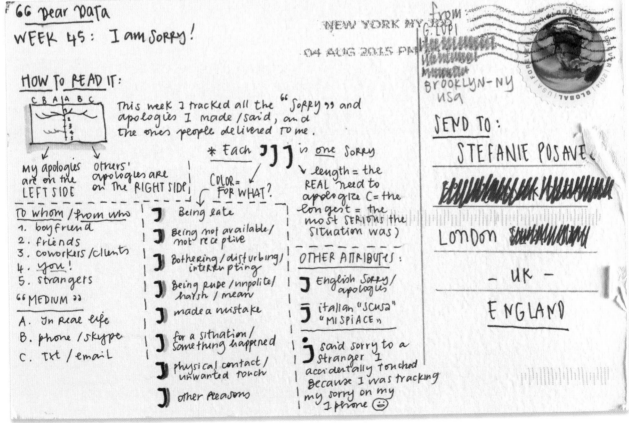

Giorgia: "This is absolutely the ugliest postcard I've ever drawn. SORRY STEFANIE!"

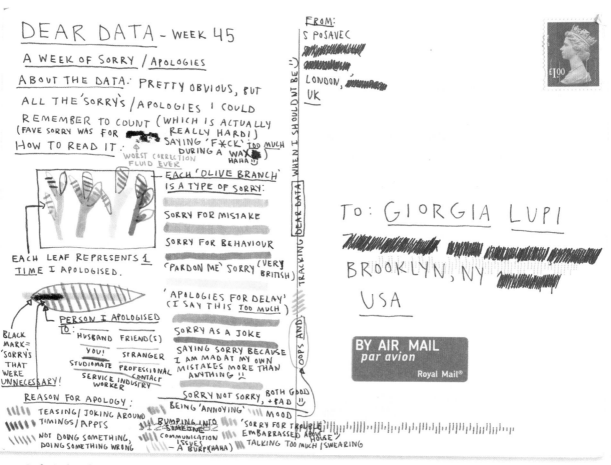

DEAR DATA - WEEK 45

A WEEK OF SORRY / APOLOGIES

ABOUT THE DATA: PRETTY OBVIOUS, BUT
ALL THE 'SORRY'S / APOLOGIES I COULD
REMEMBER TO COUNT (WHICH IS ACTUALLY
(FAVE SORRY WAS FOR ███████ REALLY HARD!)
HOW TO READ IT: ▢ SAYING 'F✳CK' TOO MUCH
WORST CORRECTION   DURING A WAX
FLUID EVER   HAHA!!)

EACH LEAF REPRESENTS 1
TIME I APOLOGISED.

BLACK
MARK =
'SORRY'S
THAT
WERE
UNNECESSARY!

EACH 'OLIVE BRANCH'
IS A TYPE OF SORRY:

SORRY FOR MISTAKE

SORRY FOR BEHAVIOUR

'PARDON ME' SORRY (VERY BRITISH)

'APOLOGIES FOR DELAY'
(I SAY THIS TOO MUCH)

SORRY AS A JOKE

SAYING SORRY BECAUSE
I AM MAD AT MY OWN
MISTAKES MORE THAN
ANYTHING !!

SORRY NOT SORRY, BOTH GOOD
+ BAD !!

PERSON I APOLOGISED
TO:
HUSBAND   FRIEND(S)
YOU!   STRANGER
STUDIOMATE PROFESSIONAL
SERVICE INDUSTRY CONTACT
WORKER

REASON FOR APOLOGY:
TEASING / JOKING AROUND
TIMINGS / APPTS
NOT DOING SOMETHING,
DOING SOMETHING WRONG
BUMPING INTO
SOMEONE
COMMUNICATION
ISSUES
— A BURP (HAHA)
BEING 'ANNOYING'   MOOD
'SORRY FOR TROUBLE'
EMBARRASSED ABOUT
HOUSE'
TALKING TOO MUCH / SWEARING

TRACKING 'DEAR DATA' WHEN I SHOULDN'T BE !

OOPS AND

FROM:
S POSAVEC
███████████████
███████████████
LONDON, ████████
UK

TO: GIORGIA LUPI
████████████ ████████████████████
BROOKLYN, NY ████
USA ████████████

BY AIR MAIL
par avion
Royal Mail®

Stefanie drew her apologies in the form of olive branches she would like to hand out to "make peace" throughout the week.

IM█PERFECTION

is a *sign* of

NOT AGAIN.

EXPLORATION.

SIGH.

250

A year ~~trying~~ of

MISTAKES

means ~~[scribbled out]~~ a year of

OOPS.

TRYING

SOMETHING NEW.

week forty-six
a week of
BOOKS WE OWN

Stefanie and Giorgia figured that surveying the books they own could be a further entry point to each other lives.

Sharing our bookshelf is sharing a part of ourself: our travels, the things we're interested in, our aspirations, our pasts…

I WISH I HAD you ALL HeRe WITH Me

This week reminded Giorgia of all of the books that she left in Italy when moving overseas, and of the painful process of selection – "what to ship and what to leave" – while emptying her apartment in Milan.

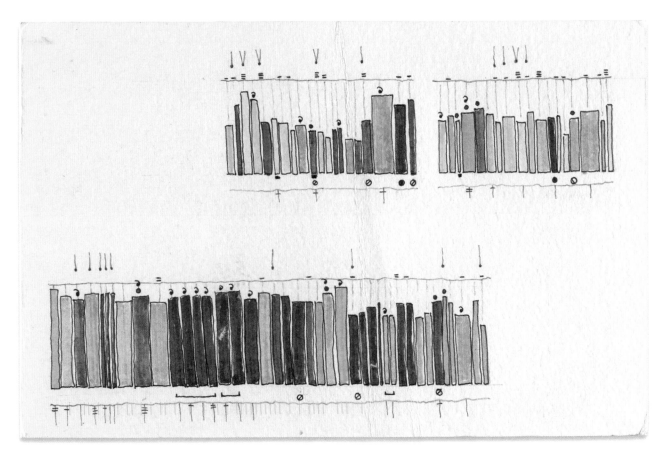

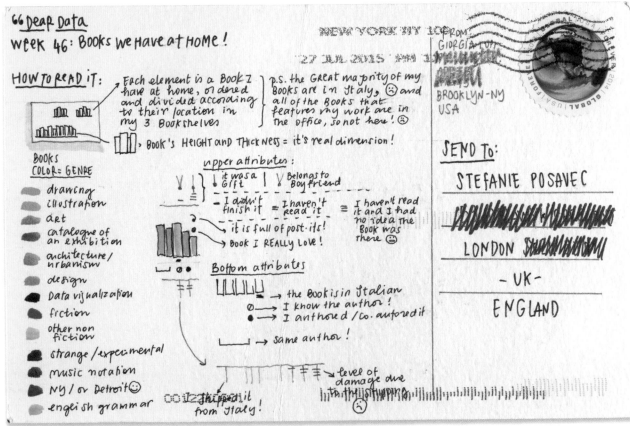

For Giorgia, this week recalled the funny (but painful) wait for her books to arrive in New York: the boxes shipped got here one after the other in a random way, each one more and more damaged as days passed.

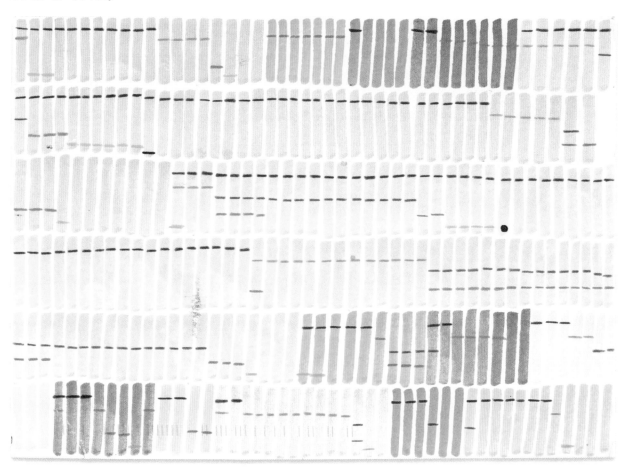

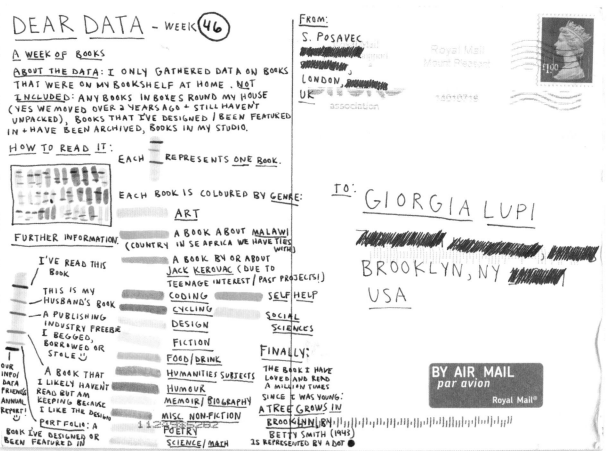

DEAR DATA — WEEK (46)

A WEEK OF BOOKS

ABOUT THE DATA: I ONLY GATHERED DATA ON BOOKS THAT WERE ON MY BOOKSHELF AT HOME. <u>NOT INCLUDED</u>: ANY BOOKS IN BOXES ROUND MY HOUSE (YES WE MOVED OVER 2 YEARS AGO + STILL HAVEN'T UNPACKED), BOOKS THAT I'VE DESIGNED / BEEN FEATURED IN + HAVE BEEN ARCHIVED, BOOKS IN MY STUDIO.

HOW TO READ IT:

EACH ▮ REPRESENTS <u>ONE BOOK</u>.

EACH BOOK IS COLOURED BY GENRE:
- ART
- A BOOK ABOUT MALAWI (COUNTRY IN SE AFRICA WE HAVE TIES WITH)
- A BOOK BY OR ABOUT JACK KEROUAC (DUE TO TEENAGE INTEREST / PAST PROJECTS!)
- CODING
- CYCLING
- DESIGN
- FICTION
- FOOD/DRINK
- HUMANITIES SUBJECTS
- HUMOUR
- MEMOIR/BIOGRAPHY
- MISC. NON-FICTION
- POETRY
- SCIENCE/MATH
- SELF HELP
- SOCIAL SCIENCES

FURTHER INFORMATION:
- I'VE READ THIS BOOK
- THIS IS MY HUSBAND'S BOOK
- A PUBLISHING INDUSTRY FREEBIE I BEGGED, BORROWED OR STOLE ☺
- A BOOK THAT I LIKELY HAVEN'T READ BUT AM KEEPING BECAUSE I LIKE THE DESIGN
- PORTFOLIO: A BOOK I'VE DESIGNED OR BEEN FEATURED IN
- OUR INFO/DATA FRIENDS ANNUAL REPORT!

FINALLY: THE BOOK I HAVE LOVED AND READ A MILLION TIMES SINCE I WAS YOUNG: A TREE GROWS IN BROOKLYN BY BETTY SMITH (1943) IS REPRESENTED BY A DOT ●

FROM: S. POSAVEC, LONDON, UK

TO: GIORGIA LUPI, BROOKLYN, NY USA

BY AIR MAIL / par avion / Royal Mail®

"Our info/data friend's annual report": a joke referencing our friend Nicholas Felton and his wonderful self-tracking project again.

A WEEK OF

SMELLS

AND

scents

This week, Giorgia and Stefanie sniffed the air
to capture the perfumed scents and pungent smells
that wafted through their weeks. Could they paint a
picture of their week through gathering data on such
an intangible, subtle aspect of daily life?

WAYS TO PREVENT
MOTHER-IN-LAW DISCORD:
NEVER MENTION YOU
DON'T LIKE THE SMELL OF HER
(ADMITTEDLY VERY CHARMING)
DOG IN A POSTCARD!

STEFANIE CAN'T DRAW DOGS. SORRY

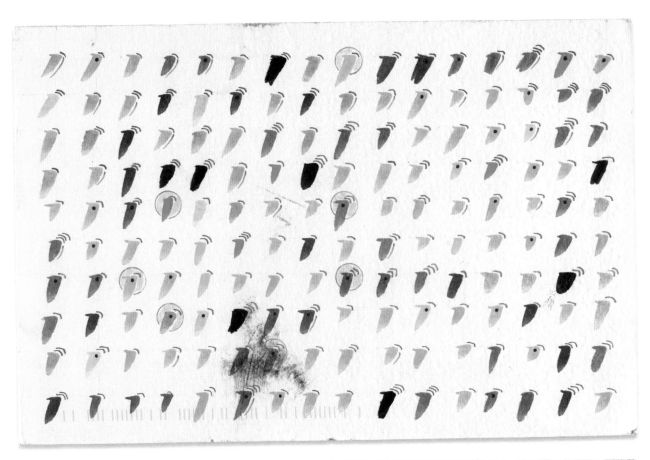

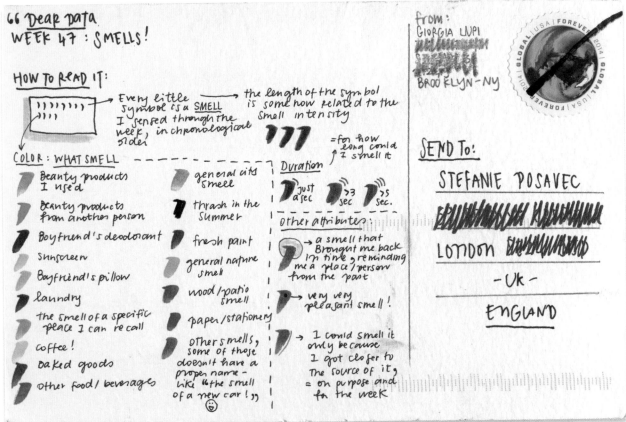

During these kind of weeks, Giorgia is reminded of how data can grasp the routine and ordinary moments of our lives: they are the backgrounds of our habits and journeys through our days.

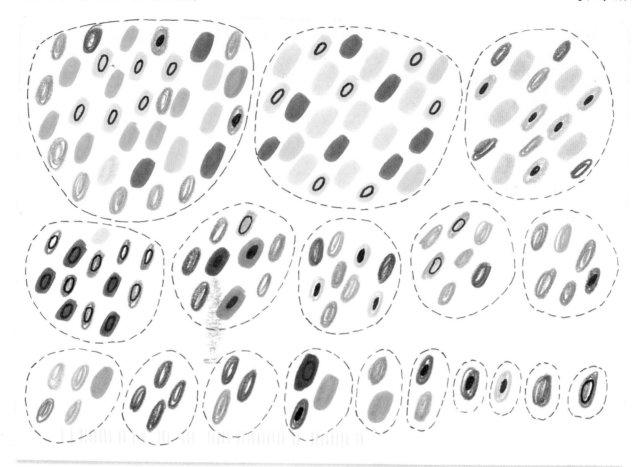

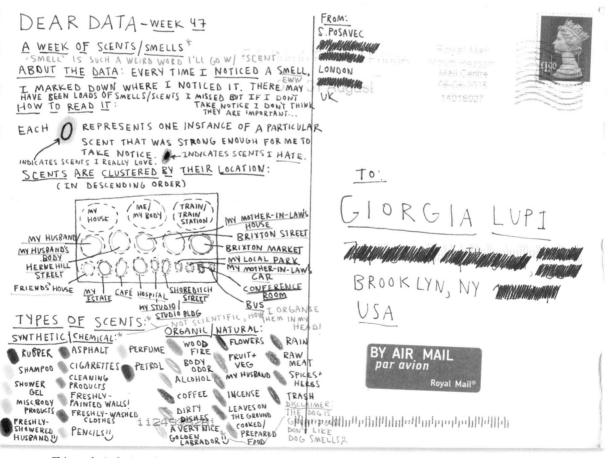

This week, Stefanie realized she surrounds herself with more synthetically made scents than she had thought. Why so many "Freshly painted walls"? Her house was painted the week before!

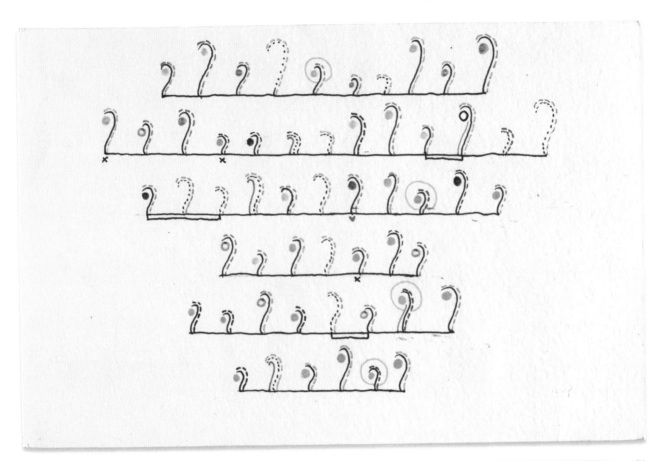

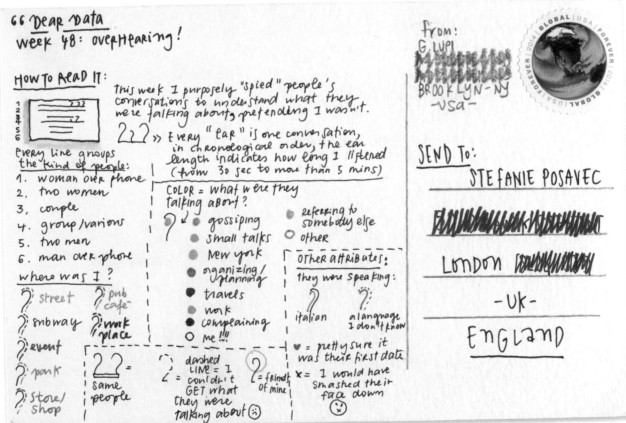

66 Dear Data
week 48: overhearing!

HOW TO READ IT:

1 2 3 4 5 6

this week I purposely "spied" people's
conversations to understand what they
were talking about, pretending I wasn't.

ʔʔʔ » Every "ear" is one conversation,
in chronological order, the ear
length indicates how long I listened
(from 30 sec to more than 5 mins)

Every line groups
the kind of people:
1. woman over phone
2. two women
3. couple
4. group/various
5. two men
6. man over phone

where was I?

ʔ street   ʔ pub/cafe
ʔ subway   ʔ work/place
ʔ event
ʔ park
ʔ store/shop

ʔʔ = same people

COLOR = what were they
talking about?

ʔ ◖ gossiping
  ◔ small talks
  ● New york
  ◕ organizing/planning
  ● travels
  ◑ work
  ● complaining
  ○ me!!!

◔ referring to
  somebody else
○ other

OTHER attributes:
they were speaking:

ʔ italian   ʔ a language
                 I don't know

♥ = pretty sure it
was their first date

ʔ dashed
 LINE = I
 couldn't
 GET what
 they were
 talking about ☺

ʔ = friend
    of mine

x = I would have
    smashed their
    face down ☹

from:
G.LUPI
~~~~~~~~
BROOKLYN-NY
-USA-

SEND TO:
STEFANIE POSAVEC
~~~~~~~~~~~~~~~~~
LONDON ~~~~~~~~
-UK-
ENGLAND

For Giorgia, the nicest note of the week was catching two Italian women clearly commenting on her outfit: as often times
happens when you speak a foreign language, they were sure she couldn't understand them.

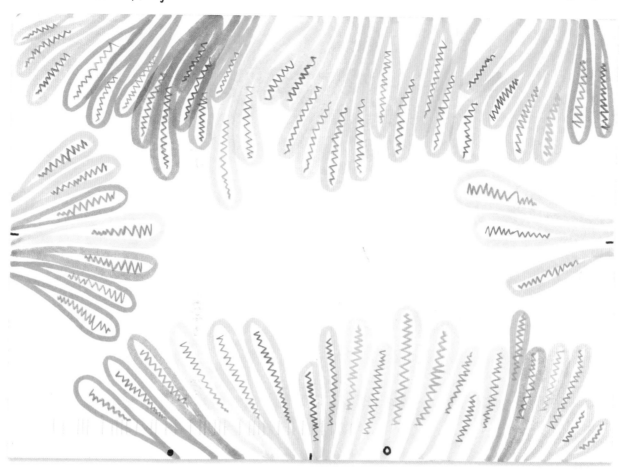

DEAR DATA WEEK 48

A WEEK OF EAVESDROPPING

ABOUT THE DATA: I WENT OUT OF MY WAY TO
LISTEN TO OTHER PEOPLE'S CONVERSATIONS,
THOUGH WHAT I'VE REALISED IS THAT MOST
OF THESE CONVERSATIONS ARE BORING".
NOTE: ONLY STRANGERS WERE TRACKED AS WITH
COLLEAGUES, ETC. IN THE SAME SPACE AS ME,
WE ALL ACCEPT WE WILL HEAR EACH OTHER'S CONVERSATIONS
FROM TIME TO TIME!

HOW TO READ IT: EACH ~~~ REPRESENTS ONE
OVERHEARD
CONVERSATION.
CONVERSATIONS SPILL ONTO
THE POSTCARD FROM THE SIDES; EACH POSTCARD SIDE
REPRESENTS A DIFFERENT LOCATION:

FROM:
S. POSAVEC
~~~~~~~~~~~
~~~~~~~~~~~
LONDON
~~~~~~~~~~~
UK

TO:
GIORGIA LUPI
~~~~~~~~~~~~~~~~~
BROOKLYN, NY ~~~
USA

BY AIR MAIL
par avion
Royal Mail®

FAVOURITE
FINDS:
• SOMEONE
BOOKING A
BRAZILIAN WAX !!
• RANDOM
CONVO ABOUT
STEPHEN
HAWKING (???)

HERNE
HILL -
CAFÉ -

TUBE/TRAIN OR TUBE/TRAIN STATION
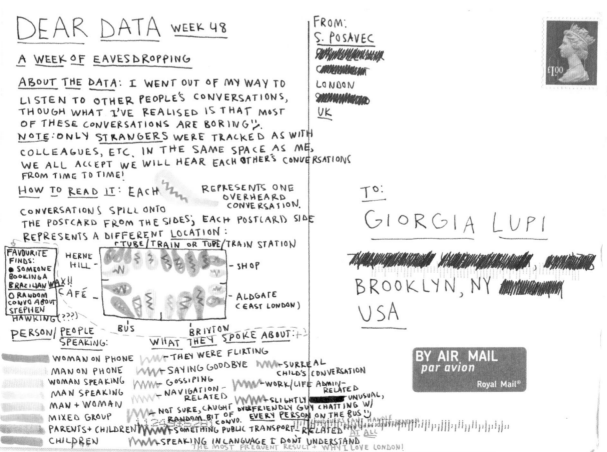
- SHOP
- ALDGATE
(EAST LONDON)

BUS   BRIXTON

PERSON/ PEOPLE
SPEAKING: WHAT THEY SPOKE ABOUT:

—— WOMAN ON PHONE   ~~~ THEY WERE FLIRTING
| MAN ON PHONE   ~~~ SAYING GOODBYE ~~~ SURREAL
WOMAN SPEAKING   ~~~ GOSSIPING   CHILD'S CONVERSATION
MAN SPEAKING   ~~~ NAVIGATION-   ~~~ WORK/LIFE ADMIN-
MAN + WOMAN   RELATED   RELATED
MIXED GROUP   ~~~ NOT SURE, CAUGHT   ~~~ SLIGHTLY ~~~~ UNUSUAL,
                     RANDOM BIT OF   OVERFRIENDLY GUY CHATTING W/
PARENTS + CHILDREN   CONVO. ~~~ SOMETHING PUBLIC TRANSPORT-RELATED AT ALL
CHILDREN   ~~~ SPEAKING IN LANGUAGE I DON'T UNDERSTAND
                     THE MOST FREQUENT RESULT + WHY I LOVE LONDON!

Stefanie's drawing alludes to speech bubbles, with conversation creeping onto the postcard from its edges,
and her listening in. Her favourite data this week: the scores of languages spoken in London!

SO EXCITED!
LET'S SPY!

GIORGIA's EXPECTATIONS of OVERHEARING interesting conversations

" ... YES I HAVE BEEN TO JAPAN, BUT ONLY FOR A CONFERENCE SO NOT REALLY VISITED ... "

booooring!!

" ... MY MANICURE WAS GREAT! I TIPPED HER 20% ! "

booooring!!

" ... I HAD SUCH AN AMAZING DINNER AT THAT RESTAURANT! "

booooring!!

" THE RENT IN THE NEIGHBOURHOOD IS GOING CRAZY, WE'RE THINKING OF MOVING TO BED STUY ... "

booooring!!

I am so sorry Stefanie! I suggested such a boring topic!

OVER THE WEEK.

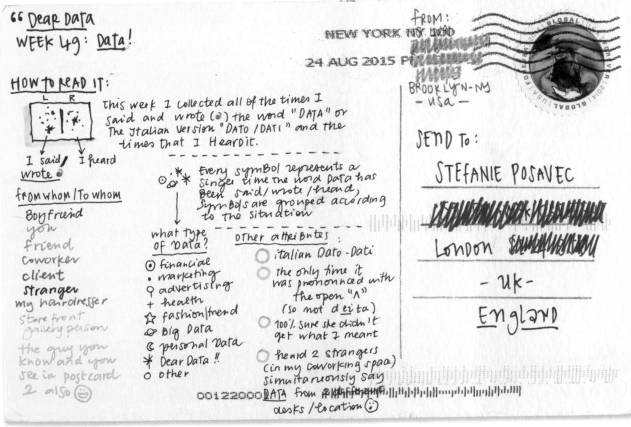

For this drawing, Giorgia didn't follow any strict rule for the organization of her data-data (ha!) but rather she was guided by her aesthetic feeling to compose a (hopefully) elegant drawing.

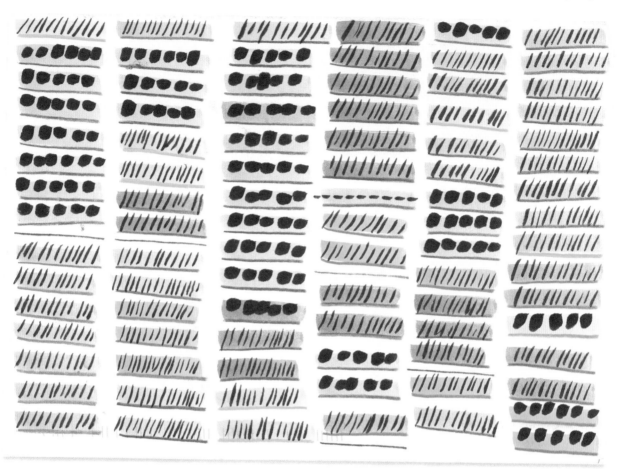

DEAR DATA ① — WEEK 49 ②ND POSTING!

A WEEK OF THE WORD 'DATA' ②

ABOUT THE DATA: I TRACKED EVERY TIME
I SPOKE OR WROTE THE WORD 'DATA' ④
HOW TO READ IT:

EACH ⚫⚫⚫⚫ IS ONE
INSTANCE OF THE WORD 'DATA'. ⑤
INSTANCES ARE ORGANISED
L→R, TOP→BOTTOM, AND
ARE IN CHRONOLOGICAL ORDER.
(UH-OH, YOU CAN SEE HOW LATE
   I POSTED THE CARD THIS
                WEEK !!)

PENCIL LINES = ⑥
NEW DAY OF DATA

FROM:
S. POSAVEC
~~████████~~
~~████████~~
~~████████~~
LONDON
UK

WHO I WAS 'SPEAKING' TO:
- NO ONE
- FAN OF DEAR DATA ⑦
- INTERNET PUBLIC ON SOCIAL MEDIA
- FRIEND(S)
- **YOU!**
- COLLEAGUES
- INTERNET PUBLIC ON THE WEB
- MY HUSBAND

WHERE I SAID/ WROTE THE WORD 'DATA': ⑨
- IN REAL LIFE
- ON THE DEAR DATA ⑨ WEBSITE
- ON A POSTCARD
- OVER EMAIL
- ON PHONE/OVER VIDEO CHAT
- IN A SPREADSHEET
- ON SOCIAL MEDIA/ IN A SEARCH ENGINE
- OVER MESSAGING

TOPIC OF CONVERSATION:
- ///////// DEAR DATA: I TALK ABOUT IT TOOOOO MUCH!
- ⚫⚫⚫⚫⚫ WORK PROJECTS
- •—•—•—•—
- AN ARTIST USING DATA ⑪

TOTAL NUMBER OF
MENTIONS OF DATA ⑫
THIS CARD: **12**

TO:
GIORGIA LUPI   MORE SMUDGES :(
~~████████████████████~~,
BROOKLYN, NY ~~██████~~
USA

BY AIR MAIL
par avion
Royal Mail®

One of Stefanie's favourite postcards she drew this year, so *of course* this postcard went missing and
she had to re-draw and re-send.

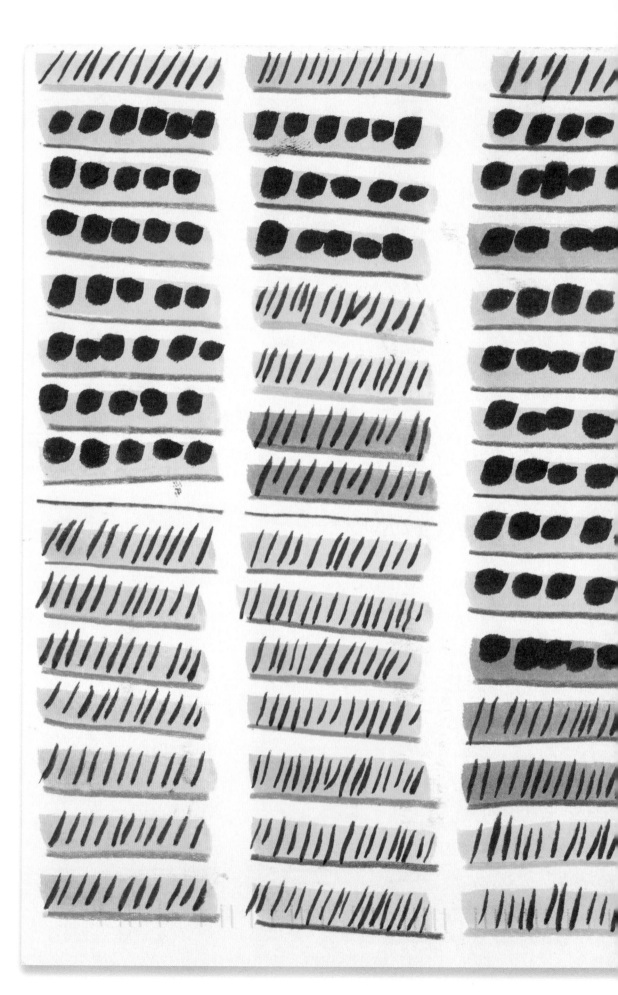

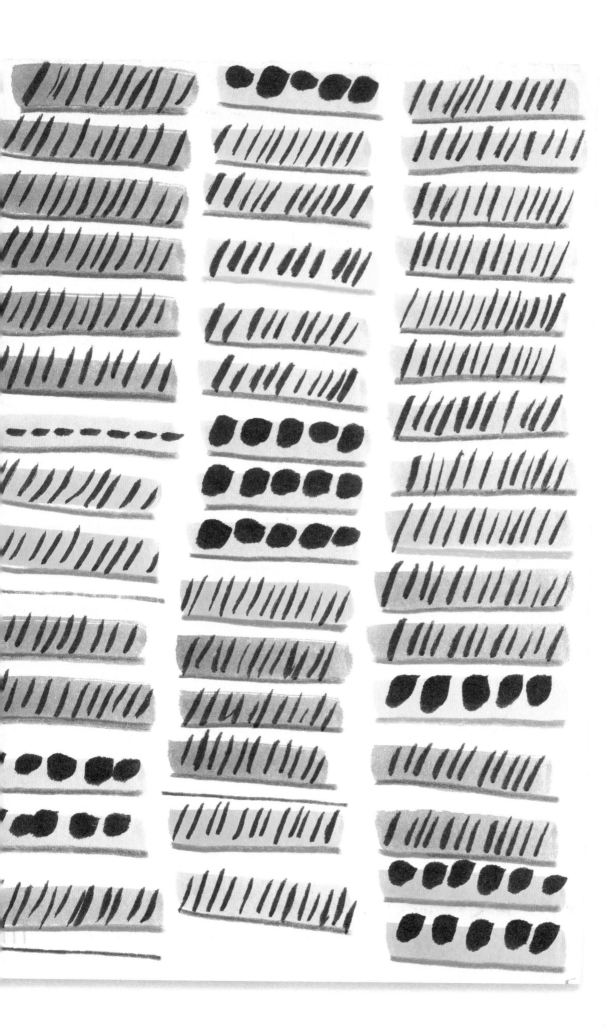

AN EMOTIONAL JOURNEY

OR, A VERY PUBLIC APOLOGY TO STEFANIE'S HUSBAND

START

Stefanie and her husband plan to cycle to an exhibition. They prepare by putting on sunscreen, and Stefanie's husband consolidates two bottles of sunscreen into one. Stefanie throws this bottle into her backpack, and off they cycle.

All is forgiven (phew). Stefanie tiptoes away in quiet remorse and with thanks for such a patient husband.

The beginning of Stefanie's many apologies to her husband, as she knew she had been completely unreasonable.

HOME

Stefanie opens her laptop and double-checks that her data was backed up: all safe, except for weeks fifty and fifty-one ... so not so bad.

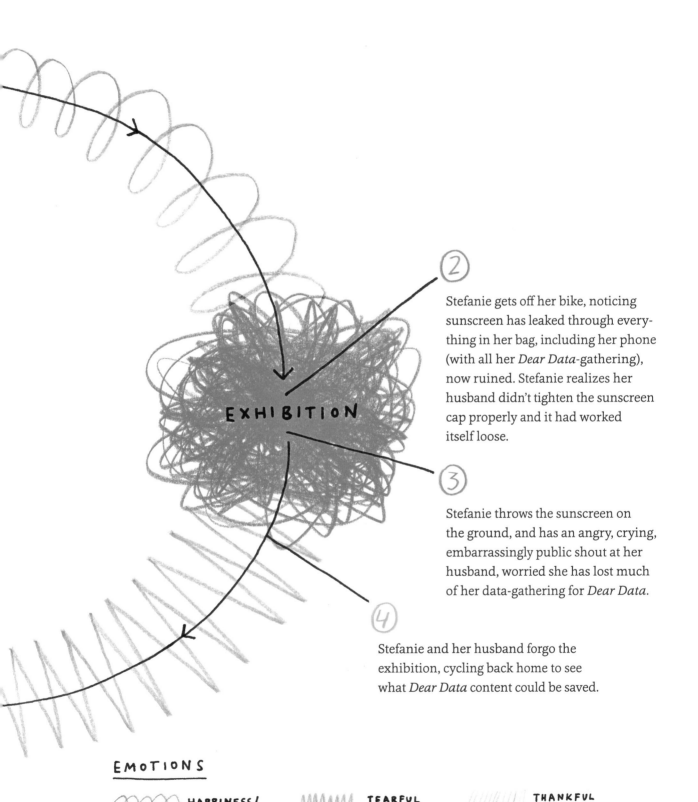

②

Stefanie gets off her bike, noticing sunscreen has leaked through everything in her bag, including her phone (with all her *Dear Data*-gathering), now ruined. Stefanie realizes her husband didn't tighten the sunscreen cap properly and it had worked itself loose.

③

Stefanie throws the sunscreen on the ground, and has an angry, crying, embarrassingly public shout at her husband, worried she has lost much of her data-gathering for *Dear Data*.

④

Stefanie and her husband forgo the exhibition, cycling back home to see what *Dear Data* content could be saved.

EXHIBITION

EMOTIONS

HAPPINESS/ ANTICIPATION

TEARFUL ANGER

THANKFUL RELIEF

IRRATIONAL FURY + WRATH

EMBARRASSED REMORSE

SIZE = EMOTION'S INTENSITY

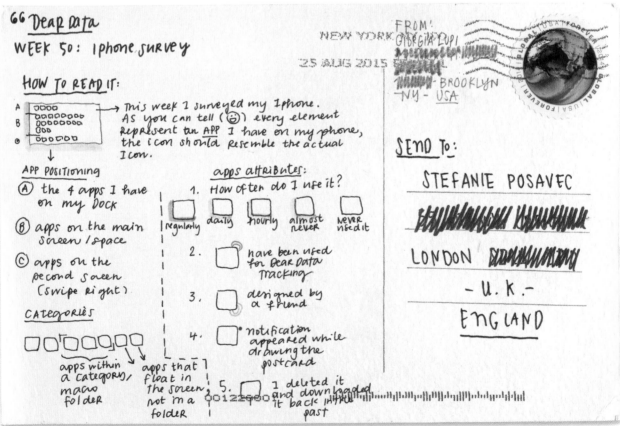

66 Dear Data
WEEK 50: Iphone survey

HOW TO READ IT:

A — This week I surveyed my Iphone. As you can tell (☺) every element represent tan APP I have on my phone, the icon should resemble the actual icon.

APP POSITIONING

(A) the 4 apps I have on my Dock

(B) apps on the main screen / space

(C) apps on the second screen (swipe right)

CATEGORIES

apps within a category / macro folder

apps that float in the screen, not in a folder

apps attributes:

1. How often do I use it?
   regularly   daily   hourly   almost never   never used it

2. have been used for Dear Data Tracking

3. designed by a friend

4. notification appeared while drawing the postcard

5. 00122000   I deleted it and downloaded it back in the past

FROM:
NEW YORK   GIORGIA LUPI
25 AUG 2015   ~~~~~~~
                ~~~~~~~
                ~~~~~ - BROOKLYN
                NY - USA

SEND To:

STEFANIE POSAVEC

~~~~~~~~~~~~~~~~

LONDON ~~~~~~~~

- U. K. -

ENGLAND

Before the end of the project, for once, Giorgia added illustrated details to her data-drawing to portray her phone to Stefanie in a more explicit way. (But she hates how the postcard looks) :(

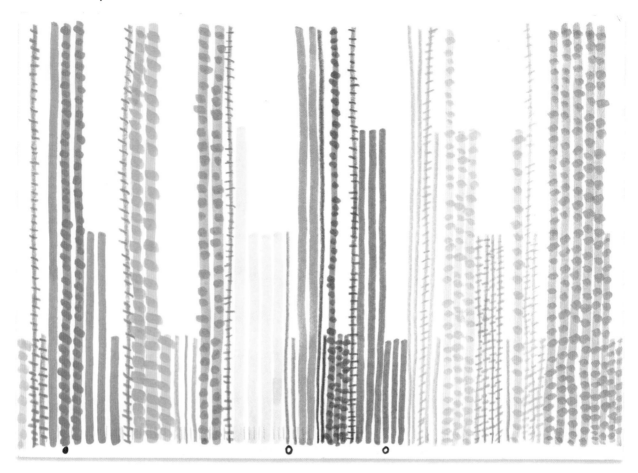

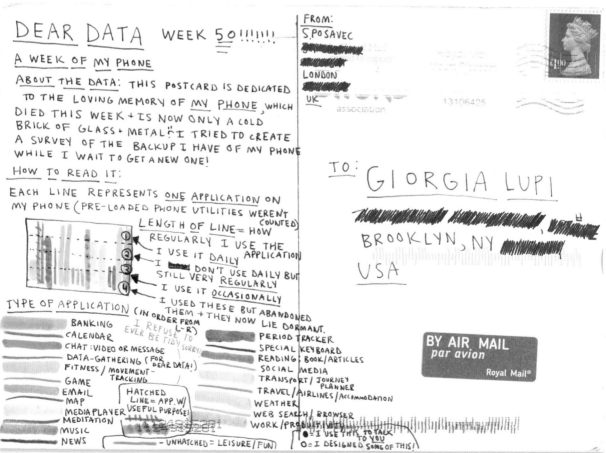

DEAR DATA   WEEK 50!!!!!!!

A WEEK OF MY PHONE

ABOUT THE DATA: THIS POSTCARD IS DEDICATED
TO THE LOVING MEMORY OF MY PHONE, WHICH
DIED THIS WEEK + IS NOW ONLY A COLD
BRICK OF GLASS + METAL. I TRIED TO CREATE
A SURVEY OF THE BACKUP I HAVE OF MY PHONE
WHILE I WAIT TO GET A NEW ONE!

HOW TO READ IT:

EACH LINE REPRESENTS ONE APPLICATION ON
MY PHONE (PRE-LOADED PHONE UTILITIES WEREN'T COUNTED)

LENGTH OF LINE = HOW
① REGULARLY I USE THE APPLICATION
② I USE IT DAILY
③ I DON'T USE DAILY BUT STILL VERY REGULARLY
④ I USE IT OCCASIONALLY
I USED THESE BUT ABANDONED THEM + THEY NOW LIE DORMANT.

TYPE OF APPLICATION (IN ORDER FROM L-R)
I REFUSE TO EVER BE TIDY SORRY!

BANKING
CALENDAR
CHAT: VIDEO OR MESSAGE
DATA-GATHERING (FOR DEAR DATA!)
FITNESS / MOVEMENT - TRACKING
GAME
EMAIL
MAP
MEDIA PLAYER
MEDITATION
MUSIC
NEWS

HATCHED LINE = APP W/ USEFUL PURPOSE)

PERIOD TRACKER
SPECIAL KEYBOARD
READING: BOOK/ARTICLES
SOCIAL MEDIA
TRANSPORT / JOURNEY PLANNER
TRAVEL / AIRLINES / ACCOMMODATION
WEATHER
WEB SEARCH / BROWSER
WORK / PRODUCTIVITY

— UNHATCHED = LEISURE / FUN

● = I USE THIS TO TALK TO YOU
O = I DESIGNED SOME OF THIS!

FROM:
S. POSAVEC
LONDON
UK
association

£1·00
13106425

TO: GIORGIA LUPI

BROOKLYN, NY

USA

BY AIR MAIL
par avion
Royal Mail®

Since Stefanie's phone had died, she used a back-up of all of her applications to piece together which ones she was using at the time of its demise.

A WEEK OF PRIVACY

Data can reveal everything about a person, and "big" data – with its billions of data points – is often used to paint a picture of ourselves and our buying habits (and more) without us ever realizing it.

Since the beginning, *Dear Data* has been a project of trust, where Stefanie and Giorgia have agreed to reveal their very personal data to each other. But what about the moments in their lives that they would prefer to keep private and not to share with each other, their families and their partners?

This week, Giorgia and Stefanie focused on gathering data on the moments they wouldn't feel comfortable drawing on a postcard and sending to the other.

COVERING UP STEFANIE'S
MOST PRIVATE MOMENTS

I WAS
UNKIND

I WAS
CRYING

I

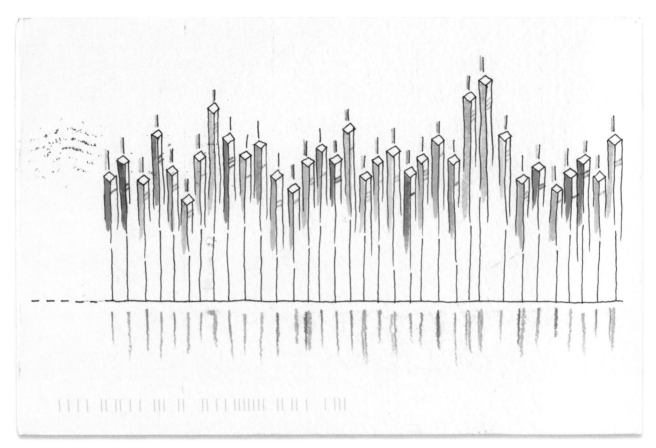

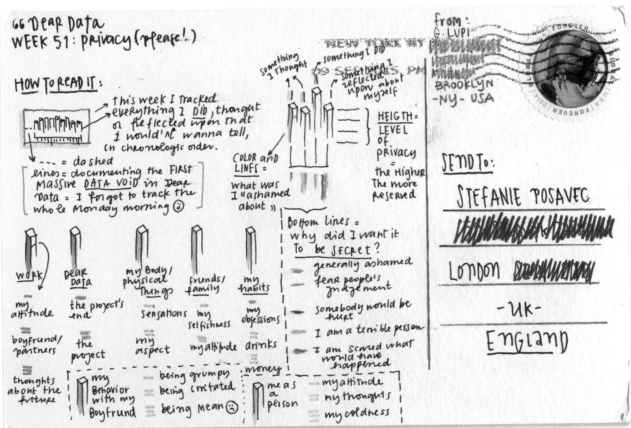

Giorgia's card starts with dashed lines from the left, before displaying her private logs chronologically: her very first massive data void. As a matter of fact, she forgot to track the whole of Monday morning, argh!

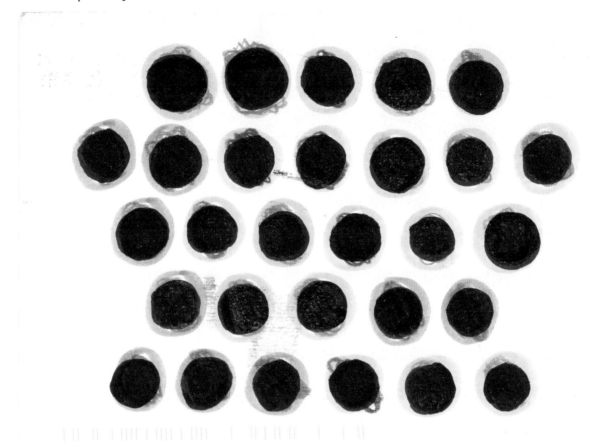

DEAR DATA — WEEK 51

A WEEK OF PRIVACY

ABOUT THE DATA: ORIGINALLY I WAS TRACKING
EVERY MOMENT I WOULDN'T WANT TO SHARE WITH
YOU (OR ANYONE ELSE) BUT MY PHONE DIED + I
LOST MY DATA. SO, THIS IS A LIST OF MOMENTS
THAT I WOULD PREFER TO KEEP PRIVATE FROM
LAST WEEK, BUT MADE FROM MEMORY.

HOW TO READ IT: EACH ⬤ IS ONE MOMENT FROM
'CENSORED' SYMBOL   THE WEEK THAT
                           I WOULD PREFER
                           TO KEEP PRIVATE.

SYMBOLS ARE ORDERED BY HOW
EMBARRASSED / UNCOMFORTABLE I
WOULD FEEL IF YOU KNEW WHAT
            THESE MOMENTS
            WERE!
ORDERED FROM ①→⑤
WITH ① = I WOULDN'T BE TOO EMBARRASSED
     ⑤ = I WOULD BE VERY EMBARRASSED/
                             UNCOMFORTABLE

TYPE OF MOMENT I
WANTED TO KEEP PRIVATE:

⬤ A THOUGHT
   I HAD

⬤ ONE OF MY
   ACTIONS

⬤ MY INTERACTIONS
   WITH OTHERS

⬤ MY BEHAVIOUR

IF I HAD TO SHARE THIS
MOMENT, WHO I WOULD
BE WILLING TO SHARE IT
WITH:

MORE
PRIVATE   ⬤ NO ONE BUT
                   ME.

                 ⬤ MY HUSBAND

                 ⬤ MY FRIENDS
                   (+ ALL ABOVE)

LESS PRIVATE   ⬤ MY PARENTS
                   (+ ALL ABOVE)

FROM:
S. POSAVEC
▓▓▓▓▓▓▓▓▓▓
▓▓▓▓▓▓▓▓▓▓
UK

Royal Mail
Mount Pleasant
Mail Centre
02-09-2015
34102357

TO: GIORGIA LUPI
▓▓▓▓▓▓▓▓▓▓▓▓ , ▓▓▓▓▓▓
BROOKLYN, NY ▓▓▓▓▓▓
USA

BY AIR MAIL
par avion
Royal Mail®

Stefanie intentionally obscured her data by describing it in a very basic fashion, then covered her drawing with
black ink to make her data even more private. Sorry, Giorgia, these secrets are hers!

I don't want anyone to know that ~~████ ████ ████ ████~~
~~████ ████ ████~~. ~~████████~~ I would keep it ~~████████ ████~~
~~████ ████ ████ ████ ████ ████ ██ ████~~ she would think I
~~████████ ████████████~~. I wouldn't want Stefanie to learn that ~~██~~
~~████████ ████ ██ ████████ ████████ ████ ████████████ ████~~
and my obsession for ~~████████~~. I am ashamed of my ~~████ ██~~
~~████████ ████ ████████~~. ~~████████~~ otherwise they will think
that ~~████ ████ ████████████ ████~~. ~~████████ ████████~~
~~████████~~ it's hard to admit that ~~████ ████ ████~~. I cried
because ~~████████ ████████ ████████~~. only my boyfriend knows
that ~~████ ████ ████~~. ~~████ ████ ████████████ ████ ████~~
~~████ ████ ████ ██ ████ ████ ████ ████████████~~
~~████~~. I needed to apologize for ~~████ ████ ████~~. ~~████ ████~~
~~████████ ████ ████ ████████~~ Because I feel ashamed about
~~████ ████ ████ ██ ████ ████████~~. ~~████ ████ ████████~~
~~████████~~ I never told anyone that ~~████ ████ ████████████ ████~~.
~~████████ ████████ ██ ████ ████ ████ ████████████ ████~~
and how horrible I am ~~████████████ ████ ████ ████ ████~~
~~████ ████████████ ████ ████████~~ I also have a DEAR DATA secret
that is ~~████ ████████ ████ ████████~~. ~~████████ ████ ████~~
~~████████ ████ ████~~ I will never get over that ~~████ ████████████~~
~~████ ████████ ████ ████ ████ ████████████ ████~~. ~~████████~~
secret because she would ~~████████ ████████ ██ ████ ████ ████~~
~~████ ████ ████ ████ ████████████ ████~~. ~~████████ ████~~

276

▮▮▮▮▮▮▮▮▮▮▮▮▮▮▮▮▮▮▮▮▮▮▮▮▮▮▮▮ . ▮▮▮▮▮▮▮▮▮▮▮

I feel terrible to have ▮▮▮▮▮▮▮▮▮▮▮▮▮▮▮▮▮▮▮▮▮▮▮▮ .

▮▮▮▮▮▮▮▮▮▮▮▮▮▮▮▮▮▮▮▮▮ I am ashamed of my

▮▮▮▮▮▮▮▮▮▮▮▮▮▮▮▮▮▮▮▮▮▮▮▮▮▮▮▮ ▮▮▮▮▮▮▮▮▮▮

▮▮▮▮▮▮▮▮▮ . I wouldn't want ▮▮▮▮▮▮▮▮▮▮▮▮

▮▮▮▮▮▮▮▮ . only my boyfriend knows that ▮▮▮▮▮▮▮

▮▮ and how horrible I am ▮▮▮▮▮▮▮▮▮▮▮▮▮▮▮▮▮▮

▮▮▮▮▮▮▮▮▮▮▮▮▮▮▮▮ . ▮▮▮▮▮▮▮▮▮▮▮▮

▮▮▮▮▮▮▮▮▮▮▮▮▮▮▮▮▮▮▮▮▮▮ ▮▮▮▮▮▮▮▮▮▮

▮▮▮▮▮▮▮▮▮▮▮▮▮▮▮▮ . ▮▮▮▮▮▮▮▮▮▮▮▮▮▮▮▮▮

▮▮▮▮▮▮▮▮▮▮ ▮▮▮▮▮▮▮▮▮▮▮▮▮▮▮▮▮▮▮▮

▮▮▮▮▮ I realized how much ▮▮▮▮▮▮▮▮▮▮▮▮▮▮▮

▮▮▮▮▮▮▮▮ . ▮▮▮▮▮▮▮▮▮▮ because I feel ▮▮▮▮▮▮▮▮▮▮

▮▮▮▮▮▮▮▮▮▮▮▮▮▮▮▮▮▮▮▮▮▮▮▮▮▮▮▮▮▮▮

▮▮▮▮▮▮▮▮▮▮▮▮▮▮▮▮▮▮▮▮▮▮ ▮▮▮▮▮▮▮▮▮▮

I never told anyone that ▮▮▮▮▮▮▮▮▮▮▮▮▮▮▮▮

▮▮▮▮▮▮▮▮▮▮▮▮▮▮ . ▮▮▮▮▮▮▮▮▮▮▮▮▮▮▮▮▮▮▮

Giorgia ended up revealing most of her
censored feelings and secrets to Stefanie
after *Dear Data* was over.

▮▮▮▮▮▮▮▮▮▮▮▮▮▮▮▮▮▮▮▮▮▮▮▮▮▮▮▮▮▮▮

▮▮▮▮▮▮▮▮▮▮▮ how horrible I am ▮▮▮▮▮▮▮▮▮

▮▮▮▮▮▮▮▮▮▮▮▮▮▮▮▮▮▮▮▮▮▮▮▮▮▮▮▮▮▮▮

▮▮▮▮▮▮▮▮▮▮▮▮▮ Because I feel ashamed about ▮▮▮▮ .

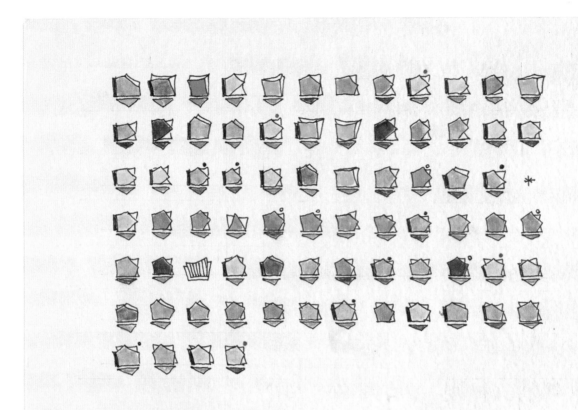

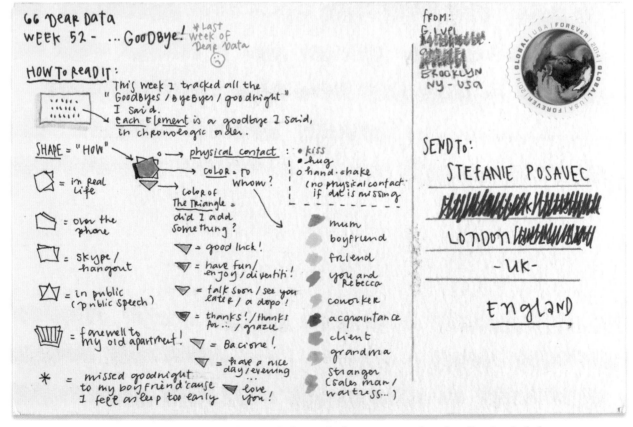

The most shameful revelation. Of course, the last week of *Dear Data* was about "goodbyes", to include a special goodbye to *Dear Data* in their postcards. Guess what Giorgia forgot to add? :/

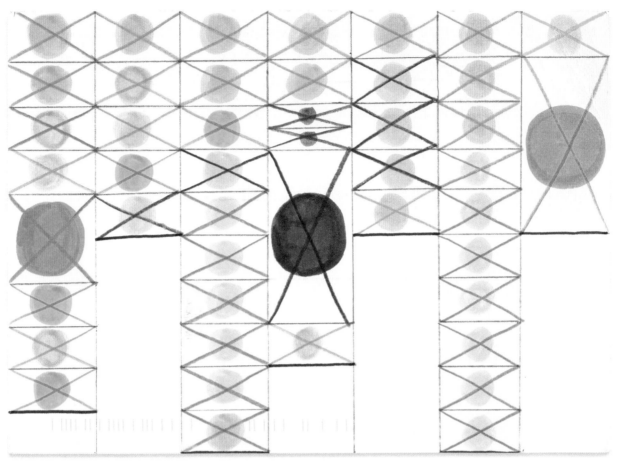

DEAR DATA – WEEK (52)

A WEEK OF GOODBYES :')

ABOUT THE DATA: SAYING GOODBYE, BOTH FOR AWHILE AND FOREVER.

HOW TO READ IT: EACH ⊠ IS ONE GOODBYE.

GOODBYES ARE ORGANISED IN CHRONOLOGICAL ORDER FROM L-R AND TOP-BOTTOM.

TYPE OF GOODBYE/ LEVEL OF EMOTION:

BEING POLITE, WE WONT MEET AGAIN

"UNTIL WE MEET AGAIN"

NEARLY A FINAL GOODBYE

A FINAL GOODBYE.

HOW/WHERE I WAS SAYING THE GOODBYE:
PHONE/ VIDEO/ MESSAGE
IN SHOP
AT HOME
AT STUDIO (NEW + OLD)

AT NOTTING HILL CARNIVAL
AT PUB (INCL. MY AMAZING PUB CRAWL!)
— ON SOCIAL MEDIA

WHO/WHAT I WAS SAYING GOODBYE TO:
COLLEAGUE   MY HUSBAND
STUDIOMATE   SHOP-WORKER
FRIEND   MY OLD STUDIO "
YOU!   DEAR DATA

AND A FINAL LEFT-HANDS MUDGE HAHA

THANKS FOR SUCH A GREAT PROJECT!! WE DID IT!!!! :')

FROM: S POSAVEC ~~~~~ LONDON ~~~~~ UK

National Letter ~~~~~ week
14 - 18 September 2015

Royal Mail
Mount Pleasant
Mail Centre
16-09-2015
44009732

£1·00

TO:
GIORGIA LUPI
~~~~~~~~~~~~~~~~~~~~~~~~
BROOKLYN, NY ~~~~~
USA

BY AIR MAIL
par avion
Royal Mail®

"My amazing pub crawl": Stefanie hit ten pubs in an afternoon and was feeling pretty proud. "My old studio": the pub crawl was in honour of the disbanding of the studio she shared with friends.

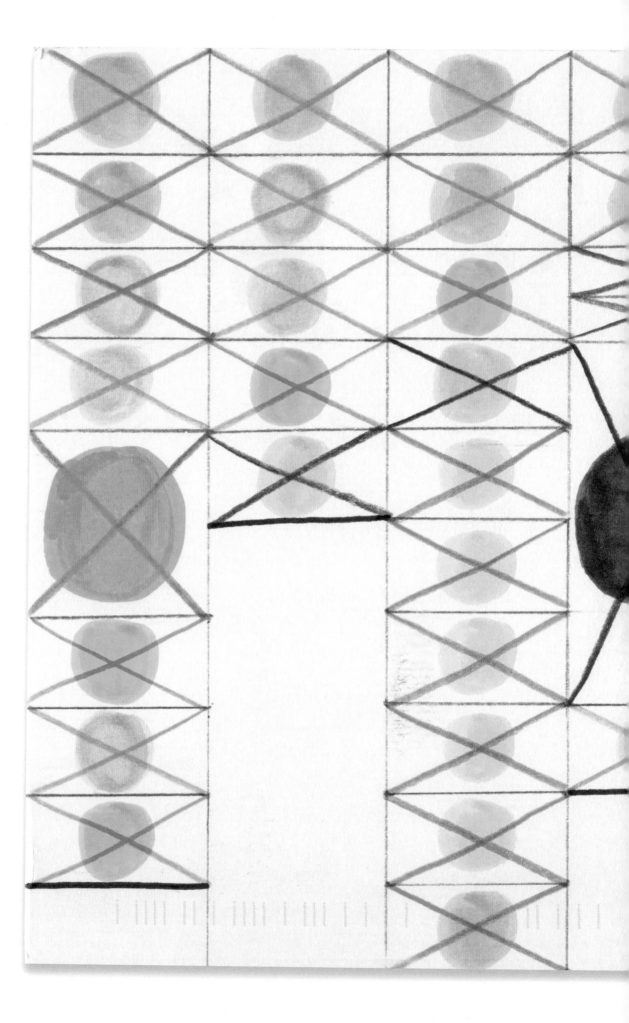

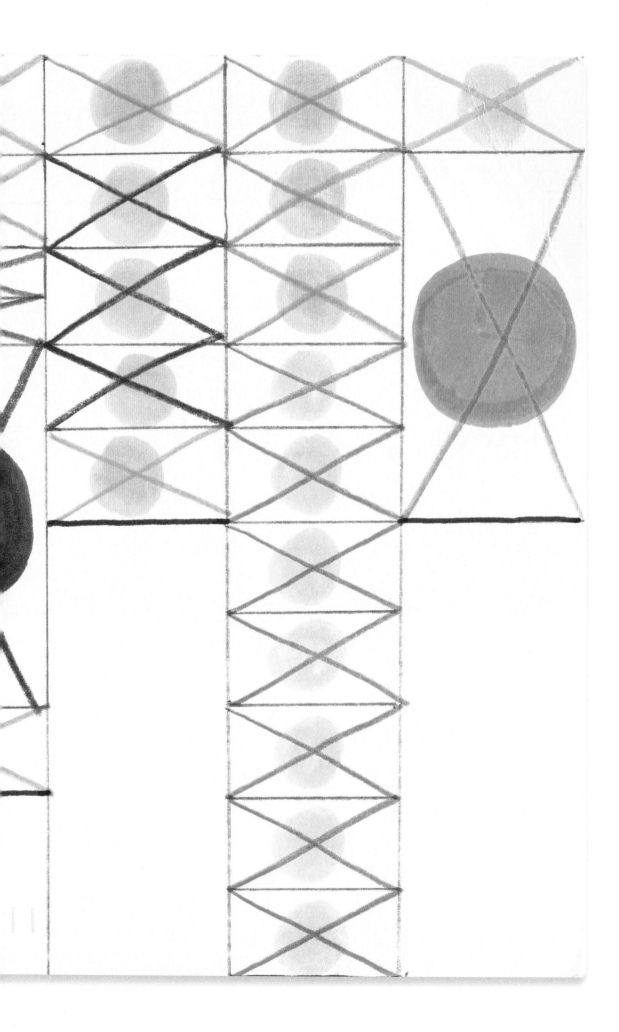

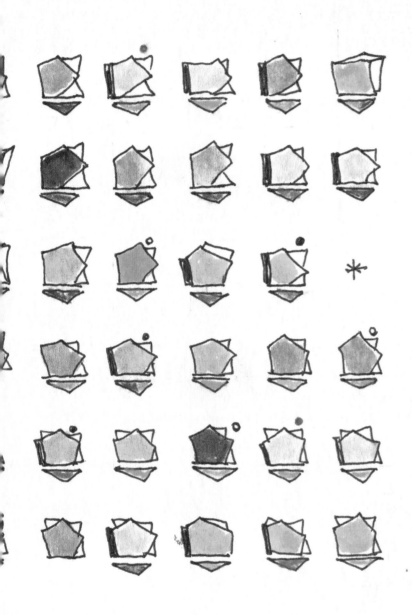

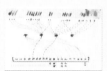

To **Draw** is To

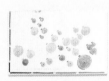

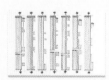

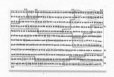

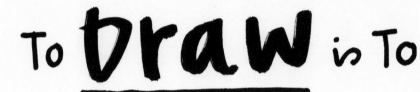

284

   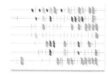 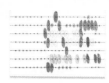 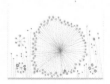

REMEMBER.

 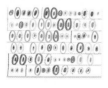    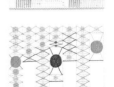

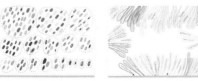  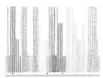

IT'S NOT THAT HARD!

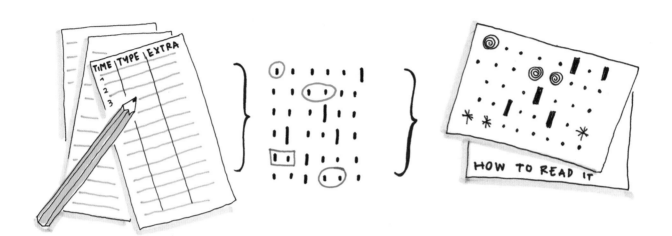

SEE THE WORLD AS A DATA COLLECTOR

Data permeates our days and our lives, it's just a matter of learning how to recognize it.

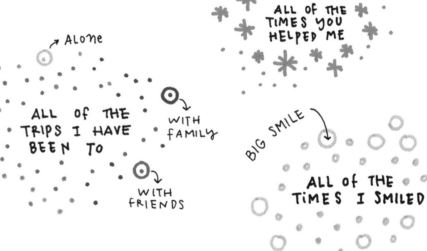

Alone

ALL OF THE TRIPS I HAVE BEEN TO

WITH FAMILY

WITH FRIENDS

ALL OF THE TIMES YOU HELPED ME

BIG SMILE

ALL OF THE TIMES I SMILED

BEGIN WITH A QUESTION

Begin with a primary question: what do you want to know and explore? Then enrich the data (and give the drawings depth) by asking additional smaller, contextual questions.

ALL OF THE TIMES I COMPLAIN:

⊙	WHAT IS MY COMPLAINT ABOUT?
++	IS IT REALLY NECESSARY?
++	WHO DO I COMPLAIN TO?
++	WHAT DOES IT SAY ABOUT ME?
++	(...)

① MAIN QUESTION

② ADDING FURTHER DETAILS and CONTEXT.

GATHER THE DATA

Thank goodness for modern technology: input manually-gathered data into note-taking or data-gathering apps on your phone, all the while being immediate, truthful, and consistent with your data-gathering.

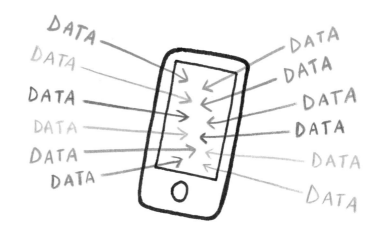

SPEND TIME WITH DATA

Before starting to visualize, always analyze and spend time with your data, searching for patterns and trying to understand it at a deeper level.

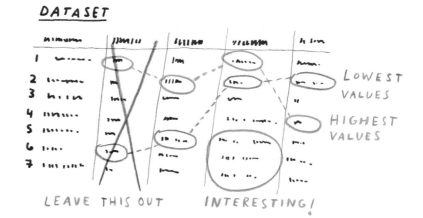

DATASET

LOWEST VALUES

HIGHEST VALUES

LEAVE THIS OUT   INTERESTING!

ORGANIZE AND CATEGORIZE

Often it's good to simplify the data by grouping it into larger categories based on what will best communicate the story.

FEMALE FRIENDS

NATALIE BLAISE SARAH MIRIAM

ANIMALS

DUCK ELEPHANT CAT SQUIRREL DOG FOX

LEISURE ACTIVITIES

READING CYCLING GARDENING COOKING RUNNING

FIND THE MAIN STORY

Starting with the patterns discovered in the data, decide what the main story is for the drawing. Finding the data's focus helps decide the layout of a data drawing.

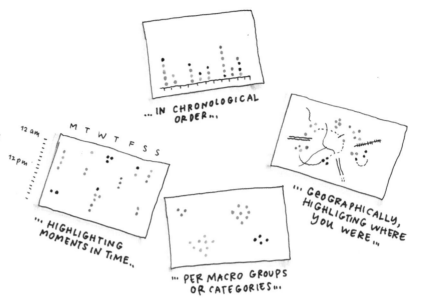

... IN CHRONOLOGICAL ORDER ...

" HIGHLIGHTING MOMENTS IN TIME "

" PER MACRO GROUPS OR CATEGORIES "

" GEOGRAPHICALLY, HIGHLIGTING WHERE YOU WERE "

VISUAL INSPIRATION TO BUILD YOUR PERSONAL VOCABULARY

Lose yourself in images, using the aesthetic qualities of the features you are attracted to as visual inspiration for the drawing.

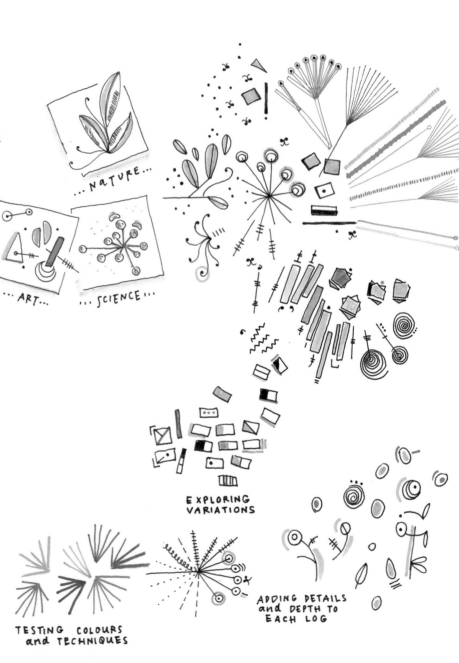

... NATURE ...

... ART ...

... SCIENCE ...

SKETCH and EXPERIMENT WITH FIRST IDEAS

Explore ideas by sketching and playfully experimenting with form, colour, and materials in a freehand fashion as you decide the visual elements that will represent every part of the data.

EXPLORING VARIATIONS

TESTING COLOURS and TECHNIQUES

ADDING DETAILS and DEPTH TO EACH LOG

DRAW THE FINAL PICTURE

After sketching and testing ideas for a data-drawing, you'll find an approach that works. Then create your drawing, ensuring it includes all the tiny details, trying to make it as beautiful (and as understandable) as you can.

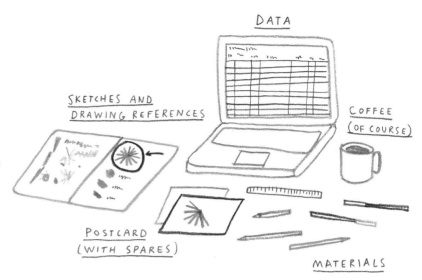

DRAW THE LEGEND

Creating a legend starts with a question: "What does someone need to read my data-drawing?" In the legend, every design element that represents data is listed so the recipient understands what everything means.

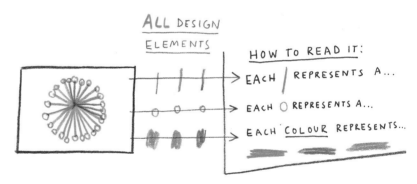

AND FINALLY, SEND IT ON ITS WAY!

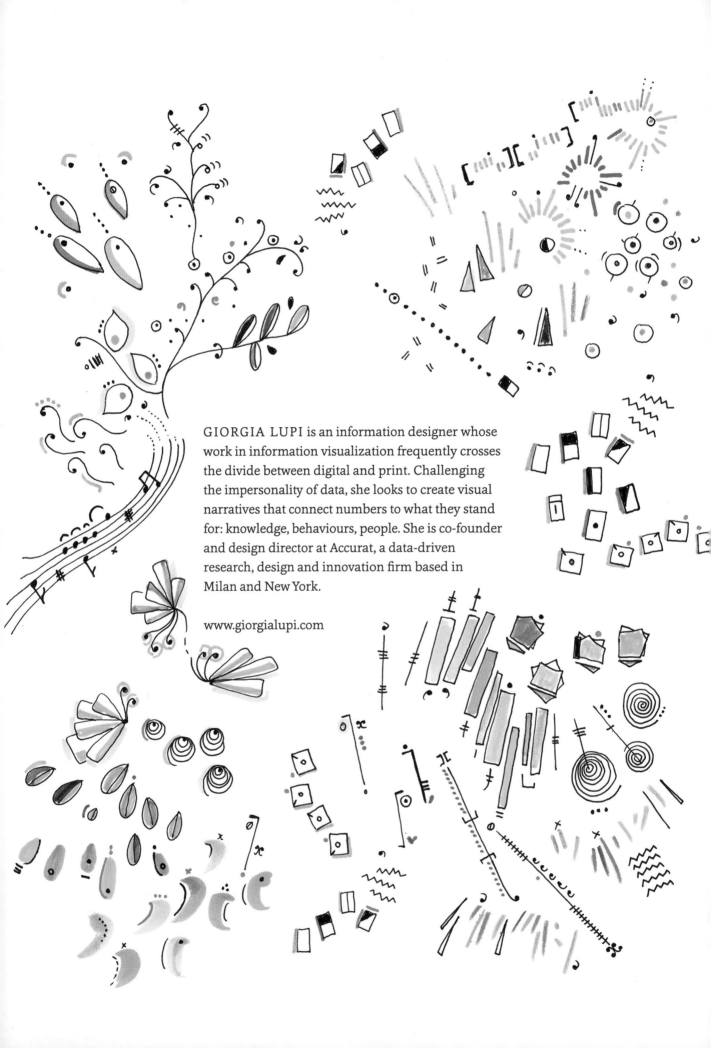

GIORGIA LUPI is an information designer whose work in information visualization frequently crosses the divide between digital and print. Challenging the impersonality of data, she looks to create visual narratives that connect numbers to what they stand for: knowledge, behaviours, people. She is co-founder and design director at Accurat, a data-driven research, design and innovation firm based in Milan and New York.

www.giorgialupi.com

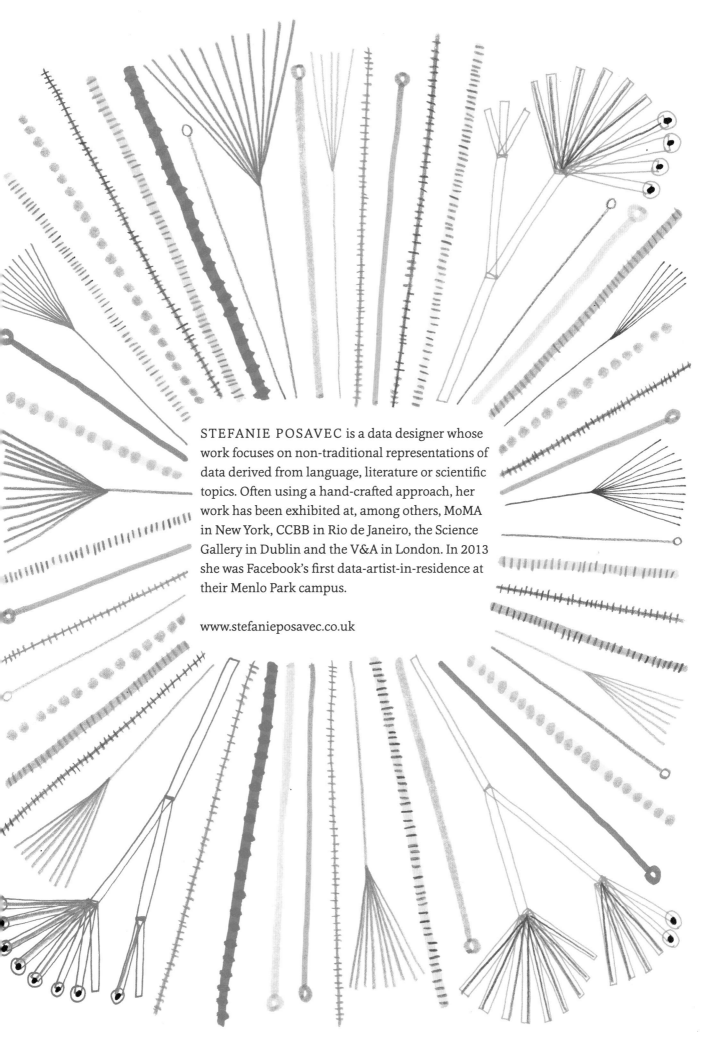

STEFANIE POSAVEC is a data designer whose work focuses on non-traditional representations of data derived from language, literature or scientific topics. Often using a hand-crafted approach, her work has been exhibited at, among others, MoMA in New York, CCBB in Rio de Janeiro, the Science Gallery in Dublin and the V&A in London. In 2013 she was Facebook's first data-artist-in-residence at their Menlo Park campus.

www.stefanieposavec.co.uk